Restructuring Higher Education in India

Restructuring Higher Education in India

Sudhanshu Bhushan

RAWAT PUBLICATIONS
Jaipur • New Delhi • Bangalore • Mumbai • Hyderabad • Guwahati

ISBN 81-316-0304-0

Published by
Prem Rawat for **Rawat Publications**
Satyam Apts, Sector 3, Jawahar Nagar, Jaipur 302 004 (India)
Phone: 0141 265 1748 / 7006 Fax: 0141 265 1748
E-mail: info@rawatbooks.com
Website: www.rawatbooks.com

New Delhi Office
4858/24, Ansari Road, Daryaganj, New Delhi 110 002
Phone: 011 2326 3290

Also at Bangalore, Mumbai, Hyderabad and Guwahati

Typeset by Rawat Computers, Jaipur
Printed at Chaman Enterprises, New Delhi

Contents

IV
Plan Support and Financing

Preface

Higher education in India is undergoing a big transformation, which is reflected not only in the choice of students with respect to the programme and institutions, but also in the methods of teaching and learning from instruction mode to student-centred learning. The learning resource now is varied from print material to e-learning. A change is also evident in the assumption of higher education from public to private good. Internationalization of higher education adds a newer dimension to it. There is also an entrepreneurial dimension to the governance of higher education. Similarly, in the area of financing, there is a change in the shift of burden upon students to pay for it.

The process of change calls for a debate to understand the dimensions of the problem along quantity and quality axes. The quantitative expansion has an important dimension in terms of inclusive growth. The debate on quality, too, has to be not in terms of meritocracy but in terms of diversified providers, learners, methods, resources etc. The competition rather than control and autonomy and innovation rather than protection and inbreeding are the hallmarks of quality in higher education.

This book is an attempt to analyze issues relating to privatization, emergence of foreign education providers and issue of foreign direct investment in higher education. At the level of practices various providers have appeared on the scene due to high demand for higher education. But, unfortunately, there is no policy framework to deal with the changing phenomenon. As a result, certainly, there is risk of commercialization of education, which may adversely affect the objectives of quality and inclusiveness in higher education. There may also develop an imbalance in the growth of basic and applied disciplines. Hence regulations to deal with these issues need to be considered. The present work throws light on this.

Regulation alone, however, is not sufficient. It needs to be supplemented with academic reforms. Such reforms are to be seen from two perspectives. First, the neo-liberal reforms, which call for pro-market strategies, include less regulation, less barriers to entry and greater freedom to institutions and individuals. On the other hand, institutional reforms initiated by the state take into account the societal needs and priorities. Thus, not only a planned approach to academic reforms initiated by the state needs to be percolated down at the institutional level, but a challenge also lies in synthesizing the two approaches in a constructive manner.

While the regulated growth is desirable, it is also necessary to expose the higher education system to greater competition. Transparency and accountability should be inbuilt into the system. Choice-based credit system should, therefore, be given a big push to improve quality. Reforms in governance also need to be promoted. While the bureaucratic reform is necessary, it is also advisable to have entrepreneurial mode in the functioning of university. Besides, research base through doctoral programme should be strengthened. Old ways of doing things should give way to innovative ways.

The book also makes an attempt to understand the directions and growth process of higher education. It calls policy makers to initiate regulations that could bring higher education on to socially desirable path and explore institutional reforms that will motivate the stakeholders—teachers, administrators and planners—to institutionalize new practices to deal with change.

It has been the modest effort of the author to understand the regulatory aspect of policies in his professional career. He was immensely benefited from discussions at the level of senior academic and administrative leaders of higher education. However, consultative meets and workshops in different areas of higher education were based on experiences. The objective analyses and deeper analytical understanding on various themes required to be developed. The collection of papers in the book is author's endeavour to present a systematic thinking on the past developments and bring out a vision for future development trajectory in higher education. Papers were presented in seminars, workshops and policy discussions. The book is, therefore, an outcome of synthesis of ideas of the participants and the author.

It is indeed difficult to trace the influence of a single person or the group on the author's mind. However, I am indebted to each and everyone with whom I had the opportunity to interact on various themes. In particular, I would like to acknowledge the faculty of National University of Educational Planning and Administration (NUEPA) for providing an academic ambience that helped me in shaping this volume. Throughout the period Dr Vijay Vrat Arya has been working with me in research projects and has facilitated in completing the work.

CHAPTER 1

Introduction

Prime Minister Dr Man Mohan Singh, in his opening remark at the launch of the Knowledge Commission, on August 2, 2005, posed a challenge for the Knowledge Commission: How to create a second wave of institution-building and of excellence in the field of education, research and capability building in India so that we are better prepared for the 21st century? His reference to the first wave of institution-building in higher education by the first Prime Minister of India Pt. Jawahar Lal Nehru was a reminder of his vision to prepare the youth of India in higher education institutions for meaningful participation in the industrial revolution that he launched in the second plan. Prime Minister Singh's reference to the past makes us believe that higher education needs to be reconstructed from the past. His reference to the second wave means that something new needs to be reconstituted to prepare the youth now to meaningfully participate in the emerging knowledge economy by reconstructing the past. He thus implicitly assumes that state will once again come forward to invest in institutions of excellence. This provides a great hope and basic assumption for the book for setting the agenda for the future.

An immediate challenge is to present a vision for the future. If second wave is interpreted to mean paradigm shift, as it is sometimes argued, how does the past legacy support or inhibit the progress on the second wave? What needs to be given up? What elements of the past need to be remodelled? What needs to be introduced afresh? Reflections on these questions will provide insights to the issue of institution-building, new sets of policies, role of state and planning, new initiatives and programmes. Needless to say, components of second wave require us to learn from past, in fact, evaluate the past development, assess the present strengths and weaknesses and given this understanding plan for the future on the basis of realistic assumptions for preparing India for knowledge economy.

The objective of the book is to analyse the post-independent phase of institution-building and provide some inputs to the second wave of institution-building in higher education. Higher education policy direction in India cannot afford, in changing times, to fight old ideological battle and be influenced by political judgements alone. It must take into account the changing realities of the present and the present realities be understood through an academic discourse. These discourses should lead us through to arrive at policy decisions to meet the challenges of future. The book is an attempt to give an account of discourse on some dimensions of higher education so that policy and practices provide a direction that could carry us through to build a strong India.

I
Future Trajectory over Past Growth: Quantitative Dimension

An important point is to visualize a future trajectory of higher education in India observing the past growth and current demand. The fact that enrolment in higher education in India is around 14 million, approximating a Gross Enrolment Ratio (GER) of over 10 per cent, through a vast network of over 20,000 colleges affiliated with universities is a tremendous feat of success. However, the vision of a strong India should take us very far from the present, as the industrialized world witnesses at present the gross enrolment ratio well above 50 per cent. Such target may be visualized in the next 20 years or so. However, near unanimity of 15 per cent GER in the terminal year of the 11th Plan (2011–12) amounts to raising enrolment from around 14 million to 21 million. It amounts to increasing the existing institutional capacity by one and a half time. The expansion of colleges and universities should be the foremost priority. The fundamental principle in the expansion should be the recognition of the primary responsibility of state. The private institutions should also play a role in expansion. However, a dominating role of private would create an imbalance. Such imbalance should not be allowed to creep in. Imbalance would aggravate divisiveness in society, as lesser participation of socially deprived sections in higher education would halt the upward social and economic mobility of such sections.

The future trajectory requires a substantial step up in the growth rate of enrolment, something like a compound growth rate of 9 per cent per annum during 11th Plan to realize the target GER of 15 per cent. The real challenge for the policy maker is to realize the large quantitative expansion and along the trajectory of growth to upgrade quality and also create inclusiveness. A critical mass of research workers need to be produced. There is no doubt that this requires an efficient and competitive higher education system where accountability of highest order needs to be maintained. Hence, a discussion on reform philosophy is called for.

Reform Philosophy

As the need for quantitative expansion of higher education is felt, the expansion must have some philosophy of education reforms. Should it be guided by institutional reform measures as determined by appropriate authorities or higher education should follow neo-liberal approach of education reform? In the former case the university system initiates reforms and the state actively supports the reforms through public investment. It is suggested that government should base its higher education reform in terms of institutionalizing the agenda of reforms relating to inclusion, quality, excellence, relevance and values to be created in the society. In the case, of latter, state is guided by the market principles of reform. In this case, market principle will achieve efficiency in the allocation of scarce resources. The competition is the mechanism to ensure the efficient allocation of resources. The notion of quality is closer to the concept of efficiency, performance and productivity.

The central theme of higher education recommendations of the National Knowledge Commission (NKC) is guided by the neo-liberal theories. The restructuring of higher education that it suggests is aimed at creating a synthesis of state with market. What is missing here is the element of synthesis of state with society's needs and priorities. University system in any country is guided by the ethics of maintaining a critical voice to the dominant order of the society. It is supposed to guide the society towards a social order that cares for the subordinates. The market paradigm that supports the dominant status of the people needs to be controlled through some reform agenda. State guided by the market principles, as under neo-liberal doctrine, will perpetuate the differentiation and hierarchy. Indian society is traditionally hierarchical and there should be efforts to reduce the hierarchy. Higher education system in India cannot afford to perpetuate the hierarchy. It is for this reason that neo-liberal recommendations of NKC cannot at present find favour. It is not the efficiency guided by the rules of market but the efficiency in terms of social priorities or goals that should form the basis of higher education reform (Jain, 2004).

The reform philosophy in higher education should, therefore, have strong plan component. The 11th Plan has given a well-deserved priority to the higher education sector. The size of the 11th Plan on higher education is expected to be roughly 10 times the size of the 10th Plan on higher education. In absolute terms, it amounts to an increase from around Rs 4,000 crore to around Rs 40,000 crore. Given an allocation of this magnitude, the institutional reform agenda needs to be properly understood.

Institutional Reform

Institutional reform is needed to upgrade quality. Quality is not a technical or efficiency related issue. Quality is a value related issue. It is also a social issue. It must reflect how efficiently higher education institutions promote diversity as a relevant social goal, employability as a relevant economic goal and democratic values as relevant political goal. Efficiency, competition and accountability are necessary. However, these categories need to be looked at not only from market principles.

Efficiency, competition and accountability are values that need to be deliberated upon and higher education system should adhere to these principles and ideals.[1]

The neo-liberal doctrine for quality improvement is driven by managerialism. The NKC argues that an expansion of higher education which provides students with choices and creates competition between institutions is going to be vital in enhancing accountability. Accountability is then supposed to improve the quality of higher education institutions in India. These include stringent information norms for educational institutions. Internal systems of evaluation, evaluation of teachers by students, peer evaluation of teacher by teacher are suggested to strengthen accountability in the teaching-learning process. It prefers hierarchy in the cadre of teachers through salary differential to attract talent. Level playing field for foreign and domestic institutions is supposed to enhance quality through competitiveness. It is noted that "information, along with competition, fostered by increased supply, will close the accountability loop". It thus favours individual rationality and denies collective rationality of the state. State can, however, create conditions for managerial rationality.

The above neo-liberal way of institutional reform is based on certain assumptions. It assumes that all actors (all students and all teachers) are homogeneous. It also assumes that all institutions (all colleges and all teachers) are homogeneous. Given market signals in terms of information, students will make choices about courses and colleges. Choice theoretic framework will promote courses and colleges through the demand and supply mechanism. Competition will then allow quality course and institutions to survive. Teachers too will respond to the information in terms of evaluations and adjust their behaviour and conduct through better choice of actions. It also assumes that all teachers have uniform facilities and privileges and there is no distinction between a teacher posted in a rural college and a teacher posted in an urban college.

As can be easily observed, above neo-liberal way of looking at higher education is not correct.[2] Perfect information does not exist. Students are from different backgrounds. They need differential support in terms of preferential treatment in admission, financial support and even pedagogic support. Rural and urban scenario needs to be differentiated. Students and teachers in both these set-ups may not respond to market-based signals. They need institutional support in varying manners. Students coming from agricultural labour families and those coming from high class families may arrive in the same college. This diverse situation will always require differential strategies.

The basis of institutional reform, therefore, has to be in terms of institutional mechanism. It has to be in terms of understanding diverse needs and priorities of the individual and the society. University Grants Commission (UGC) in the past has relied on scheme-based interventions. These interventions should be based on research input and implemented efficiently. In a country where differentiation and inequality is very high only institutional mechanisms can mitigate them. State have to be an active partner in institutional reform. Resources earmarked for the 11th Plan require strong institutional reform measures and it cannot be left on the vagaries of market.

Structural Reform

What enabling structure and strategy would facilitate expansion of such a high order? Can we carry on with the existing structure of higher education? Do we need to replace some of the older structures? It may be argued that institutional reform also requires structural reform. Knowledge Commission argues that multiple councils have functioned in the past as mere instruments of control without facilitating the expansion of quality institutions. Multiple councils lacked complete coordination among themselves resulting in license raj that presumably created obstruction for the growth of private institutions of high quality.

It is suggested by the Knowledge Commission to remove the entry barriers. "Entry through legislation alone, as at present, is a formidable barrier. The consequence is a steady increase in the average size of existing universities with a steady deterioration in their quality. The absence of competition only compounds problems" (NKC, 2006). The structural reform that it suggests relates to establishing an Independent Regulatory Authority for Higher Education (IRAHE). IRAHE shall be responsible for setting the criteria and deciding on entry. It would, in addition, license agencies to take care of accreditation.

Another structural change relates to affiliating system. It is said to be outdated. It is said to be cumbersome to manage. Affiliated colleges have hardly any autonomy. Universities find it difficult to assess performance of such a large number of students. A large restructuring is suggested by the Knowledge Commission in terms of Undergraduate Board of Education controlling undergraduate colleges. Structural reform is suggested to create large number of universities, large number of autonomous colleges, cluster of colleges as universities. The principle in restructuring is to remove entry barriers, remove control and provide autonomy so that a large space is created for innovativeness.

It is important to understand whether large restructuring on the lines suggested by the Knowledge Commission can be a practical solution. Can it be sustained? Should the restructuring in favour of decontrol not act against the deprived sections? The underlying idea in restructuring is decontrol and freedom in the entry and exit of educational institutions, entry subject only to the licensing conditions to be fulfilled. The idea of the restructuring of affiliated colleges is to reduce the university to the optimum size. Besides if large number of educational institutions are independently pursuing their goals then there will be greater choice of programmes and institutions for the students. On the other hand, the institutions' responsiveness to the students will increase and with this the accountability of teachers will also grow.

The structural reform is required for the second wave of institution-building. This can be hardly questioned? However, the structural reform is needed to build not only the post-industrial structure but also to reproduce the agricultural and industrial society. As different forms of structures—post-industrial, industrial and agricultural—exist the higher education structure has to be directed to meet the diverse needs. This societal and economy-based higher education needs to be constructed and not left to be determined through choice and competition model. The model of education required for a perfectly flexible labour market as in the case of a post-industrial society may require research universities. It may require the flexible curricula. It may also require student-centred learning strategies and networking among institutions. This education structure may require different governing principles guided more by managerialism. However, for a large agriculture and industrial structure that requires different levels of skill, the education structure has to provide for institutions that prepare students to be successfully integrated into the agriculture and industrial structures. The need for vocational courses, the need for specific profession-based courses can be fulfilled by directed efforts. The directed efforts for institutions may also be required for balanced geographical distribution. The challenge in the second wave of institution-building is to create differential structure to support a highly differentiated labour market. A higher education structure cannot be built to serve high wage and high skill labour market alone, even though creating a high skill is in itself a challenge. It means the state has to mediate the needs of market and the needs of society. This creates sometimes a dilemma for the state. Structural reforms needed for an education structure to meet the needs of a perfectly flexible market may be different and sometimes in conflict with the education structure that is needed to serve the diverse economic structure of the society. Strategies may also be quite different. For example, the strategies for private participation in higher education may vary in both the cases. Seeking private sector participation may be much easier in the former case, as the prospective high wage jobs will enable the private sectors to extract high fees from the students. It means that state has to restructure the institutions very carefully in serving through market-based reform process and through institution-building.

II
Chapter Outline

The book is divided into four sections. The first section is on growth patterns of higher education. The second section deals with emerging issues in higher education. The third section highlights the issues relating to reform process in higher education. The last section analyses the plan and finance of higher education in India.

Section I notes the growth patterns of higher education in India. Chapter 2 looks at the supply side in terms of institutional capacity, institutional mode and diversified disciplines in which university system has so far developed. It also looks at the distribution of general and professional colleges in different states. Enrolment by levels and disciplines are examined. The issue of inequitable access by social class and gender is examined. The chapter thus sums up the important issues arising from the quantitative expansion of higher education in India.

If the quality of higher education is not guaranteed along the path of expansion it would indeed be difficult to sustain the internal growth and the meaningful participation of India in a global economy. In the context of knowledge economy, university system needs to meet new challenges. The present set-up of university system needs to promote quality through competitiveness. Perspectives to promote quality differ widely. Chapter 3 examines varying perceptions of quality. The assessment of quality in Indian higher education is presented and the new perception in promoting quality through competition is analysed. The newer dimensions to the quality debate in international perspective that has percolated down to the higher education needs a systematic understanding. Understanding the context of newer quality debate is necessary to tune the higher education institutions and, in particular, to prepare the academic community to stand up to face new challenges.

Section II on 'Emerging Issues' appears from the policy perspective. The discourse on higher education in India has to understand and analyse the trends towards privatization, internationalization and liberalization. These emerging trends have their own dynamics. They threaten the public nature of higher education. However, no one can deny their presence in today's context. The best way to deal with these emerging issues is to present a right policy environment so that benefits are maximized and threats are put to the minimum.

In the second section three emerging issues are being analysed. The first deals with the process of privatization in higher education. From the point of view of policy there has been a failure to regulate private universities in India. Another sensitive issue relates to fees and admission in self-financing institutions. There has been legislative inaction resulting in judicial activism on these two issues. Chhattisgarh legislation in the year 2002 allowed the flood of private universities of sub-standard quality. Later, The Supreme Court of India (2005) in its historic judgment announced the closure of a large number of private universities which were found to be inferior in quality. Students enrolled in those universities suffered a great deal. Although the Government of India has published a Gazette Notification on December 27, 2003, UGC Establishment and Maintenance of Standards in Private Universities Regulations, 2003, yet the government has not been successful in regulating the standards and fees and admission. There are at present 23 private universities in India established under different Acts of state governments. There is a dilemma before UGC to recognize the private university as soon as it is established under the state act even without knowing much about the standard of such private university. The chapter highlights the legal and other dimensions of regulation of private universities with a view to sort out the issue with a consistent set of rules. The legislative action is needed sooner rather than later as the phenomenon of private universities is growing at a rapid pace.

Growth of self-financing professional colleges in India is a desirable trend in so far as government is not able to meet the growing demand for professional courses. However, the inelastic nature of the demand for professional courses gave rise to practices in admission and fees that cannot be justified beyond a point. For example, discriminatory admission practices and exorbitantly high fees charged from the students may have socially harmful effects in denying admission to meritorious and poor students. There is a long history of judicial intervention trying to settle the issue, each time with a new set of issues. The legislative inaction has again necessitated judicial activism. The fourth chapter under the emerging issues also brings to light fees and admission controversies for a settlement through a central legislation.

The second section then analyses the issues relating to internationalization of higher education in Chapter 5. Internationalization of higher education in India has led to the emergence of foreign universities in India. Quite often in partnership with private institutions in India foreign education providers are imparting education. The chapter reviews the genesis and growth of foreign universities in India. The findings of research study bring to light the mechanics of their operation and geographical and coursewise presence of foreign programmes in India. The analysis of their rationales and concerns shows that with suitable legislation, joint venture with reputed and accredited universities may be promoted. What is important from the point of view of public policy is to check the unrestricted growth, as it may distort the structure of higher education in favour of the elite. The issue is under active consideration of the Government of India as the draft bill on the entry of foreign universities is being discussed. From a policy perspective the important point is to develop a meaningful participation of reputed foreign universities with some of the central and state universities in India rather than allow the unrestricted growth in partnership with unrecognized private institutions.

Chapter 6 analyses another issue relating to foreign direct investment (FDI) in education. Those who argue in favour consider that FDI is necessary to supplement the public finance. They point out that both from the point of view of quality and competitiveness the foreign investment is desirable. The opponents argue that this will pose a threat to the public system as the FDI will promote commercialization.

There is an ambiguity in education policy over the issue of foreign direct investment (FDI) in education. At present, there is 100 per cent FDI in education through automatic route. Almost 100 per cent FDI in education is continuing with regulatory controls in education making it practically impossible to attract private foreign investment in education. Another fundamental issue is that private investment associated with FDI is not neutral. It challenges the public good nature of education and distorts the non-profit character of education. Hence, there is a contradiction in policy. In principle, there is no restriction in private foreign investment in education. Private foreign investment will flow in the country in order to secure a profit which is, however, not permitted in India. Another problem is that the empirical estimates on FDI in education are also not available, as RBI does not have classification by education with respect to FDI.

The emerging issues discussed in section two provide a different turn and twist to higher education. Even if a policy regime to regulate the activities exists there are certain effects that have permeated over to the public system of higher education. These call for a reform process in the Indian higher education. The reform agenda may be influenced by a philosophy of neo-liberal reform. National Knowledge Commission favours the approach and hence a discussion on the neo-liberal reform process is necessary. There are three major issues of reform—reform in governance of universities, academic reforms and improving the standard of doctoral research. The third section on reform process has four chapters which critically analyses the neo-liberal reform agenda and then takes up the issue of governance, academic reform and doctoral research one by one.

There is a neo-liberal reform agenda of higher education given in the recommendations of the National Knowledge Commission. Chapter 7 takes up the philosophy underlying the recommendations of Knowledge Commission. It provides the choice and competition model to improve the quality of higher education. It advocates the reduction in the barriers to entry and to improve the choice among students. Given the perfect information and market-induced system of accountability, it is expected that competition will improve the efficiency of higher education. Given this philosophy there are wide-ranging recommendations. The chapter critically examines the neo-liberal reform philosophy and the recommendations emanating therefrom.

The Yashpal Committee Report appointed by the Ministry of Human Resource Development has presented its report in June 2009. It is interesting to understand the comparative perspective within which the restructuring of higher education in India is being conceptualized in these reports. Chapter 8 shows how a complex picture is looked at from two different perspectives. In fact, the two world views of restructuring of higher education are presented in these reports. It indeed poses a serious policy dilemma in Higher Education in India. The report notes that dichotomies of higher education are precisely because there has been fragmentation of knowledge and hardly has there been attempt to understand the principle of universal knowledge. Unless this epistemological understanding of knowledge is clear, the renovation and rejuvenation of higher education cannot be even conceptualized.

Another issue of reform process relates to governance of universities, which is discussed in Chapter 9. Transformation from elite to mass higher education has led to the governance of universities through the bureaucratic machinery normally headed by the person of academic repute. The appointment of vice chancellor takes place through a committee appointed by the government. Government has, however, not put a competitive process of selection and as a result university is not always headed by the right person. The problem of governance of universities begins precisely from here. The bureaucratic governance of university then suffers from the usual problem of delays in decision-making. The university system is too centralized and too much effort is wasted in controlling the admission, examination, finance and so on. There is hardly a system of autonomy and accountability to generate internal pressure to improve quality in the colleges and university departments. There is a need to have a close look to change the system of governance of universities. Now universities have become a knowledge enterprise. The academic role of a teacher is fast-changing towards a learner centred approach. This demands a change in governance towards clear-cut autonomy and accountability. The leader heading the institution has to be innovative. Chapter 9 analyses some governance issues that need to be introduced.

The academic reform should be the top agenda in the restructuring of higher education. The choice-based credit system has many advantages. It provides flexibility with which a student can think of combining various optional subjects. The emerging knowledge paradigm requiring interdisciplinary ability can be fulfilled under choice-based credit system. Besides, quality of education may be substantially enhanced if a student gets the chance to acquire partial credit from reputed institution in which it has specialization. It provides an up-to-date record of progress towards a degree and a plan for student's entire educational experience. It is thus cost-effective system that reduces dropouts and raises the internal efficiency of the education system. The teaching learning process needs a paradigm shift in terms of learner centred approach. Teachers through the training programmes need to be exposed to the paradigm shift in the teaching learning process. A two-pronged approach to enhance the quality should be taken up—promotion of excellence in select institutions and institutional reform measures—to prepare the ground for promoting excellence in average institutions. Future directions in higher education call for investment in quality on the basis of institutional assessment and planning. State commitment to provide financial resources for the same should be total. Chapter 10 analyses the process of academic reform in higher education in India.

The place of doctoral study in the research management assumes importance in the context of knowledge society. Doctoral level research is the chief instrument through which universities allow to cultivate knowledge and disseminate it through two domains—teaching and research. The research emerging from universities should be viewed as primarily contributing to national development. The objective of the present chapter is to examine the doctoral practices in universities in India. Given the primary role of doctoral research, the recognition of the importance and enhanced funding at the policy level is desired. Of great importance is the fact that universities plan a structural reform and introduce best practices to promote the standards of doctoral research. This would provide a firm basis to support the quality of teaching and research in universities and support the knowledge management of a country in a much more fundamental way. The last chapter in section three on academic reform explores the various facets of doctoral programme and suggests some ways in which the doctoral research can be improved.

Section IV analyses the plan support and financing of higher education. Deceleration in the public financing of higher education is symptomatic of a systemic crisis caused by the fiscal policy of the state. Its roots can be traced to the neo-liberal policies of the state. Deceleration in public funding has led to a huge investment gap in higher education and is affecting quality adversely. The shift in public policy in higher education requires new ways to approach issues of planning and finance of higher education. UGC should help to invest in strategic and priority areas and innovate instruments and institutions to mobilize resources for higher education. Institutional planning and finance should be the strategy to encourage institutions to intervene in the management of quality.

Notes

1. For a diagnostic understanding of higher education in India, see Jayaram (2007).
2. See Lauder et al. (1994); See Williams and Echols (1992) for the argument that choice and competition tend to lead to social class polarization and working class students will be trapped in schools and find themselves unable to enter university. It means marketization of education without strong state intervention will tend to produce low skill rather than high skill which is required for second wave of institution-building in the context of knowledge economy (see Hasley et al., 1980).

References

Halsey, A.H., A. Heath and J. Ridge (1980), *Origins and Destinations*, Clarendon, Oxford.

Jain, S.K. (2004), Education, Economic Efficiency and Social Values, Contemporary Issues and Ideas in Social Sciences, accessed from the website www.ciiss.net/ on February 15, 2005. Paper presented at Core Group Workshop on Science Education in India, held on March 22–24, 2007, at Homi Bhabha Centre for Science Education, Tata Institute of Fundamental Research, Mumbai.

Jayaram, N. (2007), "India", in James J.F. Forest and Philip G. Altbach, *International Handbook of Higher Education*, (Part two: *Regions and Countries*), Springer Netherlands.

Lauder, H. et al. (1994), The Creation of Market Competition for Education in New Zealand, Wellington Ministry of Education.

Williams, J. and F. Echols (1992), "Alert and Inert Clients: The Scottish Experience of Parental Choice of Schools", *Economics of Education Review*, 11, 339–350.

I

Growth Patterns of Higher Education

CHAPTER 2

Growth in Indian Higher Education System

Directions of development in higher education in the past were set by the commissions, committees and the national policies on higher education. The important components of development are the growth of universities and colleges that provide the institutional capacity of higher education. Institutional capacity of higher education is reflected in the growth of enrolments. The enrolments—aggregate as well as discipline-specific and by levels of education—the most important developments that need to be analysed. The role of women's participation in the development process is also reviewed. Another component is the growth of teachers in proportion to the growth of student enrolment. In short, the review of the quantitative aspects of the growth in Indian higher education system and issues arising therefrom are the central aims of the present chapter.

I
Directions of Development

Higher education in India has two phases. Pre-independence colonial phase set the beginning of modern higher education in 1854 with Wood's dispatch and creation of universities at Calcutta, Madras and Bombay in 1857. Higher education remained elite institutions with a view to fulfil colonial agenda—social, political and economical. The post-independence phase marks the transition from elite to mass higher education. The first commission on higher education in the post-independence phase, popularly known as Radhakrishnan Commission (1950), that completed its task in a short span of time from December 1948 to August 1949, is a truly remarkable piece of literature on higher education with its recommendations covering all aspects of higher education right from the aims of university education in independent India to the standard of teaching, courses of study, postgraduate training and research, professional education, rural education, women's education, examination and finance. It provided a definite direction amidst uncertainties as even the Constitution of India was not adopted by the time the report was published. Significantly, the recommendations of the first commission for the formation of University Grants Commission (UGC), to regulate the standards of higher education, was later fulfilled with UGC Act, 1956, granting UGC, established in 1953, a statutory status. Since then the history of higher education at the policy and planning level was, in a way, the history of initiatives and programmes of UGC based on numerous committees, Kothari Commission recommendations and the government policy on education. The period between 1956, the statutory status to the UGC and the establishment of Education Commission in 1964 under the chairmanship of D.S. Kothari was the period of supporting the expansion of colleges and universities established under central and state legislation.[1]

Another important event in the history of education and higher education, in particular, was the establishment of Kothari Commission (1964–66) that made its recommendations on all aspects of higher education—both academic and administrative, as well as on the roles of the UGC. What directions were set by the commission? The detailed discussion on higher education is covered Chapter XI to Chapter XVI. The major issue in the wake of expansion was the issue of 'governance of universities' that could facilitate quality in teaching, research, extension as well as the development of science, vocational and technical education that could successfully support the industrial development of the country. The issue of the autonomy of university, the role and appointment of the Vice-chancellor and expansion of affiliated colleges to fulfil the demand and the coordination and maintenance of standards were issues of critical importance. In particular, Kothari Commission recommended closing up any fragmentation that occurred within higher education and suggested professional councils in agriculture, engineering, medicine to coordinate the developments within a particular sector and coordination between different councils and UGC. Kothari Commission felt that "in view of the magnitude and importance of the problem facing the Commission considerably larger funds will have to be made available to enable it to deal effectively with them" (p. 345). It suggested that 6 per cent of the national income be devoted to education—a point that was endorsed by the National Policy on Education, 1968—but a dream that is yet to be realized. The National Policy on Education, 1968 also endorsed the 10+2+3 pattern of education. It noted very briefly, yet emphatically, the provision of essential facilities for maintaining high standards of universities, promotion of postgraduate courses, centres of advanced study and increased support to research in universities.

Various committees set up by the governments and the UGC also determined the directions in which the higher education moved. Sen Committee (UGC, 1974) submitted its report on the issue of minimum qualifications for lecturers and their pay scales. V.S. Jha Committee (1974–77) reviewed the functioning of UGC with regard to coordination and determination of standards of higher education. There were also a number of conferences of Vice-chancellors convened by the UGC and the government to decide a number of issues such as admission and facilities for weaker sections, role and responsibility of teachers, autonomous colleges, on women's participation etc. Committees that deserve mention in the area of management of universities were D.S. Kothari on Model Act for Universities (1964), P.B. Gajendragadkar Committee on Governance of Universities and Colleges (1971), A. Gnanam Committee on Towards New Educational Management (1990), Soneri Committee on Review of Gnanam Committee Recommendations (1995) and P.C. Alexander Committee on the Role of the Governor as Chancellor of the Universities (1997) (Approved, 2003).

Consultation with the state governments was ensured through the Central Advisory Board of Education, an apex body, which constituted various committees from time to time to consider their recommendations. The latest two such committees were on the financing of universities and on the issue of autonomy in higher education.

In the financing of higher education two committees—one on central universities, under the chairmanship of Justice K. Punnayya (UGC, 1993), and another on technical education institutions under the chairmanship of D. Swaminathan (AICTE, 1994), to outline methods of mobilization of resources for higher education deserve special mention. Both committees stressed the importance of state financing of higher education and suggested ways for non-governmental sources of finance. Other recommendations that attracted the attention of the government include: (i) raising fee levels, (ii) raising of resources by the institutions through consultancy, and sale of other services, (iii) introduction of self-financing courses and (iv) introduction/revitalization of student loans. The trend towards privatization reflected in the approach to financing was rather supported by Ambani and Birla (2000) that vehemently supported out and out privatization of higher education.

An important milestone and the last word is the prevailing National Policy on Education, 1986. Concept of autonomy was given a big push through developing autonomous colleges and postgraduate department's autonomy. Greater flexibility to the courses was permitted. Teaching methods, teachers' orientation, assessment of teachers were to receive priority. Delinking of degree from job and the rural university were to be set up.

It is no secret that the official policy treats higher education as a non-commercial and social activity, yet the current trends defy it. The conflict came to the surface when attempts were made to contain commercialization. The Supreme Court had to interfere time and again to allow privatization without commercializing education. Recently, the Supreme Court of India (2005) created another controversy on the issue of reservation in private unaided institutions. There seems to be tension and the official policy on higher education demands a fresh round of discussions in the wake of events overtaking higher education in recent years on the grounds of commercialization, internationalization of higher education, potentials of knowledge economy and also to realize the potentials of ICT revolution.

II
Assessing the Past

Access

Expansion of Institutional Capacity

At the time of independence in 1947 there were only 20 universities in the country and this increased to 440 in 2007 denoting a 22-fold increase over the period of 60 years. During the 10th Plan period, the expansion of institutional capacity in terms of the increase in universities is given in Table 2.1. During the 10th Plan, six central universities, 73 state universities, 52 deemed universities and 23 private universities have been added. State universities have grown at the rate of 41 per cent whereas the deemed universities have grown at the rate of 100 per cent. The expansion of deemed and private universities is the marked feature of the recent years during 10th Plan (see Table 2.1).

Table 2.1

Growth of Universities in the 10th Plan

No.	Category	Universities: As on March 31, 2002	Universities: As on September 2007
1.	Central	18	24
2.	State	178	251
3.	Deemed	52	104
4.	Institutions (Est. by State Legislative Act)	05	5
5.	Institutions of National Importance (Est. by Central Legislation	12	33
6.	Private University		23
7.	Total	265	440

Source: UGC Annual Reports 2002–03, UGC, New Delhi and MHRD (2007–08).

Universities by Types of Disciplines

Distribution of central and state universities into major disciplines show that out of 237 universities, 126 universities are in general disciplines, although some of them may have affiliating technical and professional colleges as well. There are 35 agricultural universities followed by 14 technological, 11 language, 11 open, 9 medical, 6 law, 5 women, 4 animal and fishery universities (see Table 2.2). It shows the university system has diversified into many disciplines—a trend that needs to be encouraged. Furthermore, the government must support the large scale expansion of state universities to have a balanced growth of universities, public as well as private and general as well as professional.

Among the deemed universities there is greater diversification. Apart from majority being in technological disciplines, there are universities in specific research areas such as English and foreign language, yoga, brain research, dairy research, mines, basic science, neuro science, physical education, fisheries, economics and politics, development research, armament technology, population science, social science, IT, management, education, home sciences, rural studies, music, veterinary research, forest research, drama, planning and architecture, foreign trade, educational planning and administration.

Growth of private deemed universities has been lately the result of restricted growth of state universities, however, the diversification of deemed universities in diversified disciplines has been, in a way, a new sign of growth in a knowledge society. In the context of promotion of deemed universities, the University Grants

Table 2.2

Distribution of Central and State Universities into Types of Disciplines

Type	*Number*	*Per cent*
General	126	54
Agricultural	35	15
Technological	14	6
Language	11	5
Medical	9	4
Law	6	2.6
Woman	5	1.3
Animal and Fishery	4	1.7
Open	11	5
Others	16	5.7
Total	237	100

Source: UGC Annual Report, 2004–05, UGC, New Delhi.

Commission needs to take the utmost care in the selection of quality institutions and further monitoring the progress in the maintenance of standards.

Optimum Size of a University

The average deviation in enrolment of Indian universities is very high. There are some universities with over half a million enrolments and some with even enrolments in hundreds and thousands. The average deviation in the number of colleges in state universities is also very high ranging from over 500 colleges to few colleges. There is no standardization in the size of universities as regulated structure of higher education did not allow market forces to operate to achieve standardization or the optimum size of universities both in terms of enrolment and in the number of affiliated colleges.

The 11th Plan notes that UGC in consultation with stakeholders determine the optimum size of university. Optimum size of a university leads to achieving efficiency in resources, besides, small size of university helps in effective monitoring of the colleges. A college may be granted autonomy and universities may effectively monitor through performance indicators.

Research finding tells us very little on the optimum size of university or the college. Hence, a norm may be considered to determine the optimum size of university. At all-India level, as

Table 2.3

Number of Universities Required

Criteria		*Restructuring, 2005*		*Projection by 2012*	
		Total	*Additional*	*Total*	*Additional*
Enrolment Criteria	(i) 20,000 per university	646	309	1072	735
	(ii) 30,000 per university	430	93	715	378
College Criteria	(i) 20 colleges per university	585	248	—	—
	(ii) 30 colleges per university	389	52	—	—
Population Criteria	(i) one university per 2 lakh population in 18–24 year age	619	282	715	378

Note: The year for restructuring is taken to be 2005, as enrolment figure was available till 2005.

per Selected Educational Statistics (SES) 2005–06, the total number of universities was 337 and total enrolments 12.9 million, yielding an average enrolment of 38363 students. Statewise range in average enrolment per university was 4060 in Arunachal Pradesh to 60,224 in Andhra Pradesh. No doubt, if we look at the range universitywise, it will be much higher than statewise range in average enrolment per university. Different norms may be considered for optimum size of university.

Under enrolment criteria using norm (i) and norm (ii), it was estimated that the numbers of universities required were 646 and 430 respectively by 2005. Hence under restructuring of university, additional 309 universities and additional 93 universities under norm (i) and (ii) respectively will be required under present restructuring. Required number of additional universities, after restructuring, during the 11th Plan will be 735 by norm (i) and 378 by norm (ii). On the basis of number of colleges per university criteria under norm (i) and norm (ii), 248 and 52 additional universities respectively will be required.

If we take population criteria, 282 additional universities under restructuring by 2005 and 378 additional universities by 2012 will be required.

Under restructuring, the larger number of state universities should be created by any of the following strategies:

1. Large universities should give rise to few independent universities.
2. Smaller universities should be merged to form a single university.
3. Cluster of colleges may come together to form a university.
4. Private deemed university and private state universities may be established.

An important point that follows from the above analysis is that in the restructuring of universities there should be an effort towards optimizing the size of university to have effective governance. It should be kept in mind that quantitative estimates of expansion on the basis of optimality has its own limitation. Optimality should be broadly looked of from the point of view of critical number of teachers, departments, disciplined within a university for knowledge generation and sharing.

Number and Distribution of Colleges

Table 2.4 shows the growth of colleges during the 10th Plan. There were 15,437 colleges in 2002 and this increased to 18,064 in 2006. Of these, about 14,400 colleges (79%) of arts, science and commerce are under the purview of the UGC. However, only 42 per cent of these colleges falling under the purview of UGC are included under the 2(f) and 12(B) of the UGC Act and are entitled for funding support under UGC plan grant. Nearly 92 per cent of the colleges included under 12(B) of the UGC Act received X plan grant support. It is also important to note that only 2,780 colleges have been accredited by National Assessment and Accreditation Council (NAAC) by March 2005.

Table 2.4

Number of Colleges in 2002 and 2006

S.No.	*Category*	*As on January 1, 2002*	*As on March 31, 2006*	*Per cent of Previous Row*
1.	Total	15,437	18,064	
2.	Under UGC purview (Arts, Science and Commerce)	11,128	14,400	79.72
3.	Included u/s 2(f) UGC Act		6,109	42.42
4.	Included u/s 12(B) UGC Act		5,525	90.44
5.	Funded by UGC X plan		5,068	91.73
6.	Accredited by NAAC		2,780	37.1

Source: UGC (undated).

It may be noted from the above table that a vast majority of the colleges are under the purview of the UGC but not recognized by UGC under section 2(f) of UGC Act. Limited coverage of the colleges recognized by the UGC poses a great challenge for the UGC in respect of maintenance of standard.

Distribution of Colleges in Terms of Management

There is no published information on distribution of colleges in terms of management. There are colleges fully funded and managed by the government, colleges partly funded and privately managed and the colleges fully funded and managed by the private. All such colleges have to be affiliated by the universities.

Guesstimates suggest that majority of colleges in technical and professional disciplines in recent years have been under private management as well as fully financed by the private. In general education, majority of colleges are government and private but aided by the government. However, in recent years, the resource constraint has forced the government to restrict the expansion of colleges under general education.

Distribution of Colleges in Different States

There are some distinguishing features in the distribution of colleges in different states. There is a north-south imbalance in the number of colleges in general, technical and professional disciplines.

Three categories of the institutions have been identified in Table 2.4. States having chronic deficit of colleges in (i) arts, science and commerce colleges; (ii) engg., tech., and arch. colleges; and (iii) medical colleges (allopathy/ayurvedic/homeopathy/unani/nursing/pharmaceuticals) have been identified. Further, states having moderate deficit of colleges in above disciplines have also been identified. To remove regional imbalance, chronic and moderate deficit states need to be given proper focus in respective disciplines.

The following conclusions emerge:[2]

1. There are few states/UT, which do not have higher education institutions in respective disciplines.
2. States/UTs like (i) Sikkim, Daman & Diu, Delhi, Tripura, West Bengal, Jharkhand, Jammu & Kashmir are having chronic deficit in arts, science and commerce colleges; (ii) Bihar, Chhattisgarh, Assam, Jharkhand, Uttaranchal, Himachal Pradesh, Tripura, Jammu & Kashmir, Manipur are having chronic deficit in engineering, technical, and archeological Colleges; and (iii) Chhattisgarh, Uttaranchal, Uttar Pradesh, West Bengal, Assam, Bihar, Tripura, Jharkhand, Haryana, Manipur are having chronic deficit in medical colleges (allo/ayur/homeo/unani/nurs./pharm.)
3. States/UTs like (i) Uttar Pradesh, Andman & Nicobar Islands, Uttaranchal, Tamil Nadu, Haryana, Gujarat, Punjab are having deficit in arts, science and commerce colleges;

(ii) Uttar Pradesh, Orissa, West Bengal, Gujarat, Rajasthan, Madhya Pradesh, Arunachal Pradesh, Delhi are having deficit in engg., tech., and arch. Colleges; (iii) Orissa, Rajasthan, Madhya Pradesh, Delhi, Jammu & Kashmir, Andhra Pradesh, Gujarat are having deficit in medical colleges (allo/ayur/homeo/unani/nurs./pharm.).

Teachers

The total number of teachers in 2005–06 is 4.88 lakh and the student-teacher ratio works out to be 23. The student-teacher ratio is 18 in the university departments and colleges and 23 in the affiliated colleges. The average enrolment per college is 532 (see Table 2.5).

Table 2.5

Number of Teachers and Institutions of Higher Education, 2004–05

Institution	*Enrolment*	*Teachers*	*Colleges*	*Student-teacher ratio*	*Students per college*
University Depts and University Colleges	14,26,793	78,819		18	
Affiliated Colleges	96,01,227	4,09,184	18,064	23	532
Total	1,10,28,020	4,88,003	18,064	23	

Source: UGC Annual Report, 2005–06, New Delhi.

The distribution of student-teacher ratio in some of the NAAC accredited colleges show that the distribution is highly uneven among high and low grade colleges. For example student-teacher ratio in A and above grade colleges is 20.4, whereas it is as high as 28.5 in all C grade colleges. The student-teacher ratio of permanent teachers is 29.8 in A and above grade colleges. It goes upto 38 in B grade colleges (see Table 2.6). It clearly suggests that there is the shortage of permanent teachers in even high grade colleges. The availability of highly qualified teachers is the most important index of high access and quality. There is the need to reverse this situation by recruiting permanent teachers to the colleges.

Table 2.6

Distribution of Student-Teacher Ratio in the NAAC Accredited Colleges

	NAAC Grades					
Indicators	*A & Above*	*B++ & B+*	*B only*	*C++,C + & C*	*Non-Accredited*	*Total*
No. of Sample Colleges	110	547	298	233	285	1473
STR (Student-Teacher Ratio)	20.4	31.8	28.6	28.5	25.2	25.0
STR by Permanent Teachers	29.8	31.8	38.1	35.8	35.6	33.5

Source: UGC (Unpublished) Analysis of Self-Assessment Report of NAAC Accredited Colleges.

Enrolment

Growth of higher education in India can be looked at both from supply as well as the demand side. In terms of the supply side what needs to be ascertained is that all those who have passed senior secondary and are eligible and willing to join higher education must have an access to the institutions of higher education. Secondly, the growth of higher education, both in terms of number and diversification, must meet the growing manpower needs of the economy and society. This means that higher education has supply side backward linkages with school education and forward linkages with economy in terms of supplying skilled manpower to the economy including the well-qualified teachers to the education sector itself. NSS 55th round (1999–2000) informs that 55 per cent of all those eligibles who have passed senior secondary get entry into higher education whereas large number of students do not find themselves in the temples of higher learning. This section sums up the growth of higher education in terms of enrolment by levels and disciplines.

There are three different sources of enrolment/attendance in higher education institutions:

(a) Selected Educational Statistics (SES), MHRD, Government of India: It provides annual enrolment of students by levels (doctorate, postgraduate, graduate, diploma/certificate) and streamwise enrolment (arts, science, commerce, engineering and technology, medicine, teacher education and others) in colleges and universities and enrolment in diploma/certificate courses in polytechnics, teacher training schools and institutions such as arts and crafts including industrial trade for boys and girls. It also reports enrolment in distance education in IGNOU and 11 state open universities.

(b) Census: It provides decennial information on persons of specific age attending college education (UG and PG) in universities or private institutions (recognized or unrecognized) and vocational education. Vocational education includes degree, diploma and certificate in technical/professional courses. Census definition of higher education is very wide and embraces all types of education—public, private, distance, certificate, diploma and degree.

(c) National Sample Survey (NSS): It provides data on educational attainment and enrolment in its different rounds—38th (1983), 43rd (1987–88), 50th (1993–94), 55th (1999–2000) and 60th (2003–04). The different rounds may not be strictly comparable due to definitional variation.

Enrolment by Levels and Major Disciplines (SES)

Table 2.7 sums up the enrolment by levels of education from selected educational statistics. The total enrolment in higher education is 13.6 million that gives a GER of over 10 per cent in 2005–06. The total enrolment in doctorate and postgraduate is 36,519 and 8,64,862 respectively. It shows a rather low research base in relation to the total enrolment in higher education. Technical education has grown at 29 per cent as compared to a declining growth rate of 1.4 per cent for general graduate education during the period 2001–02 to 2005–06. Enrolled technical graduates are 21.8 lakh as opposed to 67.41 lakh general education enrolment in 2005–06. Added to this is the 6.9 lakh diploma enrolment.

Table 2.7

Enrolment by Levels and Major Disciplines

Year	*Ph.D.*	*PG*	*General Graduate (Art, Science & Commerce)*	*Technical Graduate (Engg., Medical, B. Ed)*	*Total Higher Education Degree (2+3+4+5)*	*Diploma (Polytechnics, Teacher Training Schools, Tech. Indus., Arts & crafts school)*	*Total Higher Education (Degree, Diploma) (6+7)*
1	2	3	4	5	6	7	8
1980–81	25,417	2,91,341	18,86,428	2,39,267	24,42,453	4,30,126	28,72,579
1990–91	32,468	3,54,216	32,85,776	4,16,828	40,89,288	7,96,686	48,85,974
2000–01	45,004	6,47,338	72,44,915	6,88,625	86,25,882	9,87,279	96,13,161
2001–02	53,119	6,47,016	71,39,497	7,90,050	86,29,682	11,04,594	97,34,276
2002–03	65,357	7,82,590	76,33,125	10,35,701	95,16,773	11,99,785	1,07,16,558
2003–04	65,525	8,06,636	80,26,147	11,10,840	1,00,09,148	11,91,447	1,12,00,595
2004–05	55,352	7,90,267	67,28,029	11,08,549	86,82,197	12,54,890	99,37,087
2005–06	36,519	8,64,862	67,41,592	21,87,097	1,29,28,180	6,90,959*	1,36,19,139

Includes only polytechnic.

Source: MHRD (various years) Selected Educational Statistics, Government of India, New Delhi.

Table 2.8 sums up different percentages that present a glimpse of growth pattern in different disciplines as well as the levels of higher education. The graduate enrolment as a proportion to total enrolment is increasing except for the last year, the postgraduate enrolment as a proportion to total enrolment is decreasing in the past 25 years. The proportion of doctorate to postgraduate enrolment is also declining indicating a lower level of transition to research. Science and technology graduates as a proportion to total graduates has declined from 32 per cent in 1980 to 29 per cent in 2003 and has gone up in the last two years as a result of surge in technical graduates. Recent years, however, show a decline in science graduates to total science graduates including technical ones. The ratio of technical to total graduates was 8 per cent in 1980 and it has gradually gone upto 22 per cent as a result of increasing enrolment in engineering. It is important to note that the demand for teachers is high, yet the proportion of B.Ed. enrolment to total general graduates is declining and is currently at 3 per cent. The fall in vocational enrolment to total higher education enrolment is yet another area of concern for the planners and managers of higher education.

Table 2.8

Enrolment Ratios by Levels and Major Disciplines (%)

Year	*Graduate/ Total*	*PG/ Total*	*Ph.D/ PG*	*Science Graduate (B.Sc.+B E+ MBBS)/ Total Graduates*	*BSc/Total Science Graduate*	*Technical Graduates/ Total Graduate*	*B.Ed/ (B.A+ B.Sc+ B.com)*	*Diploma Vocational/ Total Higher Education*
1980	87	12	9	32	75	8	4	18
1990	91	9	9	29	70	9	3	19
2000	92	8	7	25	71	7	2	11
2001	92	7	8	27	68	9	2	13
2002	91	8	8	28	63	11	2	13
2003	91	8	8	29	62	11	2	12
2004	90	9	7	31	61	12	2	13
2005	69	7	4	40	44	22	3	5

Note: Above percentages are calculated from the figures in SES, MHRD, Government of India.

Source: MHRD (various years).

Statewise Enrolment in Higher Education

Another interesting aspect of enrolment projection is its statewise disaggregated target. At present, there is a large

Table 2.9

GER for All States in 2005 and 2012

	2005 Actual GER	*2012 Projected GER*
States having less than 10 per cent GER	D & N Haveli (0%), Lakshadweep (0%), Daman Diu (1.9%), A & N Islands (5.6%), Bihar (5.7%), Tripura (6.3%), Arunachal Pradesh (6.6%), Assam (6.7%), Rajasthan (7.1%), Jammu & Kashmir (7.2%), West Bengal (7.8%), Jharkhand (8.1%), Chhatisgarh (8.5%), Orissa (8.9%), Uttar Pradesh (9.1%), Nagaland (9.4%) and Kerala (9.9%)	D & N Haveli (0%), Lakshadweep (0%), Daman Diu (2.3%), A & N Islands (7.6%), Bihar (7.8%), Tripura (9.2%), Arunachal Pradesh (9.6%) and Assam (9.6%)
States having GER between 10 to 15 per cent	India (10.4%), Haryana (10.5%), Madhya Pradesh (10.9%), Mizoram (11%), Punjab (11%), Gujarat (11.2%), Sikkim (11.4%), Goa (11.6%), Maharashtra (12%), Manipur (12.4%), Karnataka (12.4%), Andhra Pradesh (12.9%), Meghalaya (13.7%), Himachal Pradesh (13.9%) and Tamil Nadu (14%)	Rajasthan (10%), J & K (10.3%), West Bengal (11.5%), Jharkhand (11.6%), Chhatisgarh (12.1%), Uttar Pradesh (13%), Orissa (13.1%), Nagaland (13.6%), Kerala (14.6%) and Haryana (14.9%)
States having GER between 15 to 20 per cent	Uttaranchal (15.1%)	India (15%), Madhya Pradesh (15.5%), Mizoram (16%), Punjab (16%), Gujarat (16.1%), Sikkim (16.7%), Goa (16.7%), Maharashtra (17.3%), Manipur (17.9%), Karnataka (18.1%) and Andhra Pradesh (19.2%)
States having GER greater than 20 per cent	Pondicherry (21.8%) and Delhi (32.2%)	Meghalaya (20%), Himachal Pradesh (20.2%), Tamil Nadu (20.6%), Uttaranchal (21.5%), Pondicherry (31.4%) and Delhi (45.8%)

Note: Calculated from different rounds of Selected Educational Statistics.

variation in the GER of different states. If we assume an annual enrolment growth rate of 7.5 per cent across all states, still many states will not be able to achieve even 10 per cent GER by 2011–12. The overall scenario is presented in Table 2.9. The point to note is that in achieving over all GER of 15 per cent, statewise disaggregated target should not be overlooked.

Census Enrolment Ratio

Census provides information on the attendance of higher education in colleges and vocational education. Census results show that on a wider definition of higher education (degree, diploma and certificate in post senior secondary stage) the GER in higher education has gone upto a level of 13.82 per cent in 2001 (Table 2.10).

Table 2.10

Enrolment in Higher Education (Census)

Year	*College (lakh)*	*Vocational (lakh)*	*Total (lakh)*	*GER (18–23 years) per cent*
1991	102.2	3.8	106	10.95
2001	144.3	16.6	160.9	13.82

Note: UGC (undated) Results of unpublished research studies (unpublished), New Delhi.

NSS Enrolment Ratio

As per the NSSO figures, the total enrolments in higher education in 2003–04 are 161.1 lakh, giving GER of 13.22 per cent (Table 2.11). NSS results show the enrolments in technical

Table 2.11

Enrolment in Higher Education (NSS)

Year	*Graduate & above*	*Technical/ Vocational*	*Total*	*GER*
1983	51.1	7.8	58.9	7.67
1987–88	65.0	9.17	74.1	8.57
1993–94	65.7	24.55	90.2	8.85
1999–00	85.7	25.23	110.9	10.08
2003–04	NA	NA	161.1	13.22

Note: NA: Not available.

Source: UGC (undated) Results of unpublished research studies (unpublished), New Delhi.

education have shot up in the 1990s. Aggregate enrolment in higher education given in NSS is closer to the census result.

Rural-Urban disparity in higher education is no less glaring. As per NSS estimates, the GER in rural area was 7 per cent as opposed to 27 per cent of GER in urban area in 2003–04. The disparity needs to be addressed by promoting rural colleges and universities for a balanced development of higher education in India.

Problems with Different Databases

The SES under-estimates enrolment rates because of the under-reporting of enrolment in private (recognized and unrecognized) institutions and also due to non-reporting of enrolment data on an annual basis by some of the state governments and other ministries and councils. Extrapolations are used to fill the gaps arising from non-reporting by some of the states. The problem with the NSS and also census data is that it is collected from households and it is likely to overestimate the student enrolment in colleges and universities as it might include those who are doing diploma or training programmes (e.g., computer training) in unrecognized institutions also. A further problem with the population census data is that it does not distinguish between enrolment in professional degree and diploma programmes. Database of higher education needs to be reliable in terms of coverage of all disciplines as well as reporting from various sources.

Table 2.12

Gross Enrolment Ratio in Higher Education

Country	*GER (in 2004)*
India	11
Australia	72
China	19
Malaysia	29
Philippines	29
France	56
Germany	51(2002)
UK	60
USA	82

Source: UNESCO (2006), pp. 120–129.

Comparative Scenario

The results of GER from different countries show that developing countries in South East Asia have attained much higher

GER. Developed countries have GER invariably above 50 per cent. India, therefore, cannot afford to remain in the low range of GER.

Inequitable Access to Higher Education

An important aspect of widening access is the equal participation by diverse social and economic groups.

Table 2.13 gives the Net Enrolment Ratio (NER) of different social groups in 1999–2000. It shows that at the primary level there was a wide gap in achieving universal education. The NER goes on declining at middle, secondary and higher levels of education. The important observation is the wide disparity that exists between different social groups at all the levels of education. At the higher education level, the NER of SC and ST—the most deprived social groups is 4.8 per cent and 5.2 per cent respectively. The NER of backward castes at 6.3 per cent is closer to those of SCs and STs. The NER of general category is 14.6 per cent. The extent of disparity in the participation in higher education among social groups turns out to be quite large.

Table 2.13

Net Enrolment Rates (%) Social Groups Based on NSS

	Total	*ST*	*SC*	*OBC*	*General*
6–10 (Primary)	70.8	61.0	67.3	70.1	76.8
11–13 (Middle)	44.6	35.0	38.7	43.4	51.6
14–17 (Sec.)	34.2	25.4	26.6	31.7	42.8
18–23 (Higher)	8.9	5.2	4.8	6.3	14.6

Source: Result of UGC sponsored study conducted by Shrivastava (2007), unpublished.

A detailed picture on access to higher education based on social and religious groups was also analysed recently by different authors[3] (see Sundaram, 2006; Deshpande and Yadav, 2006; Rana and Mehta, 2006). There are differences in the degree of under representation in all the three analyses. The data clearly shows that "Only a little more than 1 per cent of STs, SCs and Muslims are graduates in the age group of 20 years or above in rural India, while the figure for Hindu upper castes is four to five times higher at over 5 per cent. The real inequalities are in urban India, where the SCs in particular, but also Muslims, OBCs and STs, are way behind the forward communities and castes with a quarter or more of their population being graduates" (Deshpande and Yadav, 2006). Thorat (2006) shows that rural-urban, social group, religion and gender are the four important dimensions along which the differences in access to higher education may be noted. For example, in terms of religious group Muslims recorded an NER of 6.30 per cent, whereas Hindus registered an NER of 9 per cent. Among the rural poor the GER is 1.3 per cent, whereas the urban non-poor have achieved a level of 27.15 per cent GER—again showing a wide disparity. In terms of the category of households there may be found to exist wide disparities, say among casual labour and agricultural labour, on the one hand, and regular wage and salary earners, on the other. The gender disparity is equally discernible in the participation of higher education. Inequitable access to higher education for different groups emerges as the marked feature of higher education in India.

Women in Higher Education

The participation of women in higher education has steadily increased from 10.9 per cent in 1950–51 to 40.04 per cent in

Table 2.14

Enrolment in Higher Education by Gender (Numbers and Percentage)

Year	*Women*		*Men*		*Total*
	Number	*Per cent*	*Number*	*Per cent*	
1950–51	43,126	10.9	3,53,619	89.1	3,96,745
1960–61	1,70,455	16.2	8,79,409	83.8	10,49,864
1970–71	6,55,822	21.9	23,45,470	78.1	30,01,292
1980–81	7,48,525	27.2	20,03,912	72.8	27,52,437
1991–92	16,85,926	32.0	35,79,960	68.0	52,65,886
1995–96	21,91,138	34.1	42,34,486	65.9	64,25,624
2002–03	36,95,965	40.05	55,31,868	59.05	92,27,833
2004–05	42,34,340	40.40	62,46,702	59.60	104,81,042

Source: SES different years, MHRD, Government of India, New Delhi.

2004–05. This shows that growth of higher education has overall reduced the gender bias considerably over a period of 53 years (see Table 2.14).

By Choice of Disciplines

There have also been shifts in women's choice of disciplines in higher education. Although the share of women's enrolment in total has gone up across all disciplines over the years, there are some disciplines such as commerce and science, traditionally the male bastion, where women have registered their presence over the years. In education, women have outnumbered the men. Further in engineering and technology women have made inroads from a very low base. However, in other professional disciplines, such as in law and agriculture, women's participation needs to be further promoted (see Table 2.15).

Table 2.15

Proportion of Women Students to Total Enrolment by Discipline/Subject (1950–51 to 2002–03)

Faculties	*1950–51*	*1960–61*	*1970–71*	*1980–81*	*1991–92*	*2004–05*
Arts	16.1	24.6	31.7	37.7	41.8	51.07
Science	7.1	10.5	17.8	28.8	32.9	20.08
Commerce	0.6	0.9	3.7	15.9	22.1	16.45
Education	32.4	32.8	36.5	47.3	50.2	1.86
Engg./Tech	0.2	0.9	1.0	3.8	7.6	4.15
Medicine	16.3	21.9	22.8	24.4	33.2	3.63
Law	2.1	3.0	3.7	6.9	11.0	1.62
Agriculture*	5.8	7.0	9.5	13.6	7.1	0.25
Vet. Science*					8.0	0.08
Others*					38.3	0.81

*Agriculture, veterinary science and others are merged for the years 1950–51 to 1980–81.

Source: Chanana (2004) and UGC (2005).

Percentage Distribution in Disciplines/Subjects

The percentage of women as proportion of total enrolment of women in higher education will reveal the disciplinary choices. It is noteworthy that in teacher education, considered to be a women's profession, the percentage has decreased from 3.1 per cent in 1950–51 to 1.8 per cent in 2002–03. In medicine too there is a decline from 5.8 per cent to 3.6 per cent. In commerce, their percentage has increased from 0.4 per cent in 1950–51 to 16.5 per cent in 2002–03. In engineering and technology too there is a significant increase from less than one per cent in 1950–51 to 4.2 per cent in 2002–03 and in law from 0.7 per cent to 1.7 per cent. It is a matter of concern that both men and women have withdrawn from science in their overall choice of disciplines (see Table 2.16).

Table 2.16

Percentage Distribution by Discipline and Gender 1951–2003

Discipline	*1950–51*		*2002–03*	
	Women	*Men*	*Women*	*Men*
Arts	67.9	43.2	51.1	41.0
Science	21.0	33.4	19.9	19.8
Commerce	0.4	9.6	16.5	19.0
Education	3.1	0.8	1.8	1.2
Engg./Tech	0.04	3.4	4.2	9.7
Medicine	5.8	3.6	3.6	3.0
Law	0.7	3.8	1.7	4.3
Agriculture*	1.1	2.2	0.3	0.8
Vet. Science*			0.1	0.2
Others*			0.8	0.9

*Agriculture, veterinary science and others are merged for the years 1950–51.

Source: Chanana, Karuna (2004).

Regional Disparities

Regional disparities in women's participation in higher education are rather more glaring. There are few states/UTs where women's enrolment outnumber men. Kerala has the distinction of the highest enrolment (60%), followed by Goa (58.5), Andaman and Nicobar Islands (57.77), Chandigarh (55.5), Punjab (52.68) and Pondicherry (52.60). Those with the lowest proportion are also the most backward; namely, Bihar

(23.81); Jharkhand (30.40); Chhatisgarh (36.70); Rajasthan (32.33); Uttar Pradesh (38.40); and Madhya Pradesh (37.20). In these provinces, the proportion is less than the all-India average of 40.05 per cent.[4] Southern regions for various socio-cultural factors have shown greater participation of women in engineering and technology and medicine.

III
Issues Arising from Past Growth

Issues Relating to Access

Universities

1. The state universities have grown over the years across specific disciplines such as agriculture, language, technology, medical, law and animal and fishery. However, the diversification of deemed universities across specific subject areas is taking place at a much faster rate. The government must support the large-scale expansion of state universities to have a balanced growth of universities inclusive of general as well as professional disciplines.
2. Some of the existing state affiliated universities have overgrown in size, enrolment exceeding over 1 lakh and affiliated undergraduate colleges exceeding over 100. These universities face the problem relating to governance. It is pointed out that there is a barrier to the opening of universities, as these can be established by the State Act only. State governments should rationalize the number of universities in a manner that both enrolment and undergraduate colleges do not suffer from the problem of under-governance.
3. There are many states that do not have central universities. The establishment of central universities has been in an ad hoc manner. There is no principle in terms of excellence or balanced regional development or a model central university. Henceforth, the central government should establish one central university in each state as model university.

4. During the 10th Plan, a rapid growth almost 100 per cent, of deemed universities is a phenomenon of great interest. New state universities with state funding are difficult to be established due to resource crunch. To fill the void many private institutions find the entry through the deemed university route.
5. In the context of promotion of deemed universities, the UGC needs to take the utmost care in the selection of quality institutions and further monitoring the progress in the maintenance of standards. The private institutes and colleges that have achieved excellence may be granted deemed university status after careful scrutiny of proposals. During the 11th Plan an appropriate balance in the number of state supported universities and privately managed deemed universities should be maintained.
6. The expansion of private universities under the State Act is an interesting development in recent years. The phenomenon of private universities should be watched with great care. UGC must evolve a mechanism to maintain the standards of private universities, once the entry is permitted by an act passed by the state.
7. Another important issue is the development of universities in backward regions of the state. The central government must take initiative in greater dispersion of central universities. Central universities should play a role of model universities in promoting teaching and research in state universities.

Colleges

1. It is a matter of concern that only 40 per cent of the total number of colleges for general education are covered under 2f and 12b of the UGC Act. UGC has the responsibility to maintain standards of higher education. Hence, all the colleges need to be brought under the purview of UGC. UGC should develop a system of online monitoring of universities and colleges to keep a watch on the progress of access and quality parameters.

2. There is in all likelihood a decline in the growth of government and aided colleges under general education, given the resource constraint of the state government. The decline in growth of government and aided colleges needs to be arrested to increase access of students in general education.
3. An inter-state and inter-district imbalance in the number of colleges needs to be reduced to the minimum. There is the need to focus on some of the states/regions that lag behind other states in the number of colleges per lakh population in general, engineering, medicine and other disciplines.

Teachers

The most important issue respecting teacher in higher education in recent years relates to the shortage of well-qualified permanent teachers. Resource constraint has forced the state governments to fill up the position of vacant posts. This has resulted in the rise of low-paid temporary teachers. The central government should provide plan support to the states to create new posts of teachers in colleges and university departments in proportion to the growth in the enrolment of students.

Enrolment

1. The database of enrolment in higher education is poor. There are three sources of information on enrolment/attendance. However, they do not provide consistent results. The official statistics of MHRD need to be improved both in terms of full reporting and adequate coverage. Since this provides annual information, this is only used for analysing results and projecting the enrolment for higher education during plan periods. The online reporting of information through the higher education management information system should be developed by the UGC and it should replace the official statistics of the MHRD.
2. In terms of access with respect to levels of education the expansion of research base needs to be ensured. The enrolment levels of doctorates and postgraduates need to be

raised in the universities. At the same time, the undergraduate base of higher education in terms of its depth (higher enrolment) and width (diversified courses) too needs to be raised. Therefore, greater support to existing colleges and university postgraduate department will be required.

3. In terms of access with respect to disciplines, it is necessary to increase the base of science education in percentage terms. The B.Ed enrolment needs to be increased to meet the demand of secondary education teachers. The demand for high quality professionals is growing and increasing the number of institutions to cater to the needs of high demand needs to be established by the government.
4. Inequitable access to higher education for different groups emerges as the marked feature of higher education in India. The policy and planned support of the government should address the issue of low access by different social and religious groups.
5. Women's enrolment in higher education has improved across disciplines. However, some of the states lag behind in raising the participation of women in higher education. In such states, the facilities for women students need to be increased on a preferential basis.

Notes

1. See Sharma (2003) for a detailed analysis of developments of UGC that set the directions of development in higher education.
2. Deficit scenario is the one in which the number of institutions per lakh of population are less than the all-India average. Chronically, deficit states are the one which have extremely low number of institutions per lakh of population.
3. The analyses were presented in the context of the government's decision to reserve 27 per cent seats for the backward classes in central government institutions.

4. See Chanana (2004) for analysing the participation of women by disciplines and regions.

References

A. Gnanam Committee (1990), Towards New Educational Management.

Ambani, M. and K. Birla (2000), Report on a Policy Framework for Reforms in Education, Submitted to the Prime Minister's Council on Trade and Industry (PMCTI) on April 24.

Chanana, Karuna (2004) Gender and Disciplinary Choices: Women in Higher Education in India. Paper presented in the UNESCO Colloquium on Research and Higher Education Policy 'Knowledge, Access and Governance: Strategies for Change', 1–3 December, 2004, Paris. Online accessed from http://portal.unesco.org/education/es/files/36527/11006122283Colloquium-December04-Chanana.doc/Colloquium-December04-Chanana.doc on February 15, 2005.

D.S. Kothari Commission (1964), Report of the Education Commission (1964–66), Education and National Development, Ministry of Education, Government of India, June 1966.

D.S. Kothari (1964), Report of the Committee on 'Model Act for Universities', Ministry of Education, Government of India.

Deshpande, Satish and Yogendra Yadav (2006), "Redesigning Affirmative Action: Castes and Benefits in Higher Education", *Economic and Political Weekly*, June 17, 2419–2424.

Justice K. Punnaiya Committee (1993), Report on UGC Funding of Institutions of Higher Education, University Grants Commission, New Delhi, November.

MHRD (1968), National Policy on Education (NPE) 1968, Government of India, New Delhi.

MHRD (1986), National Policy on Education (NPE) 1986, Government of India, New Delhi.

MHRD (2007), SES 2004–05, Government of India, New Delhi.

MHRD (2007–08), Annual Report 2007–08, Government of India, New Delhi.

MHRD (various years), Selected Educational Statistics, Ministry of Human Resource Development, Government of India, New Delhi.

National Sample Survey Organisation (Various Years), Round 38th (1983), 43rd (1987–88), 50th (1993–94), 55th (1999–2000) and 60th (2003–04), NSSO, Ministry of Statistics and Programme Implementation, Government of India.

NSSO (1999–2000), NSS 55th Round: July 1999–June 2000, National Sample Survey Organisation, Ministry of Statistics and Programme Implementation, Government of India.

P.B. Gajendragadkar Committee (1971), Governance of Universities and Colleges.

P.C. Alexander Committee (1997), The Role of the Governor as Chancellor of the Universities (Approved 2003).

Radhakrishnan S. Commission (1950), The Report of the University Education Commission, Vol. I, Ministry of Education and Culture, Government of India.

Rana, Hasan and Aashish Mehta (2006), "Under-representation of Disadvantaged Classes in Colleges, What Do the Data Tell Us?" *Economic and Political Weekly*, September 2, 3791–3796.

Sen Committee (1974), Report of the Committee on Governance of Universities and Colleges Reconstituted, UGC, New Delhi.

Sharma, Kavita A. (2003), 50 Years of University Grants Commission, UGC, New Delhi.

Shrivastava, Ravi (2007), Access and Equity in Higher Education, Result of UGC Sponsored Study. (unpublished).

Soneri Committee (1995), Review of Gnanam Committee Recommendations.

Sundaram, K. (2006), On Backwardness and Fair Access to Higher Education in India: Some Results from NSS 55th Round Surveys 1999–2000, Working Paper No. 151, Center for Development Economics, Department of Economics, Delhi School of Economics, New Delhi.

Supreme Court of India (2005), Judgment: Writ Petition (Civil) No. 19 of 2004, *Prof. Yashpal and Anr vs. State of Chhattisgarh and Others*, New Delhi.

Swaminathan, D. (1994), Report of the High Power Committee for Mobilisation of Additional Resources for Technical Education

(D. Swaminathan Committee Report), All India Council for Technical Education, New Delhi.

Thorat, S. (2006), Higher Education in India: Issues Concerning Access, Quality and Inclusiveness: A Convocation Address at Shri Venkateshwara University, Tirupati on August 19.

UGC (2003), Annual Report 2002–03, New Delhi.

UGC (2005), Annual Report 2004–05, New Delhi.

UGC (2006), Annual Report 2005–06, New Delhi.

UGC (undated), Results of unpublished research studies (unpublished), New Delhi.

UNESCO (2006), Global Education Digest 2006: Comparing Education Statistics across the World, Canada, 120–129.

V.S. Jha Committee (1974–77), Report of the Review Committee on the University Grants Commission 1974–77.

CHAPTER 3

Debates on Quality in Higher Education

Quantitative expansion of higher education needs to be understood along various other dimensions of higher education. If the quality of higher education is not guaranteed along the path of expansion it would indeed be difficult to sustain the internal growth and the meaningful participation of India in a global economy. The first wave of institution-building in the post-independence phase refers to the 1950s and 1960s of plan support to higher education that led to the creation of higher education institutions on a large scale to support mass higher education in the country. The first wave led to institution-building. On the issue of quality in the first wave varying views have been expressed. Balance of opinion gives the verdict that except for islands of excellence overall quality is far from satisfactory.[1] On a mass scale the university system, it is argued, could not sustain high quality and excellence.

In the context of knowledge economy, university system needs to meet new challenges. It is necessary now to transform quickly the vast pool of information into a relevant knowledge. The issue before a teacher today is to create an intellectual climate that favours the generation and reproduction of knowledge in a seamless manner (Nigavekar, 2004). Teachers need to make efforts to transform implicit knowledge, i.e., knowledge embodied in brains into an explicit knowledge, i.e., in forms in which it can be traded. Given this new context, intervention strategies need to prepare teachers to meet the challenges of knowledge economy.

There is also an argument that the present set-up of university system needs to promote quality through competitiveness. The view is being propagated more from the trade perspective. Accordingly, the competitiveness is said to be the key to promote quality for attracting foreign students in Indian universities thereby boosting the export earnings. Educationists do not seem to have consensus on the issue of promoting quality through competition alone. Nor do they look at the issue of quality divorced from the issues of access and equity.

Perspectives to promote quality differ widely. The present chapter examines varying perceptions of quality. The assessment of quality in Indian higher education is presented and the new perception in promoting quality through competition is analysed. The newer dimensions to the quality debate in international perspective that has percolated down to the higher education needs a systematic understanding. Understanding the context of newer quality debate is necessary to tune the higher education institutions and, in particular, to prepare the academic community to stand up to face new challenges.

I
Traditional Perceptions on Quality

Varying Perceptions

In many discussions on quality, there is normative statement that quality of higher education in India is falling. There is also vulgar empiricism reflected in the statement that deterioration in quality is the result of quantitative expansion (Jayaram, 2004). Quality is also said to be related to the input parameters. It means that lack of infrastructure is responsible for low quality. Advocates of quality control and assurance framework believe that such mechanism will necessarily promote quality irrespective of the historical context in which the institutions evolved as if quality is epistemologically neutral. Thus, varying perceptions lay at the root of understanding on quality in higher education. I propose that quality needs to be understood in a historical perspective. It is necessary to understand quality as a value in itself. Besides, quality can only be understood in an institutional context as it is an embodiment of social, historical and economic environment.

Traditional Knowledge Paradigm: Elite-Based

In traditional knowledge paradigm only elites of the society had the privilege to join higher education institutions. It was also idealized that the university consists of the administration of self-governing community of scholars. Academic culture was the one in which autonomy was granted to scholars and they were free to choose the area of knowledge advancement. Students were supposed to be in active interaction and dialogue with the teacher. Knowledge was thus transferred from teacher to students who with their own independent and critical ability were free to pursue their own interests. This was evident in British tradition stemming largely from Oxbridge and harking back to the medieval origins of universities.[2]

In Indian situation, elite dominance may be observed till mid-20th century with Britishers institutionalizing university system. However, majority of students confined to the knowledge acquisition related to the running of government. Historically, it was not in the interest of the British government to develop independent critical ability. Hence, quality suffered in the sense that universities remained examining bodies and colleges affiliated to them were teaching institutions and at best individual centric knowledge was being pursued. Quality institution in traditional knowledge paradigm meant quest for knowledge by the seekers of knowledge independently. Lectures and discussions provided the platform for critical examination of a body of knowledge. Products of Indian universities, however, were able to develop ideas that provided the foundation of liberal democracy and also opposed British economic interests.

Knowledge was not standardized. Curriculum did not exist in modular form. Teaching learning process was in the form of series of lectures. Only later examination system was institutionalized to assess students' ability.

Traditional Knowledge Paradigm: Mass-Based

The conceptualization of higher education as public good prompted the state to invest in higher education and provided access to all in a liberal democratic set-up. In other words, university emerged as a public service agency provided by government with students as trainees for a range of more or less useful occupations.[3] French, Continental Europe, US and in many developing countries, this was the dominant mode. The diversification of disciplines along general, technical and professional lines developed. The boundaries of subjects were rigid. Teachers were experts in particular subject. Curriculum was subject-specific in which the teacher-centric knowledge system developed. Teacher was responsible to add knowledge to the subject through research as well as to teach the larger and larger number of students to serve the economy. Autonomy was relative subject only to the state established universities' bureaucratic procedures. Knowledge paradigm consisted of institutionalized subject-specific teaching and research. Research was supposed to add newer dimensions to the existing body of knowledge, which teachers were supposed to explain to the students. Students were the prototype of their teachers. Good teachers (rich in subject knowledge and communication skills) were supposed to produce good students and lower quality teachers can only produce lower quality students. So dominant was the role of teacher that academic standard was almost equivalent to the standards of teachers. Good departments or institutions meant quality teachers and everything else, i.e., teaching method was the one suited to teacher. Similarly, references to the books were prescribed by the teachers.[4] Naturally, this meant the diversified quality. Quality was heterogeneous as teachers were different and students were different in terms of aptitude, intelligence etc.

In this transformation from elite-based to mass-based education in a traditional knowledge system referred to above, the quality could not emerge as an all-pervasive phenomenon. However, it needs to be understood that quality cannot be viewed in technical terms alone. Mass higher education provides a context of diversity and managing the diversity is the important issue. Engagement of students in all types of discourses is the real challenge of quality emerging from mass higher education system.

III
Quality through External Assessment and Control

Role of National Assessment and Accreditation Council

The establishment of National Assessment and Accreditation Council (NAAC) in 1994 for quality assurance and accreditation of higher education institutions is the result of newer quality debate. The philosophy of an external assessment and accreditation is to introduce transparency and information to the students about the quality of institutions. For this purpose, the institutions are graded as per the standard of quality. It is also supposed that external assessment would induce the institutions to promote quality.

In its journey for a decade towards quality assurance, it began to accredit institutions on a 9-point scale on 7 criteria, viz., curricular aspects, teaching, learning and evaluation, research, consultancy and extension, infrastructure and learning resources, student support and progression, organization and

Figure 3.1

Gradewise Distribution of Colleges

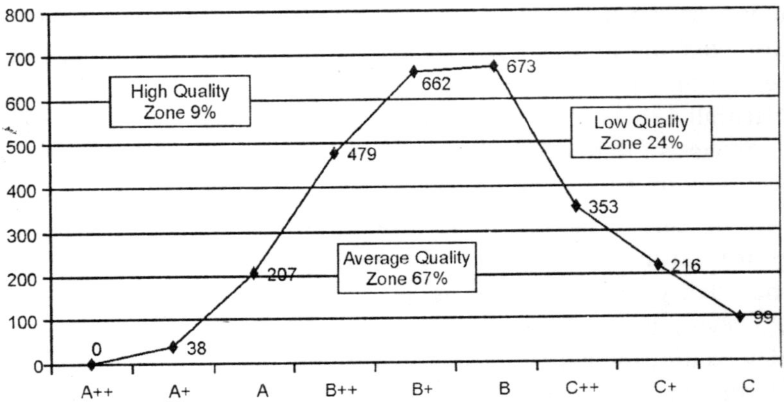

Figure 3.2

Gradewise Distribution of Universities

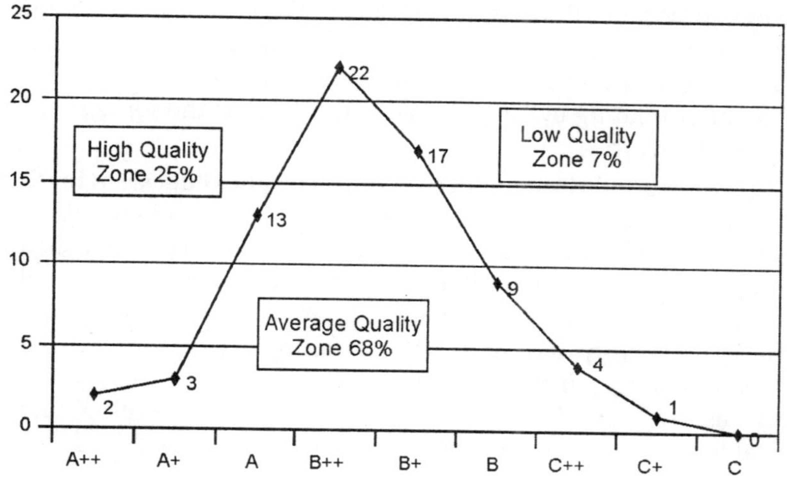

management and healthy practices. As per the NAAC assessment, three classifications of quality in colleges can be presented. There is a high quality zone in which there are 9 per cent of colleges having received all A grades. There is a zone of average quality institutions in which there are 67 per cent colleges having received all B grades. There is a low quality zone consisting of remaining 24 per cent colleges having received all C grades. With respect to the universities high quality zone consists of 25 per cent of universities and average quality zone consists of 67 per cent of universities. Only 7 per cent of universities are in low quality zones. Such a scenario presents us a picture of a large number of average quality colleges and universities on a low base of high quality colleges and universities. It produces the compulsion to invest in quality through strategic programmes and schemes.

It may be noted that accreditation developed in US in response to internal demand of the system, whereas in India, the recent quality assurance mechanism was external and purely government controlled. It did not evolve from within the system. As a result, the competitive pressure to maintain the quality did not evolve in terms of essential feature of the higher education system. Indian QA system, unlike US, is essentially unitary and centralized in character. NAAC is the only agency to conduct accreditation of all institutions. Hence, the coverage even after more than 10 years of its establishment is hardly 15–20 per cent of colleges. Accreditation is neither compulsory nor tied to the system of funding by UGC. As a result, the demand for accreditation is very low.

To assure and enhance the quality of higher education institutions, the following mechanisms need to be put in place. NAAC will have to be an apex organization and should establish few regional accreditation organizations. These regional accreditors should be recognized by NAAC and entrusted with the responsibility of compulsory accrediting the universities and college falling within the region. Once regional accrediting organization develops the capacity, they can develop and establish internal quality assurance cell at the university level. Internal quality assurance cell in turn under the guidance of regional accrediting organization could develop the capacity of detailed quality assurance of programmes of PG department and colleges and even the teachers of higher education system.

Further, with the expansion of higher education institutions, it is necessary that private higher education institutions also evolve a credible institutional mechanism, as in US, to assure and enhance the quality.

Determinants of Quality Emerging from Self-Assessment Reports of Colleges

Self-assessment reports of colleges produce some interesting information on the quality parameters. It was observed that average student-teacher ratio in all A grade colleges was 20, while it was 28 and above in colleges having obtained B and C grades. Average student-teacher ratio by permanent teachers is as high as 30 in all A grade colleges and in B grade college it is 38. The lower is the student-teacher ratio higher is the quality. The faculty needs to be increased in the colleges to upgrade the quality of institutions. Another important dimension of quality is the educational qualification of the teachers. The self-assessment report shows that higher grade of college is also associated with high percentage of teachers having Ph.D. qualification. However, only 28 per cent of teachers with Ph.D. qualification and 16 per cent of teachers with M.Phil qualification were working in the best grade colleges. Hence, to upgrade the quality of colleges teachers need to improve the qualification. The availability of books and journals in the college and organization of academic seminars and conferences are also found to be directly associated with the quality of college. Hence, these facilities should be increased to improve the quality. It has been found that higher grade colleges were the old ones and had higher student strength—around 1,600 for all A grade colleges. It means that quality is not a one-shot affair. It requires cumulative investment of resources over a period of time. Investment adds to the capacity of colleges and over a period large institutions are able to reap economies of scale and add quality. It means quality is an additive concept and lower grade colleges can improve the quality if cumulative investment in infrastructure, books, journals and in improving the research base of faculty is made.

Table 3.1

Some Aspects of Availability of Facilities and Quality in Select Institutions of Higher Education, 2002–2004

Indicators	*NAAC Grades*					
	A & Above	*B++ & B+*	*B Only*	*C++,C+ & C*	*Non-Accredited*	*Total*
No. of Sample Colleges	110	547	298	233	285	1473
STR (Student-Teacher Ratio)	20.4	31.8	28.6	28.5	25.2	25.0
STR by Permanent Teachers	29.8	31.8	38.1	35.8	35.6	33.5
Ph.D. Teachers (%)	28.1	28.0	21.9	24.9	22.4	25.6
M.Phil Teachers (%)	16.7	17.0	15,3	15.6	16.5	16.3
No. of Books per Student	9.5	10.7	6.4	7.4	7.0	8.8
No. of Books per College	15,215	13,921	7,019	6,504	6,748	9,882
No. of Journals per College	22.2	13.0	6.1	4.4	4.0	10.0
Students per Computer	145.2	143.8	251.3	546.7	202.7	258.0
Average Number of Enrolled Students per College	1,603	1,301	954	885	960	1,140

Source: UGC (2007).

Why High Quality could not be Sustained in a Traditional Knowledge System?

There existed at the national level the standard setting apex bodies but institutional framework to regulate the standard of teachers was not at all effective. Teachers once recruited to the job could not find motivating environment within institutions. Amidst life long security of job the drive for excellence could not be generated within system for a number of factors. Firstly, research was not the preferred agenda among teachers, as promotion was not linked to one's depth in research. Secondly, teaching functions predominated which amounted to reproducing written ideas. Creativity or the quest for knowledge or students' ability to translate theoretical knowledge into practical knowledge could not be developed. Thirdly, teaching became boring. In fact, students were so dissatisfied with the instructionist method of teaching that they preferred not to attend classes, turned to tuitions and passed annual examination without adding value (knowledge). Fourthly, quality was conspicuously absent and even then the teachers got awarded and promoted. There was lack of accountability on the part of teachers. There was advancement of knowledge in the form of academic collegiality but soon that gave way to internal rivalry and vested interests and destroyed the concept of self-learning community of scholars.

In a resource constrained system, autonomy without accountability cannot continue for long. Academic communities of scholars were said to be accountable to the state, society and needs of the economy. However, bureaucratic means of control were ineffective to persuade teachers to manage mass education with quality. It is in this context that a new perspective based on competitive spirit is said to be desirable to promote quality.

III
Roots of Decline in the First Wave of Institution-Building

From the assessment made in the previous section it is quite clear that in Indian higher education system quality could not become universal. It may be said that the system could utmost develop the mediocrity of research. It is intended to examine the structural factors and various implementation difficulties that led to the mediocrity of research in the university system.

Mediocrity of Research

Shah A.M. (2005) concludes that "a cumulative effect of various developments both within and outside the field of education is the declining enrolment of talented students, and therefore the declining availability of trained researchers and teachers in the basic physical sciences, the social sciences and the humanities for appointment in colleges, universities and research institutes. This development is contributing to further decline of teaching standards". He analyses the following factors for the decline of quality that arose either due to poor implementation or wrong strategies of various programmes launched by UGC: (a) personal promotion scheme became movement for mass promotions to higher ranks shorn of academic merit; (b) failure to induct a researcher into a long term commitment through M.Phil; (c) failure of Academic Staff College (ASC) to develop quality among teachers; (d) downgrading eligibility test for researchers and for recruitment of the teachers; (e) sub-standard syllabi; (f) emphasis on teaching rather than research reasserted itself in universities and growing isolation of research institutes in the style of functioning; (g) UGC's encouragement to research through centre of advanced study, departmental assistance, award of research and teacher fellowship failed to develop quality with poor funding support to the libraries; and (h) flight of talented students to professional courses, private and foreign universities and the competitive populism within universities. Why these problems arose? The author feels that the structure of university system was unable to take the load of managing too big a system in its entire dimension. As a result, quality of teaching and research at the postgraduate level suffered. The author thus suggests a structural reform to reduce the burden of universities to manage affiliating undergraduate colleges and concentrate on postgraduate teaching and research. He would then support developing a culture of meritocracy devoid of political interference.

The point about willingness of political elite to do so is important and has been pointed out by many authors. Kapur and Mehta (2004) note that Indian higher education system has suffered, both from the state as well as market failures, and has paid the price for it in terms of sub-optimal level of higher education as reflected in mediocrity. Nonetheless, the state is the mechanism through which the reform process in higher education has to take place by understanding the new directions which define the contours of the paradigm shift. Given renewed emphasis of the Prime Minister Dr Manmohan Singh for state-induced second wave of institution-building, state needs to assume a new role of further strengthening institutions to improve quality and strategically invest in institutions and programmes and at the same time promote and regulate the market.

Institutional structure created in the phase of expansion failed to develop meritocracy as a general phenomenon. As a result, legacy presents us with mediocrity. Future vision calls for excellence in research. Restructuring of universities, narrowing the focus to manage research in a manner that develops in-built mechanism for scholastic achievement should be the corner-stone of policy. The form of such restructuring should not detain us here but the principles may clearly be laid down in terms of strict recruitment policy of teachers, reward and incentives to teachers for excellence in teaching and research, training to the teachers, freedom and resources to participate in academic programmes and infrastructural and academic support to teachers.

Failure in Coordination and Maintenance of Standards

While at the university level there developed a mediocrity of research, the respective councils at the central level could not provide the developmental assistance at the scale needed to maintain the standards of higher education. UGC and various professional bodies of higher education were established by the Union Government under Article 246 of the Constitution of India to coordinate and maintain standards in higher education.[5] At the system's level, Singh (2004) notes that "The real major lapse has been in not having set-up the National Council of Higher Education as recommended by the 1986 Policy of Education" (ibid.: 14). As a result, the task of coordination was left to the Ministry of Human Resource Development. Various professional bodies including Distance Education Council could not sit together to benchmark standards and study the developments relating to the growth of private professional colleges, issue of fake universities, upsurge of unrecognized private institutions partnering with foreign universities to confer foreign degrees illegally, the growth of correspondence and distance education and the hidden commercialization. The coordination was also required to be achieved to supervise the growth process itself—issues of required expansion in general and technical/professional courses in accordance with the demand, regional balanced development and issue of gender and social participation across different courses and various other matters that cut across different disciplines.

Not only that the benchmarking of standards was ignored, Singh (2004) also notes that the UGC, at present, is a toothless body as it has no right to give the final approval to the establishment of university nor can it derecognize the degree granted by the university, in case any violation in maintaining the minimum standards is noticed by it. Various other professional councils may have some difficulties or the other in terms of needed statutory support to maintain standards. The whole issue, therefore, is to empower, statutorily and financially, the professional councils and asking them to coordinate. The accountability of professional councils needs to be ensured at least in maintaining the minimum standards for the postgraduate department, research, professional and technical courses, recruitment of quality teachers, if not all the undergraduate colleges. The role of NAAC and NBA as accrediting agencies will then be to promote quality above the benchmarked standards in preferential areas and institutions and to encourage all undergraduate colleges to progressively improve the quality. Accrediting agencies role should be to create awareness and motivation among teachers to improve the quality and to inform the students about the standards of particular institutions. For a large country like India, accrediting agencies need to evolve appropriate mechanisms for accreditation.

Thus, if we take stock of the first phase/wave of institution-building, the strength of higher education is large and diversified structure of institutions with few institutions of excellence. The weakness of the system is that quality is not only poor, there seems to be systematic erosion of quality, particularly in research and teaching. Furthermore, the dominance of private and foreign institutions offering programmes that have high market demand may adversely affect equity if the monitoring mechanism is not created. Hence, the strategy as emerging from past experience should be to introduce reforms at the level of universities by narrowing the focus of management to improve research and teaching and evolve suitable structures to regulate admission, fees, examination etc., that at present overburden the university system. The second set of strategy should be restructuring and empowering the professional councils, evolving a system of benchmarking of standards and constant monitoring of the developments in higher education.

IV
Theoretical Framework of Competition

Competition as Market Phenomenon

The present-day context of globalization adds new dimension to the issue of competitiveness. Competition as a market phenomenon refers to entry of private institutions, free mobility of teachers, setting of fees, i.e., price of education by the forces of demand and supply and free choice of students to choose courses and institutions. The notion of competition as a market phenomenon cannot be sustained in higher education, as it has been traditionally regarded as a public good. It is dominantly supplied through subsidy by the government. There is also restricted mobility of teachers due to institutional factor. The recent trend towards privatization has, however, invoked in a limited sense framework of competition as a market phenomenon. It is not our purpose here to examine the complexity of introducing competition as a market phenomenon in higher education.[6] The different perspective of competition is presented below in a restricted sense to reflect on the strategy to induce quality as an inbuilt process and as a process to generate greater accountability among teachers. The three varying perspectives derive ideas from scholars of repute—Adam Smith, Thorstein Veblen and Buchanan and Devletoglou.

Competition Based on Student Consumerism

The context of the decline of British universities during Adam Smith's time in the late 18th century may have been different from today, yet Adam Smith in the *Wealth of Nations* argues for "competition based on the reputation of students who are free to choose and who pay in large part the incomes of their professors" (Raines and Leathers, 2004: 115). Smith thus noted that the performance of the faculty members would be greatly enhanced if the students demand in return for what they have to pay. Smith gave further insight into effective teaching by the men of letters by repeated encounter of the topic with the students and also affirmed the relevance of appropriate curriculum for competitive spirit. Smith favoured to set incomes to faculty out of the fees of students and not out of endowment provided by the state. According to him, endowment provides protection to the teachers and ensures less accountability among teachers. He made the point that without accountability responsibility to do certain work suffers (Smith, 1776, 1937).

The perspective of competition that we gain from above refers to the increasing choices made available to the students in terms of courses, learning materials, institutions etc. It also refers to the performance of the faculty being induced by the demand from students and this is possible when students are made to charge for the education.

Competition Based on Cooperation

Thorstein Veblen (1993) writing a century and a half later than Smith on the failures of American universities, however, believed in the autonomy of scholars manning universities. He argued that universities should not compete because scientific and scholarly research requires co-operation rather than competition. He noted that universities are not the business enterprise. It does not produce a marketable product and therefore the business-like competition for increasing undergraduate enrolments would go against the spirited pursuit of knowledge and is responsible for the sea of mediocrity. Thus, he preferred the strategic goal of enhancing institutional prestige through the increased endowments meant for research and payment to excellent scholars. He does not favour the effect of 'student consumerism' that defines the basis of competition.

Thus, Veblen presents a perspective missing in Adam Smith that quality research by the scholars of repute is the key to promote quality higher education. Scholars should be rewarded adequately out of state fund and reputations earned by the institutions of scholars are the key elements of quality that can be promoted only through cooperation. Schumpeter in *Capitalism, Socialism and Democracy* shares Veblen's view that only select few are both intellectually capable of being scholars and scientists and therefore free to pursue knowledge motivated by the instinct of idle curiosity.

Competition Based on Attracting Prestigious Faculty

Buchanan and Devletoglou (1970) however noted that even if the tuition fee is zero, to invoke competition for a student and for faculty teachers, universities must offer attractive packages. He centred his analysis on the competition among universities for faculty appointments as a sure way to reduce mediocrities. As the higher education scenario is changing so the role of the faculty must change for achieving scholarly achievements; their image as national and international celebrity would enhance the prestige and also the competitiveness of the university system through the 'prestigious faculty' (ibid.: 107). The point that is made here refers to the competition among universities for faculty appointments of national and international repute.

Quality through Varying Spirit of Competition

There are three perspectives on competition to promote quality. Smith favours student consumerism based on free choice and user charge. Veblen presents the role of state funding to promote research and payment to scholars and scientists. Buchanan notes that even if state subsidizes education, universities need to attract scholars of repute by offering attractive packages.

In the Indian context, the promotion of quality requires a composite strategy. Taking clue from Adam Smith, it is necessary to replace teacher's sovereignty by student centred approach, if not by student's consumerism. Student centred approach means that university system should be able to provide greater choice of curricula and courses to the students. It also means rather than only vertical mobility greater flexibility be introduced to the entry and exit from higher education providing scope for horizontal mobility of students. At a practical level, choice-based credit system needs to be introduced to promote quality. With respect to the teaching learning process, a contructivist approach rather than instructionist approach of learning needs to be promoted.

However, the role of state assumes importance in funding research and payment to the scholars out of state endowment—a perspective that derives its strength from Veblen. The reason is that market promotes a short-run perspective whereas the state provides a futuristic perspective having long-term vision. Scholarly research takes place when researchers are assured of job security and a cooperative spirit and academic collegiality is developed. Quality research from a long-term perspective is the key to quality in a knowledge economy. It is only state that can fund research in a longer term perspective.

The idea that universities need to attract reputed scholars has also its relevance in the Indian context. Indian higher education has suffered due to brain drain. There is need to develop world class university where reputed scholars from India and abroad can work together and generate knowledge. Such research universities can be the centre of quality and excellence.

Against the backdrop of theoretical understanding of competition it is necessary to understand the present position and set strategies for future change of Indian higher education. The evolution of higher education in India was primarily guided by the functional requirement of the economy. After independence, the role of state in charting out developmental path and also in creating higher education institutions was guided by the mutuality of purpose. Most observers of higher education in India feel that performance of higher education institutions has been no less satisfactory, yet a lot needs to be done to promote quality of higher education to meet global challenges of managing the knowledge economy.

V
Strategic Initiatives for Promoting Quality

Strategies in Higher Education to Meet the Demands of Knowledge Economy

Knowledge economy requires human capital base—rich in theoretical knowledge and practical and other skills such as communication, problem solving, creativity and team work. In the section that follows, it would be interesting to address Prime Minister's challenge of "creating a second wave of institution-building and of excellence in the field of education, research and capability building" in India at the level of tertiary education to meet the challenges of a knowledge economy. His reference to the first wave of institution-building by the first prime minister of India implicitly assumes that state will once again come forward to invest in institutions of excellence.

Needless to say, the University Grants Commission (UGC) in India is an apex agency to coordinate and to maintain standards of higher education. It has a number of schemes listed for promotion of standards. However, considering the fact that knowledge economy presents us with many newer issues, a set of new strategies may be required to promote quality in Indian higher education institutions to meet the demands of knowledge economy. There is need for strategic initiative for qualitative enhancement and quantitative growth.

Enhancing Overall Quality: Few with World-Class

Knowledge economy can never be sustained merely by developing islands of excellence. A dual approach of qualitative enhancement with quantitative growth in enrolment must be the strategy in higher education. In terms of this strategy, attempts must be made to improve the infrastructure and quality. (i) Few excellent institutions be developed as world class institutions, (ii) a small number of potential institutions be developed into excellent institutions, (iii) a large number of less than average institutions be developed into average institutions, and (iv) institutions that are not viable in terms of students and teachers should be merged into viable institutions or converted into some other useful institutions. An additional resource should be mobilized to develop world class and national institutions under category (i) and (ii) referred to above. Upto 2010, ten such mega universities in different regions of the country may be established with world-class infrastructure. Twenty national institutions, too, may be developed in different regions with top-class infrastructure.[7] These institutions must offer comprehensive programme of research and teaching and should emerge as 21st century institutions of excellence. Besides category (iii) and (iv) fund should be earmarked for restructuring colleges and universities.

The model to be followed essentially draws inspiration from Higher Education Project 211 launched in 1995 in China or '21st Century Centres of Excellence Plan' in Japan started in summer of 2002 and the new policy of 'Brain Korea 21' designed to elevate the quality to world-class standards in selected graduate schools and selected fields of natural sciences.[8]

Attracting Indian Professors, Researchers and Scientists Working Abroad into Indian World-Class Institutions

Dutta, Lanvin and Paua (2004) note that India ranks second in terms of availability of scientists and engineers and in domestic software companies in international markets. However, India also suffers due to brain drain as its ranking has gone upto 65 from the previous year ranking at 54. Brain drain can have a debilitating effect on national governing structures, management capacities, productive sectors, and tertiary institutions. It is estimated, for example, that at least 40 per cent of the graduates of the highly regarded Indian Institutes of Technology seek employment abroad.[9] This issue can be addressed if Indian

Professors, Researchers and Scientists working abroad could be attracted into Indian world-class institutions for a short, medium or long period by offering a chair.

University Networking

Knowledge by itself does not transform economies, nor is there any guarantee of positive returns to investments in research and development or in other products of tertiary education. World Bank (2002) notes that India, Brazil and USSR had invested heavily in building up capacity in science and technology without reaping significant returns. This is so because scientific and technological knowledge yields its greatest benefits when it is used within a complex system of institutions and practices known as a national innovation system (NIS). The report notes that an NIS is a web made up of the following elements: (a) knowledge producing organizations in the education and training system; (b) the appropriate macroeconomic and regulatory framework, including trade policies that affect technology diffusion; (c) innovative firms and networks of enterprises; (d) adequate communication infrastructures; and (e) other factors such as access to the global knowledge base and certain market conditions that favour innovation (World Bank, 1999). Tertiary education systems figure prominently in this framework, serving not only as the backbone for high-level skills but also as a network base for information sharing.

The role of the government is to create an enabling framework for NIS. It of course amounts to first providing connectivity. Currently, UGC INFONET is a nationwide communication network with the state-of-the-art university campus network. INFLIBNET is a university library network for promoting IT culture in academic sector. INFLIBNET will subscribe core academic journals in electronic form and make them accessible to academic community. The challenge in enhancing access to information is to effectively optimize and manage available bandwidth. Majority of the colleges in India must have adequate IT infrastructure and present UGC scheme provides for grants under various schemes. Grants under this head need to be augmented substantially so that majority colleges in India have enabling structures for enhanced access to information and knowledge. But much more than this is to develop university—industry interlinkages that is seriously lacking in India whereas most of the developed countries are able to make. It is expected that with UGC INFONET, university networking could be exploited. Training programmes need to be designed to sensitize the academic community on the role of networking in research and teaching. Universities need to develop a centre for knowledge management where innovations, IT integration in teaching and research, networking, collaboration with industries, training courses etc., could be planned.

Promoting Foreign Universities in Partnership with Public/Private

Indian universities should have greater collaboration with reputed foreign universities. Collaborations in joint research, teaching programmes, designing curricula, student and teacher exchange should be promoted. An enabling legislation needs to be framed to permit foreign universities to launch programme. Care needs to be taken to promote high quality foreign institutions. Besides, those institutions that bring with themselves the foreign investment may be promoted through joint venture only for selected courses and programmes. Adequate academic autonomy may be granted but the registration under trust/society and partnership condition must be invoked. In fact, selected foreign universities in selected programmes of study should be invited under attractive packages. Besides the governmental level effort, Indian universities should be given a free hand to sign MOUs with foreign universities. An advantage of promoting foreign universities is to introduce international curricula, foreign teaching method and teaching material into Indian higher education institutions and promote skilled manpower for global market. It has other important advantages such as availability of courses at cheaper costs in India than abroad; it may reduce the outflow of students and also attract foreign direct investment in India.

A proactive policy approach would mean that the government should invite Vice-chancellors of reputed universities and show interest on preferential basis to invest in India in specialized programmes on a partnership basis rather than allow autonomous liberalization in a free for all manner.

Diversified Providers of Higher Education

One of the essential conditions for promoting quality through competition is to encourage diversified providers of educational programmes within a given guiding framework. There are varied new actors and institutions that have emerged in the 'borderless' tertiary education market. Some of them are (a) virtual universities, (b) franchise universities, (c) corporate universities, (d) media companies, libraries, museums, and other institutions, and (e) education brokers (Salmi, 2001). On the heels of these new actors come software producers, publishers, entertainment firms, and others seeking to tap the potential of an emerging international market in tertiary education (Bennell and Pearce, 1998).

A policy framework needs to be evolved to accommodate new actors and institutions that bring together key facets of paradigm shift such as flexible learning utilizing distance education in a synchronous or asynchronous form[10] and providing large access. What needs to be ensured is quality certification for at least the courses/programmes offered and a certain degree of control and supervision. Policy framework should be supportive of promoting investment by private actors and initiatives undertaken by public providers of education.

ICT and Competitiveness in Higher Education

Information and Communication Technology (ICT) has tremendous potential to increase access and quality in higher education institutions at affordable cost. There is need for an enabling environment for the widespread availability and application of ICT in varied fields in higher education institutions. Critical factors for such an enabling environment are widespread availability of access devices such as telephones and PCs, connectivity to the internet through internet service providers, ICT literacy among students, teachers and educational administrators and the availability of knowledge professionals in the higher education institutions. It is also important to understand different specific areas in which efficiency can be increased through greater transparency and substantial cost reduction and quality of education can be increased through availability of reading materials, innovative delivery practices and offering web-based courses. Government of India has launched an ambitious EDUSAT project that has the capacity to create virtual classroom at all levels of education in all states through two-way video conferencing. It has immense potential to increase access and quality in education. Unfortunately, the progress in implementation of the project is very slow and the government must ensure speedy implementation in all respects.

There are following areas in which ICT coverage can be extended:

(a) admission processes can be computerized and further application and testing services can be offered online; (b) results of college and university examinations can be computerized; (c) payrolls, leave systems, accounting etc., soft-wares can be adopted as part of the e-governance; (d) use of multimedia in the classrooms can be promoted; (e) college libraries can be accessed from different points, i.e., from students' computer centres and faculty's desktops. Further, through a dedicated server and a downlink facility, networking of libraries can be assured; (f) internet, intranet and extranet facility can be promoted among students and teachers; and (g) digital campus through campus pipeline web platform and appropriate softwares and services in select institutions can be planned.

Given such scope for ICT a plan with a road map for establishing ICT and intensifying its use is suggested.

There is no estimate of present status of fully developed or partial or nil ICT infrastructures in colleges, departments or administrative set-ups of universities. Even where such facilities exist partly or fully there may not be optimum utilization of existing facilities. Two steps are suggested for improving competitiveness in higher education institutions through ICT:

- A physical projection should be made to ensure the following: (1) At least 25 per cent of colleges and university departments must have a model IT infrastructure and 25 per cent of the teachers must be trained to use it in innovative manner by 2010. A target of 50 per cent and 100 per cent may be fixed for the same by 2015 and 2020 respectively.

A Research and Training Centre for ICT Studies in Higher Education should be established by the MHRD. The objectives of the Centre would be to enable institutions for improving quality through ICT integration. The main functions would be to provide research backup, facilitate higher education institutions for ICT integration and use and provide training to teachers and administrators to operationalize ICT for distance education as well as for improving efficiency and quality.

Promotion of Selected Courses and Programmes of Study

Some selected courses and programmes of study that are related to the high knowledge end need to be promoted. At least 200 such programmes of study may be identified that require high degree of specialization. Majority of such programmes may be launched in world class and excellent institutions, while a minority of them may be launched in other institutions—public as well as private. Indian scholars working abroad may be invited to the above institutions at attractive salaries and with sufficient autonomy and research facilities. For each subject area the centre/school head must have sufficient autonomy to recruit, promote and pay the faculties of repute. Among the most significant new areas are molecular biology and biotechnology, advanced materials science, microelectronics, information systems, robotics, intelligent systems and neuroscience and environmental science and technology. Tertiary education institutions need to be able to react swiftly by establishing new programmes, reconfiguring existing ones, and eliminating outdated programmes without being hampered by bureaucratic regulations and processes (World Bank, 2002).

Diversifying Role of Academic Staff Colleges

To provide quality higher education, Academic Staff Colleges run orientation programmes for young lecturers and refresher courses for serving teachers. There should be emphasis on diversifying role of Academic Staff Colleges. First of all, the programmes run by them for the teachers should be diversified to cater to the different aspects of academic improvement such as delivery practices, learning strategies including group and multi-channel learning. An important dimension of change relates to the obsolescence of human knowledge ware. It has more to do with the updating and upgrading of learning that will be required in order to refresh and enhance individual qualifications and to keep pace with innovations in products and services. The programme may be of short duration and shall be confined to a single theme and competence. Academic Staff College should also be strengthened to meet the training requirements of the senior administrators in the colleges and universities.

National Qualifications Framework (NQF)

Last but not the least important is to develop a national qualifications framework in India. NQF will enable the recognition of skills, training institutions in or outside university and government sector. This will bring to the surface large pool of experience and knowledge embodied in human resources in unorganized sector by recognizing them under certain procedure. Levels of qualification upto the university's highest degree may be created through a classification scheme into which all the formal and non-formal education, training and experience of human resources can be integrated. This will also enable the horizontal and vertical mobility of human resource into training and education institutes through credit transfers and will facilitate truly the concept of lifelong education and training (NIEPA, 2001). NQF is thus an important tool to realize the potentials of knowledge economy.

Conclusion

In the transformation from elite to mass education in a traditional knowledge system quality could not emerge an all-pervasive phenomenon. Institutional framework to regulate the standard of teachers was not effective. Teachers once recruited to the job could not find motivating environment within institutions.

There are three perspectives on competition to promote quality. Smith favours student consumerism based on free choice and user charge. Veblen presents the role of state funding to promote research and payment to scholars and scientists. Buchanan notes that even if state subsidizes education, universities need to attract scholars of repute by offering attractive packages. A composite of three perspectives on competitiveness is suggested to promote quality. The process of accreditation as a method to promote quality has its own limitation, as it has evolved in India not as demand of the internal system, but as the imposition from an external agency. Concern for quality needs to be developed from teachers and institutions. The chapter ends with suggestions of some strategic initiatives to promote quality.

There is a need to learn from the Chinese strategies to reform higher education. China, Japan and South Korea—all have developed world-class institutions to attract faculty and students from all over the world. This will prevent the flow of qualified researchers to US and European countries. Another strategy relates to promoting the use of ICT in higher education. Multimedia and web-based learning should be promoted by appropriate pedagogic preparation of teachers. There is also the need to promote diversified providers of education that bring together key facets of paradigm shift such as flexible learning utilizing distance education. University system should establish a knowledge cell to suggest ways to transform university as knowledge enterprise.

Notes

1. See observation on quality in Mehta (2003). He notes: "We have failed to sustain a sound teaching learning process, or to provide a right kind of fodder to the job market ... we have failed to provide authentic process of certification ... people are so much uncertain about the qualities of our product that they no longer take university certification seriously" (p. 5). Another observation can be found in Jayaram (2004). He notes: "The undue emphasis on certification rather than on the teaching and learning process—a proverbial case of

the tail wagging the dog has distorted the orientation of university education" (ibid.: 93).

2. Radford, Raaheim, Vries and Williams (1997).
3. op. cit., p. 46.
4. op. cit.
5. Entry 66 of list I in the VIIth Schedule of the Constitution of India vests Central Government with the power to legislate for "Coordination and determination of standards in institutions for higher education or research and scientific and technical institutions". The Constitutional provision clearly lays down that entry 25, list III by which the state government has the power to establish university is subject to the power of Parliament to legislate under entry 66 to maintain the required standards of higher education. It is thus the constitutional obligation upon the Central government to regulate maintenance of the standards of higher education. UGC (1956) says the Constitution of India vests Parliament with exclusive authority in regard to "coordination and determination of standards in institutions for higher education or research and scientific and technical institutions". UGC Act, clause (f) and (g) of Section 26 guides UGC regarding minimum standards and its maintenance in universities.
6. Complexity arises as higher education is a non-profit activity.
7. UGC identified 5 universities in 2000 for granting status of 'Universities with Potentials for Excellence' and furthermore identified 12 universities for 'Centres of Excellence' in areas of specialization to be developed and provided financial assistance. UGC is also in the process of identifying more than 100 'Colleges with Potential for Excellence' and establishment of new 'Centres/Institutes of Excellence' for financial assistance. Different departments in Humanities/Social Sciences, Physical Sciences, Bio Sciences, Engineering and Technology are supported to achieve excellence in research and postgraduate teaching. UGC has also established 6 Inter-University Centres to address contemporary development issues with multi-disciplinary approach in nuclear science, astronomy, networking of libraries and promoting countrywide classrooms and quality in higher education. Present UGC's assistance against above schemes is a peanut when considered against $ 1.1 billion investment made by Korea during 1999–2005 under 'Brain Korea'.
8. See Lee (2004) and Kaneko (2004).

9. Number of Indian immigrants with tertiary education living in US alone is 2.25 lakh. See World Bank (2002).
10. Daniel (1997) distinguishes synchronous and asynchronous forms of distance education. Former refers to a situation in which teachers and students are linked in real time, latter to a situation in which variety of media helps students to learn in their own environment.

References

Bennell, Paul and Terry Pearce (1998), The Internationalisation of Higher Education: Exporting Education to Developing and Transitional Economies. IDS Working Paper 75, Brighton, UK: Institute of Development Studies, University of Sussex.

Buchanan, J.M. and N.E. Devletoglou (1970), *Academia in Anarchy: An Economic Diagnosis*, Basic Books Inc., New York.

Daniel J. (1997), Technology: Its Role and Impact on Education Delivery-more means better, paper presented to Commonwealth Ministers of Education Conference, Botswana, Available on http://www.open.ac.uk/OU/News/VC/Botswana.htm.

Dutta, S., B. Lanvin and F. Paua (2004), *The Global Information Technology Report: Readiness for the Networked World, 2002–03*, World Economic Forum, Oxford University Press.

Jayaram, N. (2004), "Higher Education in India: Massification and Change", in Philip G. Altbach and Toru Umakoshi (eds.), *Asian Universities Historical Perspectives and Contemporary Challenges*, The Johns Hopkins University Press, Baltimore.

Jayaram, N. (2007), "India", in James J.F. Forest and Philip G. Altbach (2007), *International Handbook of Higher Education*, (Part II: *Regions and Countries*), Springer, Netherlands.

Kaneko, Motohisa (2004), 'Japanese Higher Education Contemporary Reform and the Influence of Tradition', in Philip G. Altbach and Toru Umakoshi (eds.), *Asian Universities Historical Perspectives and Contemporary Challenges*, The Johns Hopkins University Press, Baltimore.

Kapur, D. and P.R. Mehta (2004), Indian Higher Education Reform: From Half-Baked Socialism to Half-Baked Capitalism, CID Working Paper No. 108, September.

Lee, S.H. (2004), "Korean Higher Education History and Future Challenges", in Philip G. Altbach and Toru Umakoshi (eds.),

Asian Universities Historical Perspectives and Contemporary Challenges, The Johns Hopkins University Press, USA.

Mehta, V.R. (2003), The Killing of Higher Education, UGC Golden Jubilee Lecture Series, 2002–03.

NIEPA (2001), National Qualifications Framework, Report of the National Seminar, New Delhi.

Nigavekar Arun (2004), Sustainable Quality in Flexible Higher Education in Quality Higher Education and Sustainable Development, NAAC Decennial Lectures. NAAC, Bangalore.

Radford, J., Kjell Raaheim, Peter de Vries and Ruth Williams (1997), *Quantity and Quality in Higher Education*, Higher Education Policy Series 40, Jessica Kingsley Publishers, London.

Raines, Patrick J. and Charles G. Leathers (2004), The Economic Institutions of Higher Education: Economic Theories of University Behavior, Edward Elgar Publishing Inc., Massachusetts, USA.

Salmi, Jamil (2001), Tertiary Education in the 21st Century: Challenges and Opportunity, Higher Education Management (OECD, Paris), 13 (2): 5–130.

Shah A.M. (2005), "Higher Education and Research Roots of Mediocrity", *EPW*, May 28–June 4, 2005.

Singh, Amrik (2004), *Fifty Years of Higher Education in India: The Role of the University Grants Commission*, Sage Publications, New Delhi.

Smith, A. (1976), *An Inquiry into the Nature and Causes of the Wealth of Nations*, Liberty Press, Indianapolis (Original work published 1737).

UGC (1956), The University Grants Commission Act, 1956 (as modified up to the 20th December, 1985) and Rules & Regulations Under the Act, University Grants Commission, New Delhi.

UGC (2007), Results of sponsored study, unpublished, UGC, New Delhi.

Veblen, T. (1993), *The Higher Learning in America*, New Bruswick, Transaction Publishers, NJ (Original work published 1918).

World Bank (2000), Higher Education in Developing Countries: Peril and Promise, The International Bank for Reconstruction and Development/The World Bank, Washington, D.C.

World Bank (2002), Constructing Knowledge Societies: New Challenges for Tertiary Education, World Bank, Washington DC, also available on http://www.worldbank.org.

II

Emerging Issues

CHAPTER 4

Privatization in Higher Education: Need for Legislative and Executive Action

One of the most significant features of the 21st century higher education is that it emerged against the backdrop of privatization and globalization. World over the spread of higher education was achieved through active state intervention throughout the previous century. State invested and set the directions of higher education. At the close of the previous century, public funding for higher education has been on the decline and as a conscious effort or otherwise the space seems to have been partly filled by the active intervention of private players in the higher education.

The situation in Indian higher education system almost follows the above description. In this phase of transition, the tools for policy could not evolve as fast as the change of the process itself. As a result sometimes at the level of practices situations were such that even demanded judicial interventions. Therefore, there seems to be a gap between judicial intervention and legislative and executive policy actions that might, however, reflect the compulsions of Indian civil society and democracy.

The result of course has been that the three issues such as (i) regulations of private universities; (ii) admissions and fixations of tuition fees for professional education through self-financing private institutions; and (iii) entry of foreign universities in India could not be effectively dealt with. The situation demands a solution to the issues to put an end to all uncertainties and legal battles and to generate the confidence among students, parents, management and above all the society for taking the higher education to the larger goal of achieving economic development. The difficulty lies in the fact that there has been loss in the relative autonomy to take policy decisions. There has also been an erosion of faith in regulatory disciplines. The market has pervasive influence in the minds of people.

It is against this background that the author has clarified the present situation on these issues with some historical developments. Specifically, the issue of private universities in India is the logical conclusion of the privatization. The role of any regulatory authority is to see that the larger goals of access, equity and quality are not ignored while considering any enabling framework for private university. Similarly, the issue of admission and fees in the private professional colleges need to be looked into, given the parameters set by the judicial pronouncement of Supreme Court of India (2002) in T.M.A. Pai case. It notes that the issue of autonomy of private professional colleges needs to be protected but at the same time the commercialization of higher education is to be prevented. Large uncertainties exist over the commitments to be made in higher education under GATS. The foreign universities are at present working under no regulation. The implications of foreign universities awarding degrees to the Indian students have no constitutional validity. There is the need for an effective legislation and operational framework to deal with the issues relating to foreign universities.

The objective of the present chapter is to lay bare the historical developments and throw up issues in the light of broad national objectives which higher education is supposed to address. The issue of foreign universities will be taken up in the next chapter.

I

Issues Relating to Private Universities in India

World over the trends towards private universities have gained momentum in the last decade, although as a first step towards privatization the self-financing private institutions began to operate under government control and later the self-financing programmes in the public universities were also encouraged as a way out of the crisis of public funding of higher education. Deemed to be university duly approved under UGC Act is a new variant of self-financing type of institution, which provides a model of academic autonomy with functional efficiency. It is important to note that the phase of private universities in India is one of uncertainty, legal battles and open defiance of UGC authority. The present section is an attempt to understand some of the issues relating to private universities in India and find out ways to provide the desired directions of higher education.

Present System of Universities in India

Under the constitutional provision given in entry 25 of list III under the Seventh Schedule (Article 246) central and state governments establish multi-faculty conventional universities. These are of both, unitary and affiliating types. Nearly 50 per cent of universities in India belong to this category. There are also professional universities such as technical, medical, law, agricultural, which are established by state governments. They are also of unitary and affiliating types. The third category is of open universities established by central and state governments. These offer open and flexible education through distance mode using correspondence courses/modern educational technology like interactive TV, etc.

The practice of establishing deemed to be universities under private/joint sector began in 1986. These are established under Section 3(f) of the UGC Act. Recommendation of UGC for according the status of a deemed to be university to an institution is to be accepted and notified by the central government. These may have single or multiple faculties. Apart from universities and deemed to be universities, there are also some institutions offering professional undergraduate, postgraduate and research programmes established as centres of excellence, some by an Act of Parliament such as IITs and others at the instance of the central government such as National Law Institute, National Institute of Design, Indian Institute of Management, National Institute of Fashion Technology, etc.

Move Towards Private Universities

The first move towards private universities was initiated by the central government itself when Bill No. LIX of 1995 titled The Private Universities (Establishment and Regulation) Bill, 1995 was introduced in the Rajya Sabha by the then Minister of Human Resource Development, Madhav Rao Scindia. Though the Parliamentary Standing Committee on Human Resource Development after detailed examination presented its report to the Chairman Rajya Sabha on 26th March, 1996 the Bill, however, is still pending before the Parliament.

Later Chhattisgarh state[1] promulgated an act to allow private universities to be established in the state. Chhattisgarh government may by notification in the gazette establish a university with the recognition and authorization to conduct a syllabus or to grant degrees or diplomas or awards. Such notification shall then be tabled in the Legislative Assembly. The Act allows, with the prior approval of the state government to affiliate any college or other institution or to set up more than one campus. The act allows the state government to inspect the university for the purpose of ascertaining the standards of teaching, examination and research. The Chhattisgarh Act led to the opening of 97 universities.

Gujarat notified two private universities (Dhirubhai Ambani Institute and Nirma Institute) through two separate acts of legislature in March 2003. Orissa has passed a bill, which is soon going to be introduced. Uttaranchal has already established four universities through separate Acts. A private (Zee) university was established in April 2003. Himachal Pradesh has set up the Jaypee University of Information Technology in 2002. Madhya Pradesh is ready with its own draft bill. Maharashtra, Karnataka, Andhra Pradesh and Tamil Nadu are already running private medical and engineering colleges. The number of private universities has increased upto 38.

UGC's Control through Regulation (2003)

The Government of India published a gazette notification on December 27, 2003, UGC Establishment and Maintenance of Standards in Private Universities Regulations, 2003. Some of the important features regarding establishment and recognition of private universities are:

- Each private university shall be established by a separate State Act and shall conform to the relevant provisions of the UGC Act, 1956, as amended from time to time.
- Private university shall be a unitary university having adequate facilities for teaching, research, examination and extension services.
- A private university established under a State Act shall operate ordinarily within the boundary of the state concerned. However, after the development of main campus, in exceptional circumstances, the university may be permitted to open off-campus centres, off-shore campuses and study centres after five years of its coming into existence, subject to some important conditions such as the off-campus centre(s) and/or the study centre(s) shall be set up with the prior approval of the UGC and that of the state government(s) where the centre(s) is/are proposed to be opened. UGC retains the power to monitor and close down the centres in the case of unsatisfactory performance. Any off-shore campus(es) in foreign countries shall be opened only after obtaining due permission from the Government of India and also that of the government of the host country.
- A private university shall fulfil the minimum criteria in terms of programmes, faculty, infrastructural facilities,

financial viability, etc., as laid down from time to time by the UGC and other concerned statutory bodies.

- The programmes of study leading to a degree and/or a postgraduate degree/diploma offered by a private university shall conform to the relevant regulations/norms of the UGC or the concerned statutory body as amended from time to time.
- The admission procedure and fixation of fees shall be in accordance with the norms/guidelines prescribed by the UGC and other concerned statutory bodies.

Chhattisgarh Private University Amendment Bill (2004)

Responding to criticisms, Chhattisgarh passed the Private University Amendment Bill, 2004. It provided for State Regulatory Commission on the pattern of UGC to ensure academic standard of private universities, interest of students and service condition of employees. It requires deposit of endowment fund of Rs 2 crore as guarantee. It also requires to have 15 acres of land within municipal limit and 25 acres of land outside for permanent campus. Almost 60 out of 97 universities who did not comply with requirements were denotified. Some more may be denotified when State Regulatory Commission begins to operate.

Legal Wrangles

Open Defiance of UGC Act, 1956

The controversy began with the Chhattisgarh legislation on Private University Act, 2002 that was also the first act on the establishment of private university. Section 22 of UGC Act, 1956 notes "that the right of conferring or granting degrees shall be exercised only by a University established or incorporated by or under a Central Act, a Provincial Act or a State Act or an institution deemed to be a University under Section 3 or an institution specially empowered by an Act of Parliament to confer or grant degrees". Using this provision UGC (2004a) issued a regulation by which the private university shall be established by a separate state act. This meant necessary modification was required in Chhatisgarh Act (2002). This was, however, not complied with although Chhatisgarh Act (2004) Private University Bill was passed in 2004. In fact Rajasthan came up with another ordinance in 2004 entitled Rajasthan Self-financed Private Universities Ordinance, 2004. The ordinance states that the state government may, by notification in the official gazette, establish a university with such name, location, and jurisdiction and with such conditions as may be specified in such notification. The question is: Is a separate act necessary for the establishment of every university in terms of provisions of Section 22 and Section 23 of UGC Act, 1956? It may also be asked is such a provision, if it exists, necessary? If a separate act is necessary then universities established under Chhatisgarh legislation are illegal and the Rajasthan ordinance also stands null and void. There were various other clauses in the UGC (2003) regulation relating to the infrastructure and quality norms and opening of off-campus centres and study centres that are not being implemented effectively.

Public Interest Litigation Filed by Yashpal

Eminent educationist and former Chairman of UGC, Prof. Yashpal, filed a PIL in the Supreme Court of India, challenging the validity of the Chhattisgarh Act, which allegedly allows the registration of private universities without basic education facilities. Indeed there are various newspaper reports that point to the lack of basic physical and academic infrastructure in the universities established under Chhattisgarh Act. UGC also established a committee to oversee the functioning of private universities which submitted its report that reportedly pointed to the inadequate infrastructure of the private universities. The Supreme Court of India (2005) in its historic judgment announced the closure of a large number of private universities which were found to be inferior in quality.

Delhi High Court Case of Quashing UGC (2003) Regulation

C.V. Raman University under Chhattisgarh and the Institute of Chartered Financial Analysts of India University under Uttaranchal have petitioned the Delhi High Court to quash the UGC (2004a) Establishment and Maintenance of Standards in

Private Universities Regulations, 2003. The universities argued that their status under the state law is legitimate, and as they receive no funding through the UGC, they should not be subject to its rulings. The court was informed that the UGC wanted to 'control' the private sector and not merely assure its quality. On March 22, 2004, the Delhi High Court upheld the UGC's 2003 regulations and issued notices to the governments of Chhatisgarh and Uttaranchal. The two petitioning universities were asked to file replies by April 27, 2004. The point to note is that if UGC's regulation (2003) is held as valid and also private universities continue to provide degrees then executive/legislative action may be called for to comply with the regulation.

UGC's Power to Revoke University Title or Degree Awarding Powers

It is also argued that UGC Act, 1956 does not empower the UGC to revoke university title or degree. In fact clauses to this effect were removed from the original 1951 Bill following pressure from the states. However, there is a reference to 'approval' of all the degrees by the UGC, and this has generally been the convention over the years. As a result, UGC cannot demand that private universities relinquish university title. It can only assert that its founding act gives it the right to oversee the 'minimum standard' of all universities in India whether public or private, state or federally constituted.[5] Can it be considered to give UGC more teeth by enabling UGC to provide the power to derecognize the university title or degree. Singh (2004) notes that the states would still oppose such a provision (pp. 24–25). This issue acquires greater importance now. There should be some authority to centre or state or UGC to revoke university title or degree or some alternative mechanism such as 'Fitness-to-Function Norms' to be prescribed by UGC (see Singh, 2004: 25).

Territorial Jurisdiction of Private Universities

Territorial jurisdiction is yet another feature of traditional universities. The reason must have been that in a federal set-up the jurisdiction of a university established by a state act cannot be applied to other state. Further, within a state there is no territorial jurisdiction, yet for the purposes of avoiding confusion ordinarily territorial jurisdiction is followed for each university. The Model Act of UGC (2003) states that the concept of territorial jurisdiction is no more relevant in the age of borderless education, triggered by the ICT revolution.

In the case of private university, UGC (2003) regulation prohibits off-campus and study centres of private universities in other states. The recent norm of UGC[6] states that franchising through off-campus study centres is limited only to the courses of universities conducted under distance learning.

The off-campus centres and study centres, functioning as separate entities engaged in teaching are supposed to come under the purview of Section 2f of the UGC Act. This is an open fact that universities established under State Act have their off-campus centres outside state.

The dilemma with respect to the territorial jurisdiction is that 'off-campus centres' may be desirable in the present context of cross border education, yet it throws open the problem of regulating the standards at these centres. The situation with respect to study centres with franchisee arrangement under private sector is denial of UGC regulations.

Present Concerns for Private Universities in India

As noted earlier, private universities are the logical outcome of privatization in higher education. If deemed to be universities provide an example of quasi privatization, the private universities are models of full privatization. So far as demand side analysis is concerned, there exists a middle and high income group clientele for private universities, although access to private universities will be limited due to higher fees charged by them. From the supply side, the private universities may create a niche for themselves for courses that fetch employment to attract students. The point to note is that there cannot be a market-clearing price or the output and there may not be research and quality orientation. This is what provides cause for concern. This calls for the legislative action as well as the executive action.

Policy Framework for Private Universities

There is, therefore, need to address above concerns, namely, those relating to cost and quality. A policy framework for private universities must guarantee how within a framework of constitutional provision these two concerns are addressed?

More specifically, following issues relating to the establishment and maintenance of standard of private universities in India acquire importance.

- Should there be central guidelines on the establishment of private universities?
- What are the essential conditions for the constitutional validity of private universities with respect to their establishment? Is a separate Act necessary?
- Is the issue of maintenance of standards, which is constitutionally the centre's responsibility, a separate issue unconnected with the establishment of private universities?
- If not, how is the UGC empowered to check the growth of low quality private universities?
- Should UGC be given the power to revoke university title or degree?
- Should there be compulsory accreditation of private universities by NAAC within three years of its establishment for quality assurance?
- UGC (2003) Regulation—What are the restrictive clauses for control?
- How quality private universities be promoted both with respect to teaching and research functions?
- Should Parliament legislate on the private universities?

II

Issues of Admission and Fees in Professional Private Unaided (Self-financing) Colleges in India

The Growth of Professional Colleges

There are following four characteristics of the growth of professional education in India:

(1) *Private sector dominance*: Various professional disciplines such as engineering and technology, medical and health sciences, management and teacher education were dominated by the private sector. Almost three quarters of the institutions were in the private sector (see Appendix I). It means self-financing private unaided sector is too important to be ignored in professionalization of human resources in India—so crucial a factor in the development of knowledge society.

(2) *Narrow enrolment base*: Of the total enrolment of 10.48 million in 2004–05, engineering and technology accounted for 7.20 per cent enrolment, medical accounted for 3.15 per cent and education and agriculture accounted for 1.47 and 0.59 per cent respectively (see Appendix II). It is important to note that the access to professional institutions in India needs to be raised to increase the enrolment of professional to total enrolment. A smaller base of professional enrolment is neither good for education nor for the economy. It clearly implies that higher education policy makers and the planners must address the admissions and the fees policy that supports higher participation.

(3) *Regional bias*: There is a strong regional bias in the distribution of professional institutions. Here the divide exists between the north and the south. Southern states such as Andhra Pradesh, Maharashtra, Tamil Nadu, Karnataka and to some extent Kerala account for the bulk of the professional institutions in India, mostly in the private sector. For example, out of the total 977 engineering and technology institutions above-mentioned five states accounted for 635 institutions i.e., roughly 65 per cent of total institutions in five states alone. About 64 per cent government and private and 56 per cent of private colleges in five above states account for the total engineering and technology institutions in India. It implies that north-south divide exists and this divide exists because of the dominance of private sector in India. Similar north-south divide exists in other branches of professional education in India (see Appendix IV). The growth pattern in some professional institutions in private sector in terms of institutions and intake capacity can be seen in Appendix IV. This has an important implication

for the northern states. Since most of the students from the poor northern states take admissions in the private professional institutions, higher the fees structure higher is the drain of money from the north to the south. This fact has a very important implication in terms of policy and planning design of professional institution.

(4) *Ambiguous quality*: Quality is a very important yardstick of the development of professional institutions. Hardly a research study exists that could focus on the quality aspects of the growth of professional institutions in India. There are good quality public professional institutions; some are average but a large number of less than average quality institutions exists under the government sector. So far as the private institutions are concerned some of the well-managed trusts have good institutions but most private institutions lack quality. An important argument put forward by private professional colleges in favour of the autonomy of fixing fees is that quality is dependent on the availability of infrastructural facilities such as the library, laboratories, computer facilities, classrooms, in short, the input factors. Hence, autonomy in fixing fees will help the institutions to account for input factors and maintain quality.

The four scenarios presented in the growth of professional colleges in India also present the four cardinal principles for orderly growth. These relate to the private sector participation, raising access and equity to enlarge the base of professionals, balanced regional development and the process and performance-based quality professional education in India.

Important Assumptions Setting the Directions of Growth of Professional Colleges

In recent years, there is a distinct trend in the growth of private professional institutions. For example, both in terms of institutions and the intake at the undergraduate degree level in engineering the percentage of institutions and enrolment in the private sector in total has gone up from 76 per cent in 1999–2000 to 85 per cent in 2003–04. This calls for analysis. The reasons are to be found; first, in the shift in the assumption that higher education is a non-merit good and, therefore, government could afford to withdraw subsidies (Government of India, 1997). This was an important factor in the growth of private sector. Secondly, for a long time it was felt that private sector growth would find its own equilibrium in terms of number and price. What it effectively meant that demand-supply mechanism would guide the growth of professional colleges. This was a wrong presumption. An effective, implementable and early policy guideline to manage the growth of private professional colleges was desirable. Short-term approach to solve immediate problems furthermore added to the chaotic growth scenario. This was possibly the reason that the court had to interfere time and again in the matters of admission and fees regulation of private colleges. The thinking in the mind of the policy makers that judicial intervention will ultimately settle the vexed issue of admissions and fees also did not last long, as we will see the important milestones in the judgment even today raise more questions than it sorts out.

The point to note is that public and private dichotomy is a false dichotomy. The higher education is both a public as well as private good. The externalities of higher education and research are large enough to justify it as public good and hence government's bigger commitment for professional education is essential. At the same time, benefits that accrue to an individual entitles him to a job in the corporate sector that fetches the income to the individual. Hence, there exists reason to charge for professional education. Similarly, market needs to be fine-tuned to maintain quality, raise access and follow equity. Lastly, government must act in a proactive way with certain vision such as to build a world-class professional army.

It is against this backdrop that the issue of admission and fees policy in the private professional colleges demands a state-level consultation for an orderly growth of professional colleges in India. Before elaborating on the specific issues it would be necessary to understand various judicial pronouncements as these in a certain sense not only set the directions of growth but also act as parameters for the growth as it has the legal status.

Judicial Pronouncements

Miss Mohini Jain vs State of Karnataka and Others (1992)

In the Supreme Court of India (1992) case, the petitioner had challenged the notification of the Government of Karnataka permitting the private medical colleges in the state to charge higher tuition fees from students of other states. Colleges in Karnataka contended that they had to charge fees according to the capital cost and expenditure, as they do not receive any aid from the government. The judgment noted that the denial of educational opportunities by charging capitation fees amounts to the denial of the fundamental rights in more than one ways and as such "it is not permissible in law for any educational institution to charge capitation fee as a consideration for admission to the said institution". However institutions were free to charge differential fees from foreigners and NRIs. The court, however, failed to suggest options for the funding of private institutions.

J.P. Unnikrishnan and Others vs State of Andhra Pradesh and Others (1993)

In the Supreme Court of India (1993) case, the petitioners challenged the decisions regarding charging of fees as given in the Mohini Jain case. The petitioners also challenged various state acts that prohibited the capitation fees in Andhra Pradesh, Maharashtra and Tamil Nadu. In Unnikrishnan Judgment in 1993, it was held that "Commercialization of education was not permissible and it was opposed to public policy and Indian tradition and the charging of capitation fee was illegal". In this judgment, court issued guidelines regarding admission criteria in the professional unaided colleges, ceiling of fees, process of regulation under regulatory body and also suggested mechanism for regulation. In this judgment, the issue of private aided recognized/affiliated educational institutions seems to have been settled as the power to frame rules and regulations in terms of admission and fees was already under the government or government run university/deemed to be university. The Court then formulated a scheme and directed every authority granting recognition/affiliation to impose that scheme upon institutions seeking recognition/affiliation, even if they were unaided institutions. The scheme that was framed, inter alia, postulated:

(i) That 50 per cent of the seats in every professional college, established under a trust or society act or under state act should be filled by the nominees of the government or university, selected on the basis of merit determined by a common entrance examination, which will be referred to as 'free seats', the remaining 50 per cent seats (payment seats) should be filled by those candidates who pay the prescribed fee. The allotment of students against payment seats should be done on the basis of inter se merit determined on the same basis as in the case of free seats.

(ii) That there should be no quota reserved for the management or for any family, caste or community, which may have established such a college.

(iii) That it should be open to the professional college to provide for reservation of seats for constitutionally permissible classes with the approval of the affiliating university.

(iv) That the fee chargeable in each professional college should be subject to such a ceiling as may be prescribed by the authority or by a competent court.

(v) That every state government should constitute a committee to fix the ceiling on the fees chargeable by a professional college or class of professional colleges, as the case may be. This committee should, after hearing the professional colleges, fix the fee once every three years or at such longer intervals, as it may think appropriate.

(vi) That it would be appropriate for the University Grants Commission to frame regulations under its Act regulating the fees that the affiliated colleges operating on a no grant-in-aid basis were entitled to charge. The AICTE, the Indian Medical Council and the central government were also given similar advice. The manner in which the seats were to be filled on the basis of the common entrance test was also indicated.

T.M.A. Pai Foundation and Others vs State of Karnataka and Others (2002)

In the Supreme Court of India (2002) case, the petitioner contended that the judgment of the J.P. Unnikrishnan case adversely affected the autonomy of private institutions and hence needed reconsideration. The judgment delivered by the Chief Justice of India who presided over the 11-member bench, recognized the role of private initiatives. It made the observation that "the state with its limited resources and slow moving machinery is unable to fully develop the genius of the Indian people".

T.M.A. Pai judgment in 2002 referred to the Unnikrishnan case and stated as follows, "The hard reality that emerges is that private educational institutions are a necessity in the present day context. It is not possible to do without them because the governments are in no position to meet the demand—particularly in the sector of medical and technical education, which call for substantial outlays. While education is one of the most important functions of the Indian state it has no monopoly therein. Private educational institutions—including minority educational institutions—too have a role to play".

J.P. Unnikrishnan's case presumably adversely affected the autonomy of private institutions and it noted in Para 45 of the judgment that "in view of the discussion hereinabove, we hold that the decision in Unnikrishnan's case, insofar as it framed the scheme relating to the grant of admission and the fixing of the fee, was not correct, and to the extent, the said decision and the consequent directions given to UGC, AICTE, Medical Council of India, central and state governments, etc., are overruled". Effectively can we say that the judgment held as invalid, the concept of 'free seats' and 'payment seats'? This was so as in Para 56, the judgment furthermore noted "the decision on the fee to be charged must necessarily be left to the private educational institution that does not seek or is not dependent upon any funds from the government".

In Para 57 the judgment held that "... the government can provide regulations that will ensure excellence while forbidding the charging of capitation fee and profiteering by the institution ... . There can, however, be reasonable revenue surplus which may be generated by the educational institution for the purpose of development of education and expansion of the institution". In Para 58, it was noted, "For admission into any professional institution merit must play an important role ... . Appropriate regulations for this purpose may be made keeping in view the other observations made in this judgment in the context of admission to unaided institutions". The judgment furthermore defined merit in terms of marks obtained in the qualifying examination or the marks obtained in a common entrance test.

In Para 67, "We now come to the regulations that can be framed relating to private unaided professional institutions ... it would, therefore be permissible for the university or the government, at the time of granting recognition, to require private unaided institutions to provide for merit-based selection while giving the management sufficient discretion in admitting students ... . For, instance, a certain percentage of the seats can be reserved for admission by the management out of those students who have passed the common entrance test held by itself or by the state/university and have applied to the college concerned for admission, while the rest of the seats may be filled up on the basis of counseling by the state agency ... . The prescription of percentage for this purpose has to be done by the government according to the local needs".

Supreme Court of India (2003): Islamic Academy of Education and Another vs State of Karnataka and Others

The judgment of the Supreme Court in the T.M.A. Pai case created buoyancy, which believed that they gave them the autonomy regarding fixation of fees and mode of admission although the government interpreted it otherwise. Litigations followed and in view of this the Supreme Court set-up a five-judge bench for the Islamic Academy of Education vs the Government of Karnataka case to clarify the earlier Supreme Court judgment. The following questions were taken up for consideration by the five-judge bench:

1. Whether the educational institutions are entitled to fix their own fee structure?
2. Whether minority and non-minority institutions stand on the same footing and have the same rights?

3. Whether private unaided professional colleges are entitled to fill in their seats, to the extent of 100 per cent, and if not to what extent?
4. Whether private unaided professional institutions are entitled to admit students by evolving their own method of admission?

In relation to the first question, a four-judge majority judgment clarified that the government cannot prescribe a rigid fee structure. Every institution must have the right to fix its fees in accordance with the costs. They can also generate a surplus to be used for the betterment and growth of the institution. However, there can be no profiteering and capitation fees cannot be charged. The proposed fee structure will have to be submitted to a committee headed by a retired judge to be nominated by the Chief Justice of the State. The other members of the committee will include a chartered accountant, a nominee of the AICTE/MCI and the secretary of the state in charge of technical education/medical education. Other details are as under:

1. The institutions shall charge fees only for one year, in accordance with the rules and not the fees for the entire course.
2. Care be taken that the institutions do not indulge in profiteering or otherwise exploiting students financially.
3. Fees once fixed shall not be changed for a period of three years, unless there exists an extraordinary reason.
4. The fees fixed by the institutions should be approved by the authority/body of the concerned state.
5. No institution should charge any fee beyond the amount fixed and the fees charged shall be deposited in a nationalized bank.
6. The statutory authority can frame rules for imposing penalties in case of any contravention and the penalty may be ten to fifteen times of the amount so collected and it can derecognize and cancel recognition.
7. The fee already collected for long terms should be kept in a fixed deposit in a nationalized bank and the interest accrued should be given to the students.
8. However, the management can insist on a bond from the students when they are seeking admission.

In relation to questions 3 and 4, the four-judge majority judgment pointed out that the majority judgment in the T.M.A. Pai Foundation case makes a distinction between private unaided professional colleges and other institutions. Regarding admission to various programmes it is clarified that:

1. Individual institutes cannot hold their own entrance tests. Institutions will have to make admissions on the basis of the common entrance test conducted by the state government or by an association of all colleges of a particular type.
2. The admissions should be based on merit in the common entrance test, except for the percentage given to the management.
3. The management quota, which is to be determined by the concerned government, should be filled from the students successful in the common entrance test.
4. Institutions that have been conducting their own tests for at least 25 years can approach the committee for approval for continuing such tests.
5. The states have been directed to appoint a permanent committee, which will ensure that the tests conducted by the association of colleges, are fair and transparent. A retired judge of the High Court, to be nominated by the Chief Justice of the state, should head such committees, the other members being an eminent engineer/doctor and the secretary of the concerned department.

Admission Structure Regulations AICTE (1994) and MHRD Policy Guidelines (1997)

Given two previous judicial pronouncements, it is now necessary to understand the role of AICTE in framing admission and fees regulations. AICTE was established by AICTE Act, 1987. Its functions are planning, coordination, promotion of quality and maintenance of standards of technical education system in the country. National Board of Accreditation was established in 1994 under section 10(u) of AICTE Act, 1987. It was established with a view to assess standards of quality of education, to assess and accredit institutions imparting technical education in India. It is also a recommending body regarding recognition and derecognition of institutions from the point of view of standard setting. Admission Structure Regulations AICTE, 1994 were issued under the directions of 1993 court judgment that laid down the procedure for admission and state level committee's role for determination of tuition and other fees in a professional college.

However, AICTE will have the authority to fix the number of seats in each professional college as the standard setting condition. It stands intact even after the T.M.A Pai case judgment, 2002. It means that AICTE will have the authority to fix the number of seats in each professional college but will have no authority to determine the procedure for admission of students and fixation of fees. The procedure for the allotment of seats in AICTE regulation in the light of Unnikrishnan case judgment may not hold valid as Para 45 of the T.M.A Pai case judgment quoted above overrules the scheme relating to the grant of admission and fixing of fees in Unnikrishnan case. It means to that extent the provisions of AICTE regulation, particularly relating to the distinction between free and payment seats stands overruled. Indeed AICTE's various other procedures for allotment of seats and the fixing of fees also stand overruled as autonomy to determine fees now rests with the private professional colleges.

Later Ministry of Human Resource Development (Department of Education) New Delhi, on 18th March, 1997 issued policy on fee fixation in private unaided educational institutions imparting higher and technical education including management education.[7] As we can see not only the various provisions of AICTE regulation 1994 but also the policy guidelines of MHRD, issued in 1997 approved by the President of India do not stand as valid after T.M.A Pai case judgment. More specifically we see that Clause 6 under AICTE Act under the procedure of allotment of seats relating to management seats may not hold now. This has also created uncertainty with respect to management quota. While Haryana government has fixed up 25 per cent as management quota, Kerala and Tamil Nadu's government notification fixed the management quota at 50 per cent. This is indeed a very serious matter. This has created an uncertainty as existing policy guidelines of the government itself stand as invalid. There are also disputes over the settlement of fees by the government. The Association of the Managements of Unaided Engineering Colleges (Maharashtra) has complained that private engineering colleges have the power to the determination of fees and as such, in all likehood, private colleges may defy the state government's notification.

There is a need, therefore, to think afresh on the policy guidelines considering the judgment both of the T.M.A Pai case and the Islamic Academy of Education and Another vs State of Karnataka and others case. The specific issues may be highlighted:

- Mode of entrance test: Can there be all-India and state level tests with predetermined proportion of students with adequate management quota representation?
- Fixing of the uniform management quota.
- Setting up of a permanent committee in each state to oversee the admission and fees structure.
- How should the right of private professional colleges to fix up the fees be interpreted?
- What should be the basis of charging (fixing) the fees by institutions? Can it be linked to performance indicators as well as a way to boost quality?
- How to ensure that institutions can earn the surplus but is not engaged in profiteering? This point is of utmost importance because government of India is concerned over the fact that institutions raised the fees by a very high margin almost overnight that led to protests at all-India level by student bodies.
- Should there be fresh central government policy guidelines on admission and fees?
- Does the situation call for Parliament legislation for fixing the admission norms and the fees? If so, what should be the guidelines? If not, why not?

There is also another dimension to the issue of admission and fees. The recent Supreme Court judgment in August again raised the issue of education as fundamental right. The matter also came up in the Parliament and members expressed dissatisfaction over raising fees for professional courses in self-financing private unaided institutions. There cannot be denial of the equality of opportunity as provided in the fundamental right.

Recently, on 10th–11th January, 2005, the Union HRD Minister Arjun Singh convened a conference of all the state higher and technical education ministers at Bangalore to solicit views on the issue of admission and fees in private professional colleges. All the state ministers unanimously declared that there is a need to bring central legislation with some model guidelines on admissions, reservations, fees, management quota and the principle of earning a surplus but preventing commercialization of higher education. Although the draft bill on fees and admission of private self-financing institutions was circulated for discussion in 2005, so far the government has not enacted on the issue of fees and admission in private professional colleges.

Notes

1. Chhattisgarh Niji Kshetra Vishvidyalaya (Sthapana Aur Viniyaman) Adhiniyam (2002) is one such act passed by the Chhattisgarh government. Many other states are also in the process of passing the acts allowing private universities to impart education in India.
2. 'off-campus centre'* means a centre of the private university established by it outside the main campus (within or outside the state) operated and maintained as its constituent unit, having the university's compliment of facilities, faculty and staff.
3. 'study centre'* means a centre established and maintained or recognized by the university for the purpose of advising, counselling or for rendering any other assistance required by the students used in the context of distance education.
4. 'off-shore campus'* means a campus of the private university established by it outside the country, operated and maintained as its

*additionally there were 400 private institutions offering postgraduate diploma programmes in different areas of management.

constituent unit, having the university's compliment of facilities, faculty and staff.

5. See Garrett Richard (2004a, 2004b).
6. UGC (2004b).
7. A meeting of State Higher and Technical Education Ministers was convened by the Union Minister of Human Resource Development on 10th December 1996 wherein it was decided that self-contained policy directions could be issued applicable to sectors of education, falling within the purview of the Ministry of Human Resource Development, namely higher and technical education.

References

Association of Indian Universities (2002a), Handbook on Engineering Education, 2002 AIU, New Delhi.

Association of Indian Universities (2002b), Handbook on Management Education, 2002 AIU, New Delhi.

Association of Indian Universities (2003), Handbook on Medical Education, 2003 AIU, New Delhi.

Chhatisgarh Act (2002), Chhattisgarh Niji Kshetra Vishvidyalaya (Sthapana Aur Viniyaman) Adhiniyam.

Chhattisgarh Act (2004), Chhattisgarh Private University Amendment Bill.

Garrett, Richard (2004a), "Foreign Higher Education Activity in China", *International Higher Education,* Winter. See also the website of the journal that is available online.

Garrett, Richard (2004b), "UGC's Attempt to Oversee India's Private Universities is challenged in Court, Observatory on Borderless Higher Education", *The Bulletin,* May.

Government of India (1997), Government Subsidies in India, Discussion Paper, Department of Economic Affairs, Ministry of Finance, GoI, New Delhi.

Natarajan, R. (2004), "Private Initiatives in Higher Education: Roles of Privatization in Professional Education", K.B. Powar and K.L. Johar (Ed.), Sneh Prakashan, New Delhi.

NCTE (2004), List of Recognized Teacher Education Institutions. Last visited http://www.ncte-in.org on 15th February 2004, National Council for Teacher Education, New Delhi.

Powar, K.B. and V. Bhalla (2004), *Private Inititatives in Indian Professional and Higher Education: Status and Possibilities in Private Initiatives in Higher Education*, K.B. Powar and K.L. Johar (eds.), Sneh Prakashan, New Delhi.

Singh, Amrik (2004), *Fifty Years of Higher Education in India: The Role of the University Grants Commission*, Sage Publications, New Delhi.

Supreme Court of India (1992), Judgment: Writ Petition (Civil) No. 456 of 1991, *Miss Moini Jain Versus State of Karnataka and Others*, SC, New Delhi, AIR 1992, SC 1858.

Supreme Court of India (1993), Judgment: Writ Petition No. 607 of 1992, *J.P. Unni Krishnan and Others Versus State of Andhra Pradesh and Others*, SC, New Delhi, AIR 2178, SCR (1) 594, SCC (1) 645.

Supreme Court of India (2002), Judgment: Writ Petition (Civil) No. 607 of 1992, *T.M.A. Pai Foundation and Others Versus State of Karnataka and Others*, SC, New Delhi, 8 SCC 481.

Supreme Court of India (2003), Judgment: Writ Petition (Civil) No. 350 of 1993, *Islamic Academy of Education and Another Versus State of Karnataka and Others*, SC, New Delhi, 6 SCC 697.

Supreme Court of India (2005), Judgment: Writ Petition (Civil) No. 19 of 2004, *Prof. Yashpal and Anr Versus State of Chhattisgarh and Others*, New Delhi.

University Grants Commission (2003), The Model Act for Universities of the 21st Century in India, October 2003 at the UGC Website: www.ugc.ac.in.

University Grants Commission (2004a), "Establishment and Maintenance of Standards in Private Universities Regulations, 2003", *UGC News*, 11(1): 16–18.

University Grants Commission (2004b), Franchising of Higher Education through Off-Campus Study Centres, UGC Norms, UGC News, 11(1): 38–44.

University Grants Commission (2005), Annual Report 2004–05, New Delhi.

Appendix I
Number of Private Professional Institutions, 2002

Branches	*Total*	*Private*	*Per cent of Private to Total*
Engineering and Technology	977	764	78.20
Medicine and Health Sciences*	1351	1028	76.20
Management *(Masters)	505	324	64.15
College for Teacher Education**	1541	1038	67.35

*Includes Allopathic Medicine, Dentistry, Nursing and Pharmacy and Ayurvedic Medicine, Unani Medicine, Homeopathy and Pharmacy in 2003.
**Refers to February 2004.
Source: Powar and Bhalla (2004).

Appendix II
Students' Enrolment: Facultywise 2004–05

Faculty	*Total Enrolment*	*Per cent to Total*
Arts	47,29,048	45.12
Science	21,42,325	20.44
Commerce/Management	18,85,539	17.99
Education	1,54,071	1.47
Engineering/Technology	7,54,635	7.20
Medicine	3,30,153	3.15
Agriculture	61,838	0.59
Veterinary Science	15,721	0.15
Law	3,19,671	3.05
Others	88,041	0.84
Total	1,04,81,042	100.00

Source: UGC (2005).

Appendix III

Regional Distribution of Institutions Offering Degree Programmes in Professional Courses

State	*Engineering & Technology (2002)*			*Medicine*+ *(2003)*			*Management*# *(2002)*			*Teacher Education*		
	Private	*Total*	*Per cent*$	*Private*	*Total*	*Per cent*$	*Private*	*Total*	*Per cent*$	*Private*	*Total*	*Per cent*$
Andhra Pradesh	174	188	93	77	110	70	46	64	72	260	292	89
Maharashtra	141	167	84	208	252	83	81	95	85	214	273	78
Karnataka	72	78	92	274	295	93	26	36	72	52	88	59
Tamil Nadu	137	152	90	161	183	88	56	74	76	0	28	0
Kerala	25	50	50	42	60	70	3	9	33	32	55	58
Total	549	635	86	762	900	85	212	278	76	558	736	76
All-India	764	977	78	1028	1351	76	324	505	64	1038	1541	67

$ Per cent of Private Colleges to Total Colleges in India

+ includes institutions offering Allopathic Medicine, Dentistry, Nursing, Pharmacy, Ayurvedic, Unani, Homeopathy and Physiotherapy

the data includes 25 postgraduate diploma awarding institutions that have been given equivalence with MBA degree by the Association of Indian Universities

Source: AIU (2002a, 2002b and 2003) and NCTE (2004).

Appendix IV
Growth of Technical Institutions at the Undergraduate Level

	Engineering				*Pharmacy*				*Hotel Mgmt. and Catering Tech.*				*Architecture*			
	1999–2000		*2003–04*		*1999–2000*		*2003–04*		*1999–2000*		*2003–04*		*1999–2000*		*2003–04*	
	Pvt.	*Govt.*	*Pvt.*	*Govt.*	*Pvt.*	*Govt.*	*Pvt.*	*Govt.*	*Pvt.*	*Govt.*	*Pvt.*	*Govt.*	*Pvt.*	*Govt.*	*Pvt.*	*Govt.*
Number of Institutions	510	159	1,071	194	174	30	280	40	35	6	40	9	56	22	83	24
(%)	76	24	85	15	85	14.7	87.5	12.5	85.3	14.6	81.6	18.3	71.7	28.2	77.5	22.4
Intake	1,33,811	40,307	3,25,747	55,056	8,815	1,463	14,532	1,878	1,720	310	2,230	410	2,318	2,318	2,662	746
(%)	76	24	85	15	85.7	14.2	88.5	11.4	84.7	15.2	84.4	15.5	73.7	73.7	78.1	21.8

Source: Natarajan (2004).

CHAPTER 5

Foreign Universities in India

Education in India is considered as a social service. It is accorded a status of public good. Recently, the recognition of education sector as a tradable service sector under the GATS-WTO regime has made it imperative to understand the duality of education as a social and tradable service. The phenomenon of the emergence of foreign universities imparting foreign degrees in partnership with private institutions has now been a real event in higher education. The examination of the presence of foreign universities in India is warranted, as they may have implications to influence the structure and direction of higher education possibly in terms of commercialization that may furthermore intensify the duality of education.

Given the duality of higher education as a current phenomenon, the public policy design should gear itself to deal with the phenomenon rather than evade the issue and allow the undesirable consequences to grow and then persist as a long-term irreversible trend making things difficult to control. Instruments that were relevant during early periods of active state intervention may not be as relevant as during period of dual growth of higher education institutions. Set of instruments for control may not prove to be effective. Policy instruments should be finely designed to regulate the market in such a manner that evil designs of market could be checked and policy instruments should facilitate market as per the demand of the learners. This obviously means a change in the mindset, an understanding of the situation—both national and international—and the will to implement the change in accordance with the changed circumstances.

It is in this context that the presence of foreign universities in India is being analysed. Given the context of GATS regime and various conventions and agreements of which India is a party, structures need to be established to squarely face the phenomenon of foreign universities. The objective of the paper is to highlight the mechanism and operation of foreign universities in India almost for the last 15 years and suggest strategies that government should design.

Genesis of Foreign Universities

Both public and private education has existed side by side in India since independence. This mixed model of development was allowed to grow over the years. Although at the policy-making level education was not for profit, at the operational level, higher education was increasingly a profitable venture in private sector. Even the Supreme Court, in many of its judgments, has not removed this anomaly. The ambivalence in policy and practice has resulted in growth of a large number of private providers in technical education like engineering and medical and in the nineties especially in the sector of management education. Over the years, a dual system has evolved in the higher education sector in India. The private players by nature are profit-oriented. They have not only to earn to run their institutes but also to operate institutes in a profitable way. Hence, education as a profit-oriented activity has grown over the years in spite of the central government or the Supreme Court's view that education and higher education in particular, is not for profit.

In the nineties, the private education sector in India saw an opportunity for providing foreign degrees in India. There was a huge unmet demand in India for foreign degrees. The students who could not enter into the few good public institutions in India and had money opted for the private sector. Within this section of students some were interested in getting a foreign degree but could not afford to go abroad. When the private sector came out with the idea of providing foreign degrees in India at a much lower cost, this section of the students got an opportunity to fulfil their dreams. The case of foreign universities may be looked at as another successive event in the direction of privatization. The seed of commercialization was already sown in the privatization that got accepted as there were limits to public investment in education in relation to the demand.

The key drivers of the provision of foreign education from home to the host country is the recent upsurge in the demand for transnational higher education in developing countries coupled with the likely possibility of excess capacity due to changing demographic structure in the developed countries who see excess demand in developing economies as one of trade advantage. Altbach (2003) captures this phenomenon in terms of 'centre-periphery hypothesis' indicating the strength in the export of programmes and institutions by the North to the South, i.e., from the developed to the developing countries. The phenomenon may also be captured in terms of the maintenance of international equilibrium, i.e., equality of the flow of international demand for and supply of higher education at a higher price of education, although at a given price the developing countries may still be characterized by domestic disequilibria due to supply constraint (Bhushan, 2005).

Growth of Foreign Universities

The operation of foreign education providers started in 1991–92 with study and examination centres of foreign institutions. In this phase, private institutions in India tied up with foreign partners in terms of study and examination centres. The parent foreign institutions decided the course design, curriculum, examination process and other issues. In this way foreign institutions established a 'Chain of Study and Examination Centres' in different parts of the country. As example, TASMAC, Pune, had become the study and examination centre of CSM Institute of Graduate Studies, Canada in 1991. But, in 2000, the TASMAC had a joint venture agreement with Emile Woolf International, London, offering their MBA and BA (Hons.). Oxford Brookes University, UK and University of Wales, UK validated TASMAC to offer the programmes in 2000 and 2001 respectively. The nature of collaboration was joint degree and credit transfer. Similarly, Institute of Computer and Business Management (ICBM), Hyderabad became a study centre of Kensington University, USA in 1999. TECHNA Institute, Kolkata became study and examination centre of London School of Economics, University of London in 1996. We observe that though some of the foreign institutions started their operations in collaboration with Indian partner as study centres, they developed greater collaborations in the later period. There were also those institutions, which started their operations through other modes when foreign degree gained some acceptance by industries, students and parents. At present, University of London External Programme (ULEP) has study centres for diploma in economics, management, finance and social science in Mudra Institute of Communication, H.R. College (External), Stansfield School of Business (External), Russell Square International College, Asia Pacific Institute of Technology, Panipat and School of Economics and Management Sciences (SEMS)—Rai Foundation.

The second mode of their operation can be seen through the development of twinning and teacher-student exchange. This phase may be said to have begun in 1995–96. The institutions that were interested in initiating foreign programmes in India but were rather late in responding as a partner to foreign institution in terms of study centre started with teacher-student exchange programme. Under this arrangement, students can complete part of their study in India and part in foreign university. The twinning arrangement may be optional to the students. It is one of the most preferred modes because the foreign institutions have least stakes and maximum income. In some cases, few students visited foreign institution as a part of their exposure trip completing most of the courses in India. Under this arrangement, teachers of both the partner institutions also visit each other's institute to understand the teaching-learning process. For example, EMPI, Delhi started foreign programme with Esclille, France, Fordham, New-York, and Wharton School of Business, USA through teacher-student exchange method in 1995. But they were also not restricted with these arrangements only. In 1998, EMPI established foreign collaboration with Brighton University, UK and the nature of the operation was joint degree. ITM Mumbai started their collaboration with Queen Margaret University College (QM), Edinburgh, UK in 2002–03. ITM has also 'Home Tuition Student Exchange' with Ecole Superieure des Sciences Commerciales d'Angers (ESSCA). As a part of this arrangement, ITM and ESSCA exchange about five students each year. Students pay tuition fee only in the home country and are responsible for the travel and living cost in the host country.

The third mode of their operation can be seen in terms of programmatic collaboration through the growth of joint degree. This process started in 1995–96. In fact, both the methods teacher-student exchange and joint programme started in the same period. But those institutions that established their credibility in the market moved to joint degree arrangement and the newcomers in this business were restricted with teacher-student exchange. This collaboration in terms of joint degree enables a student to complete study in India and get joint degree i.e., (foreign as well as private education institutions). It has its own attraction, as it is one of the cheapest ways to earn foreign degree. The study observed that various types of inter-institutional collaborations exist under the joint degree programme. For example, foreign institutions may support in developing the curriculum, joint course preparation, joint evaluation of the programme, teacher's visit, student summer trip etc. At the end, the student will get a joint degree of both the institutions. As example, Rizvi College of Hotel Management, Mumbai started their joint degree programme with AHLA in 2000. Skyline Business School, Delhi, established foreign collaboration with National American University, USA. The nature of collaboration was the joint programme. Dina Institute of Hotel Management, Pune with University of Middlesex, UK started joint programme in year 2001.

The fourth mode of operation can be seen through the provision of complete foreign degree in India through deeper involvement of foreign partner. This phase started in 2000. In this period, the phenomena of franchisee arrangement were also introduced in the Indian education sector. For example, Institute of International Management and Technology, Kolkata established their tie-up with Oxford Brooks University, UK in 2002. They are providing foreign-degree in India. National Insurance Academy, Pune provides degree validated by Fairfax University, USA. Manchester Business School, University of Manchester delivers (1) MBA for Financial Managers and Finance Professionals (2.5 years) and (2) MBA for Engineering Business Managers Programme in India (3 years) with Barclay Hotel Management College.

Modes of Operation

The phenomenon of internationalization of higher education opens up various modes of operation in offering the programmes. Under this arrangement, the following types of collaborations are functional in India:

1. *Twinning:* Twinning programmes are those wherein students can complete part of their study in India and part in foreign university. The twinning arrangement may be optional to the students. Students prefer this mode because it provides them the least cost opportunity to earn foreign degree with outside exposure. Of course, in many cases, students feel the difficulty of obtaining visa even when their admission under twinning arrangement is granted by a foreign university.
2. *Franchisee:* In this case, foreign institutions grant permission to an institution in another country to execute their programme with their name, curriculum, evaluation methods. In this arrangement, foreign institutions franchise a programme to an Indian organization that offers these programmes under the direct supervision of the foreign institutions. Two foreign institutions, namely Wigan and Leigh, UK and Western International University are providing degrees under franchise arrangement.

3. *Study and examination centres:* Growth of foreign degree providers started with the examination and study centres. In the initial year of the operation of such courses, most of the institutions adopted this method to provide foreign degrees in India. Under this arrangement, the foreign institution/university ties up with an Indian partner to deliver their course and also conduct the examination for the same.
4. *Multiple collaboration:* This type of collaboration is a rare phenomenon in India among the foreign degree providers. This was found only in case of Indian School of Business, Hyderabad, which has got a tie-up with Wharton, Kellog's and London Business School. These institutes are providing a one-year postgraduate diploma course in management. While all these institutes contribute in development of course material and faculty exchange, the degree is signed by all the deans, except by the Dean of London Business School.
5. *Link programme:* Link programme is another new innovative method to operate foreign degree programmes in India. Under this arrangement, an Indian institution delivers certain credit programmes in a particular time period and after that rest of the course follows at the foreign institutions. For example, a diploma in hotel management is completed with certain credits in India and a foreign degree is earned after completing certain credits abroad in foreign university. This is also twinning. But under pure twinning, the part education abroad is done for only one qualification whereas in link programme part education enables to earn another foreign degree. The time of the programme is adjusted in such a manner that after the end of first phase, the next phase will start.
6. *Programmatic collaboration:* The programmatic collaboration enables a student to complete study in India and get joint degree, i.e., (foreign as well as private education institutions). It has its own attraction, as it is one of the cheapest ways to earn a foreign degree. The study observed that various types of inter-institutional collaborations exist under programmatic collaboration. For example, foreign institutions may support in developing curriculum, joint

course preparation, joint evaluation of the programme, teachers' visit, student summer trip etc. The programmatic collaboration is a way through which new innovative courses are offered at less cost and private Indian institutions offer a foreign degree which is a way of attracting the students.

7. *Off-shore campus:* Under this arrangement, the foreign universities may open their branch either as a subsidiary or in partnership with the Indian institution. It involves large FDI inflows into India. However, no such branch campus is said to operate in India, as there is no enabling domestic regulation. In a way, off-shore campus operation is possible only when the investors are assured of no legal hurdles. It is in all likelihood, a pure commercial operation.

Presence of Foreign Education Providers

Due to the absence of regulation, it is difficult to gauge the magnitude of the foreign institutions in India. The global example of the expansion of foreign education providers in different countries shows that the process of privatization facilitates the growth of foreign institutions in the host country. During the project period in 2003–04 a number of foreign institutions collaborating with Indian partner institutions were identified. There were 131 such Indian institutions collaborating with foreign institutions. The list, however, may not be fully exhaustive. The list of such institutions was printed in a Directory (Bhushan, 2004) which was circulated on 26 August 2004 in a conference organized by NIEPA on the theme, "Internationalization of Higher Education: Issues and Concerns". However, for the detailed study on various other aspects of the institutions, only 50 institutions were selected.

Geographical Distribution in India

Spread of foreign education providers in India on the basis of the information so far collected shows that Tamil Nadu has the maximum number of Indian institutions collaborating with foreign institutions (23) and providing foreign degrees, with Chennai of course, having the highest concentration of such institutions in Tamil Nadu, followed by Maharashtra, the second largest destination of foreign education providers (20) with maximum concentration in Mumbai, the financial capital of India and Pune. Delhi registered the third largest state (19) in terms of the foreign institutions. Due to the time constraint of the project and difficulties of tracing all such foreign operators, the researchers confined the study to the number of institutions given below, although the number of such institutions may be much more than reflected in the Table 5.1.

Table 5.1

Statewise Number of Institutes having Foreign Collaboration

States	*No. of Institutes having foreign collaborations*
Andhra Pradesh	18
Delhi	19
Goa	2
Gujarat	4
Haryana	6
Karnataka	13
Kerala	3
Madhya Pradesh	3
Maharashtra	20
Rajasthan	1
Tamil Nadu	23
Uttar Pradesh	4
West Bengal	15
Total	131

Source: Bhushan (2004).

It may be observed that in different states the foreign education providers were concentrated in metropolitan cities and some other cities where the prospects of vocational courses exist on a large scale.

Presence of Foreign Education Providers by Country of Origin

It is interesting to observe that only few countries are actively involved in collaborating with private institutions in India. Information given in Table 5.2 shows that at present only USA and UK have shown their interest in making collaboration with Indian partners.

There are other potential countries such as Australia, New Zealand and Canada who are constantly watching the developments and the government's stand on any regulation regarding foreign education providers. At present, these countries are organizing educational fairs and have also representatives to attract Indian students to their respective countries. They do not show interest in educational collaboration in India, as they do not find any enabling laws for the legal operation. At the international level, many countries such as UK, USA, Canada, Australia, New Zealand, France and Germany are showing interest in providing education to other countries.

Table 5.2

Countrywise Presence of Foreign Education Providers in Different Regions in India

Name of Indian States	*No. of Countrywise Institutions Having One Foreign Collaboration With One Country*						
	UK	*USA*	*Canada*	*Australia*	*Switzerland*	*France*	*Europe*
Andhra Pradesh	7	11	—	—	—	—	—
Delhi	13	5	—	—	—	—	1
Goa		2	—	—	—	—	—
Gujarat	2	2	—	—	—	—	—
Haryana	4	2	—	—	—	—	—
Karnataka	7	6	—	—	—	—	—
Kerala		3	—	—	—	—	—
Madhya Pradesh	1	1	—	—	1	—	—
Maharashtra	7	11	2	—	—	—	—
Rajasthan	—	1	—	—	—	—	—
Tamil Nadu	6	16	—	—	—	1	—
Uttar Pradesh	1	3	—	—	—	—	—
West Bengal	11	3	—	1	—	—	—
Total	59	66	2	1	1	1	1

Source: Bhushan (2004).

Methods of Promoting Foreign Education in India

Foreign universities/institutions are marketing their programmes through different institutions, fairs, counselors and resource information centres. The internet, newspapers and magazines widely cover the advertisement for these institutions. The research team observed that the foreign universities use four different methods of enrolling students in India. One, by organizing the registration sessions through an agency in different cities of India and the other has been through tie-up with Indian institutions for offering a joint programme. The third one is setting up franchise in India and the fourth one is through correspondence or online programme. The private counsellors who facilitate the students to get admission get commission for each student. And some of the institutions have their own counsellors in different cities of India who promote the presence of the institution.

Coursewise Presence of Foreign Institutions

It is important to know how the market behaves in an unregulated scenario. It is the preference of courses in market that regulates the programmes to be offered by the foreign education providers in India.

Table 5.3

Statewise and Coursewise Operation of Foreign Institutions

State	*Professional/Vocational Courses*				*General*	*Technical Courses*	*Total*
	MBA	*Fashion Tech.*	*Mass Comm.*	*Hotel Mgmt.*	*BA/ B.Sc*	*B.Tech/M.Tech/ Medical*	
Andhra Pradesh	7	1	—	8	—	2	18
Delhi	11	2	—	2	—	4	19
Goa	—	—	—	2	—	—	2
Gujarat	1	—	1	2	—	—	4
Haryana	2	—	—	1	1	2	6
Karnataka	8	—	—	3	—	2	13
Kerala	—	—	—	3	—	—	3
Madhya Pradesh	2	—	—	1	—	—	3
Maharashtra	5	1	—	11	1	2	20
Rajasthan		—	—	1	—	—	1
Tamil Nadu	4	—	2	9	3	5	23
Uttar Pradesh	1	—	—	2	—	1	4
West Bengal	4	—	—	10	—	1	15
Total	45	4	3	55	5	19	131

Source: Bhushan (2004).

The above table shows that majority of the foreign education providers provide professional/vocational courses. Out of the total sample of 131 institutions, 107 were providing vocational courses, 19 technical courses and only five general education. The data shows that in the category of vocational courses—management courses were the most popular. Business management and hotel management constitute approximately 80 per cent of the total number of courses. The table also shows that Maharashtra has the maximum number of programmes in hotel management. Delhi has the maximum number of programmes in business management. In technical courses, at present not much interest is shown, although 19 institutions were active in technical sectors as well.

It shows that foreign institutions are taking advantage of the demand for vocational courses. As it has the potential for employment in the private sector, students prefer such courses even though they are unrecognized in India. It has the implication that unregulated structure will lead to various unrecognized courses and there may not be any standard setting institutions to monitor the quality. As such in the medium and long run, this will create chaos and confusion for the students to select the quality course and institution.

Corporate Orientation of Programmes

It may also be observed that foreign institutions are not limited only to particular age cohort in traditional courses as is the practice in Indian higher education institutions. They have both the types of programmes. One suitable for young students in different vocational courses and the other, for the corporate employees which is need-based on their job training, like use of IT software in management, tools for effective decision-making, industrial training programme to increase the efficiency of managers.

The education provided by foreign institutions in partnership with private education providers has another very interesting feature, namely, the flexibility in duration, curricula, easy credit transfer, multiple entry and multiple exit course design, imparting the greater attractiveness among the students. Thus, foreign education providers provide a practical approach to the concept of lifelong education and training which is also the need of the time. From the curriculum, course design, teaching-learning methodology of foreign education providers, it may be observed that the new education providers, foreign education providers, are preparing youth for the corporate job. The broad objective of education is preparing the youth for active participation in social, cultural, economic and the political life of a nation; so far the mandate for public university is, however, not the mandate of foreign education providers.

Rationale

An understanding of the rationale for the commercial presence of foreign educational institutions is necessary. Expected rationale should be guided by the objectives of national development. It should address some of the concerns that the Indian higher education system faces and also some of the challenges posed and opportunities arising from globalization to the higher education institution.[1]

Human Resource Development

In the global context, technological upgradation poses a challenge for educational institutions to upgrade the skill of human resources. Broadly speaking, lifelong education and training is the emerging need for which higher educational institutions must prepare themselves. The need for upgrading the skills demands prompt response in terms of developing teaching faculty, developing curricula and introducing the programmes for varying periods. Neither the regulatory framework allows nor the academia within universities realize this compelling need of the market to which university system should extend its functioning. The fact of the matter is that the demand for specialized skills exist and given the slow response of the public institutions, various private actors have become active to fill the niche market for specialized skills sometimes in partnership with foreign institutions. In the absence of no regulation to cater to the emerging demand for specialized knowledge acquisition wherever that is required, there is no systematic and institutionalized effort that greatly constraints the internal capacity of the economy to innovate and progress.

One of the most important rationales for the commercial presence of foreign educational institutions is to help develop curricula, fill the gap due to shortage of the expertise and jointly run such educational programmes in partnership with the public/private institutions. Of course the regulatory framework needs to be created for such partnership. This will have much desired impact on colleges and universities in India to learn to adapt faster to the needs of society and break the age-old practices of traditional curricula and teaching. In the running of such programmes, efforts must be made to transfer the foreign expertize and the best practices.

Arresting Brain Drain

Human resource-rich countries like India and China today face the problem of brain drain due to increased mobility of professors, researchers and scientists. Most of them move to developed country destinations. Students, mostly postgraduates and above, move to foreign country destination to study, later on to join the educational institutions or to work abroad as knowledge workers. The GATS perspective that supports trade in education furthermore promotes the possibility of increased brain drain. The Global Information Technology Report (2003) notes that India ranks second in terms of availability of scientists and engineers and also in domestic software companies in international markets. However, India also suffers due to brain drain as its ranking is 54.[2] It is estimated, for example, that at least 40 per cent of the graduates of the highly regarded Indian Institutes of Technology seek employment abroad.[3]

Important rationale for the commercial presence of foreign educational institutions could be to check the flow of students westward. Students move to advanced countries in search of quality institutions and later on prefer to take up job there itself as well. If foreign educational institutions help to build up the quality institutions or help to develop world-class institutions, then this will definitely restrict the flow of students and, to some extent, check the brain drain. As the multinational and top class companies are in India, they may be absorbed in India. What is, however, more important is that a well-thought out strategy be devised to attract foreign institutions in a way that quality transfer of education to Indian institutions could be made possible.

A related argument is "that Indians are spending between Rs 3,000–5,000 crore (roughly $ 700 million to $ 1 billion) on higher education abroad, a staggering amount for a poor country whose own educational institutions are starved of resources" (Kapur and Mehta, 2004). If the world-class national institutions are developed in partnership with highly selected foreign institutions of repute, the flight of capital as well as the outflow of students could be checked. The quality educational programmes could be offered at cheaper costs than what the same course could cost abroad. Thus, the accessibility to such course can also be enhanced. It will also lead to increased capacity of the higher education sector to generate research and produce knowledge as well as supply knowledge workers. Arresting brain drain and turning it into mutually advantageous situation of brain gain may be possible provided that institutional mobility to Indian soil is supported by appropriate policy regime.

Promoting Competitiveness

An important feature of the Indian higher education system is that, within the framework of public control, it has expanded to reach different sections of the society and that it has also a diversified structure. Yet, the quality of average institution, average teaching faculty and average student is a cause of concern.[4] In particular, the teaching faculties just like any other public sector are highly protected and the education system does not impose the need to achieve excellence. The higher education system as a whole suffers from inefficiency. There is the need to expose the system towards, if not price efficiency, various non-price efficiency factors such as upgrading the standards of teaching faculty, orienting the curricula to industrial and societal needs and promoting IT enabled teaching and learning.

It may be argued that commercial presence of foreign institutions in India will promote competitiveness in Indian higher education system. It is, however, not clear as to exactly what mechanism exists for this? It may lead to a dual growth of higher education system. Therefore, measures to promote competitiveness through foreign institutions should also focus on some such strategic factors that induce the system to be competitive. Powar (2002) recognizes that "the effect on quality can be both beneficial and detrimental". He sees the potential for quality to be improved from interaction and competition with reputable international institutions and decreased if low quality providers offer 'canned degrees'. He maintains that "quality education provided by reputed international providers will be accessible only to the privileged few that can pay for it".

Bridging Relevance Gap

Transnational education usually takes advantage of the following gaps:[5]

(i) Demand-supply gap in traditional curricula

(ii) Quality gap in terms of providing quality relevant courses

(iii) Relevance gap between content and style of curricula and what learners expect due to changing employment structure.

Usually supply-demand gap within traditional curricula should be bridged in a country by allocating more resources and should not be the preferred area of investment through the commercial presence of foreign institutions. To some extent, quality gap i.e., education of appropriate standard and quality should also be bridged by allowing teachers to acquire academic excellence and by encouraging innovation in teaching methods. However, new content and curricula may have to be designed to suit the needs of global market to bridge the relevance gap. It is in this area that internationalization of curriculum is desired. Among the most significant new areas are: molecular biology and biotechnology, advanced materials science; micro-electronics, information systems, robotics, intelligent systems and neuro-science; and environmental science and technology. One of the rationales of the commercial presence of foreign institutions should be to encourage the growth of programmes to bridge the relevance gap between content and style of curricula and what learners expect due to changing employment structure in partnership with Indian institutions.

Mobilizing Additional Resources

An important rationale for promoting the foreign educational institutions could be to attract foreign direct investment in India. While the commerce ministry favours this objective, it normally does not find favour within academic circles as the liberal approach towards foreign capital may have adverse consequences of imposing foreign curricula that may not have relevance from national point of view. Yet, foreign institutions are much better equipped than local institutions to meet the needs of foreign corporations and as the liberal FDI in other sectors have encouraged the growth of foreign corporations, there also exists the need for selective approach to promote FDI.

Under some given norms such as relating to minimum investment for opening a branch campus or the maximum equity norms, promoting FDI can be one of the rationales for the commercial presence of foreign educational institutions. An important consideration for raising additional resources through FDI is that promoting world-class institutions requires large investment. For developing a few world-class universities or specialized institutions also FDI may be allowed.

Implications

Commitments under GATS

One of the implications of commercial presence of foreign institutions now is that once commitments are made under GATS, the presence of foreign institutions is covered under mode 3 and the articles under GATS will guide trade in higher education. Hence, all the safeguards to public higher education need to be understood and provided for under national regulation or be covered under 'limitations' clause in the 'Schedule of Commitments'. What it implies is that effective regulation is necessary for the commercial presence of foreign institutions giving all safeguards to protect but, at the same time, promoting foreign institutions in terms of the priorities set by the government in a constitutionally valid manner.

Concerns

Commercialization of Education

One of the concerns expressed in promoting the commercial presence of foreign educational institutions is that the acquisition of a foreign degree will be at a price. It means education will become a commodity to be traded in the market. It goes against the conception of education as public good. The following concerns are raised against the commercialization of higher education that the commercial presence of foreign institutions might give rise to. Firstly, higher education will be limited to the select few as there will be high price for any foreign degree to be acquired. Against this, it may be argued that, in any case, only the selected students who can afford to pay high fees in foreign countries were the beneficiaries of foreign education. Commercial presence of foreign educational institutions in the host country will be accessible to rather larger segments, if not all, as the cost will be substantially lower than what it could be in foreign countries.

Another concern is that commercialization will promote privatization that will, in turn, enhance the cost of higher education and restrict the entry of the poor but meritorious students to higher education, that is, to those target groups that the government should address by financing through loans/scholarship.

Thirdly; commercialization will adversely affect the public higher education. The government may slowly withdraw from its commitments to higher education seeing that the alternate mechanism of funding is gaining support from international sources. Knight (2004) notes that while private investment in education rises, the public support will fall even more steeply. At this point in time, this is speculation only, but it is expected that this could also be a discernible trend before long. The role that trade plays in this scenario is that countries without the capacity or political will to invest in the physical and soft infrastructure for higher education will begin to rely more and more on foreign investors and providers; and that trade rules may have a heavy influence on the terms and use of the private investment and thereby on policy for education. This issue can be taken care of, provided the government is committed to its responsibility to deliver higher education as public good.

Fourthly, it is feared that developing countries may be "flooded with foreign and private providers delivering essentially profitable subjects ... and in these areas they will pose as serious competitors to local universities, leaving the latter to deal with non-profitable subjects in arts, humanities, science and technology, so vital for a country's development" (Mohamedbhai, 2003). This problem, too, can be tackled if the state lays down priorities for the presence of foreign institutions.

Conclusion

Private providers of higher education in India have added a new dimension to the higher education system. They have begun to collaborate with foreign institutions and confer foreign degrees in India. New practices have some rationales, although there is a genuine fear that new practices may promote commercialization of higher education. Besides free interplay of market may also promote foreign programmes without any check on quality. Government should consider bringing legislation on the entry of foreign universities in preferred areas promoting joint ventures with accredited and reputed Indian institutions.

Notes

1. Zhang (2003) notes five important rationales for the commercial presence of foreign educational institutions in China as implied in government policies. They are: (1) Improving the quality of human resources; (2) Upgrading China's educational system; (3) Meeting the educational demand of the country; (4) Preventing brain drain; and (5) Attracting foreign capital into education.
2. The ranking of brain drain of India has shot upto 65 in a year as per the Global Information Technology Report (2004).
3. Number of Indian immigrants with tertiary education living in US alone is 2.25 lakh (see World Bank, 2002).

4. Jayaram (2004: 99–104) notes the decline of academic profession in India reflected in the low esteem of their profession as observed by the National Commission of Teachers (NCT, 1985: 21). In spite of the reasonably good UGC pay package, the level of the professionalization of the teachers is a cause for concern.
5. See Mong (2000), 'Response to Prof. Sergio Mechado' presentation 'Introduction to the Theme of Transnational Education' in a conference held at Aveixo, Portugal, 3–4 April.

References

Altbach, Philip G. (2003), "Globalisation and the University: Myths and Realities in an Unequal World", *Journal of Educational Planning and Administration*, Vol. XVII, No. 2, 227–247.

Bhushan, Sudhanshu (2004), "Directory on Foreign Education Providers in India", NIEPA, New Delhi.

Bhushan, Sudhanshu (2005), "Foreign Education Providers in India", NIEPA, New Delhi.

Government of India (1983), Report of the National Commission on Teacher–I, The Teacher and Society, Ministry of Education, New Delhi.

Jayaram, N. (2004), "Higher Education in India: Massification and Change", in Philip G. Altbach and Toru Umakoshi (eds.), *Asian Universities Historical Perspectives and Contemporary Challenges*, The Johns Hopkins University Press, Baltimore.

Kapur D. and P.B. Mehta (2004), Indian Higher Education Reforms from Half-Baked Socialism to Half-Baked Capitalism, Working Paper for International Development at Harvard University.

Knight, Jane (2004), Cross-border Education in a Trade Environment: Complexities and Policy Implications, A background report for discussion at the AAU Workshop, Accra, Ghana.

Mohemedbhai, G. (2003), "Globalization and its Implications on Universities in Developing Countries", in G. Breton and M. Lambert (eds.), *Universities and Globalization: Private Linkages, Public Trust*, UNESCO/Université Laval/Economica, Paris, France.

Mong, Guy (2000), Response to Prof. Sergio Mechado's Presentation, 'Introduction to the Theme of Transnational Education', in a conference held at Aveixo, Portugal, 3–4 April.

Powar, K.B. (2002), WTO, GATS and Higher Education: An Indian Perspective, paper prepared for the Meeting convened by the Association of Commonwealth Universities, Perth, Australia.

The Global Information Technology Report (2003), *The Global Information Technology Report 2002–2003: Readiness for the Networked World (Economics)*, World Economic Forum, S. Dutta, B. Lanvin and F. Paua (eds.), Oxford University Press, USA.

The Global Information Technology Report (2004), *The Global Information Technology Report 2003–2004: Towards an Equitable Information Society*, S. Dutta, B. Lanvin and F. Paua (eds.), Oxford University.

World Bank (2002), Constructing Knowledge Societies: New Challenges for Tertiary Education, Wold Bank, Washington DC, also available on http://www.worldbank.org

Zhang, C. (2003), Transnational Higher Education in China: Why has the State Encouraged its Development? Monograph, International Educational Administration and Policy Analysis, Stanford University
http://www.stanford.edu/dept/SUSE/ICE/monographs/Zhang.pdf

CHAPTER 6

Foreign Direct Investment in Education

One of the contemporary debates in education since the liberalization of the economy pertains to the issue of foreign direct investment in education. The debate is confined to the discussion in media. Opinions on FDI in education are speculative in nature and are divided. Those who oppose FDI raise various issues relating to concerns and the people who favour FDI point out various benefits accruing from liberalization in education. The ambiguity in education policy over the issue of FDI in education is equally responsible for the confusion, as 100 per cent FDI in education through automatic route is continuing with regulatory controls in education making it practically impossible to attract foreign investment in education. The empirical estimates on FDI in education are also not available, as RBI does not have classification by education with respect to FDI.

The issue of FDI in services, particularly in education sector, has come to acquire importance, as domestic capacity in education needs to meet the challenges posed by the internationalization of education. Broadly speaking, development being dependent on knowledge, nations cannot simply remain isolated. In an interdependent world of knowledge the international mobility of programmes and institutions brought about through FDI is assuming greater proportions. Given such compulsion, there is the issue of understanding implications and policy regimes.

Common argument is that FDI primarily should be viewed as financial proposition and inflow of private finance in education would ease constraints on the capacity to expand. However, FDI as a financial proposition, though important, is a secondary consideration. The primary and fundamental issue is that private investment associated with FDI is not neutral. It challenges the public good nature of education and distorts the non-profit character of education.

The central objective of the chapter is to understand the context of FDI in education with recent phenomenon of increasing mobility of programmes and institutions. The contradiction resulting from FDI policy in education and the control regime is analysed. The supposed rationales for FDI in education are examined. It is then argued that FDI in education raises various concerns raising social costs higher than private returns. In the context of sectoral approach to FDI in education, there arises a case for a very cautious approach to FDI in higher education. The present uncertainty that gives rise to unregulated flows of FDI due to absence of regulation on the entry of foreign universities in India needs to be put up with. The thrust of the paper is to focus light on issues that confronts us in determining the sectoral policy on FDI in education.

What is Foreign Direct Investment (FDI)?

According to OECD, an FDI enterprise is an incorporated or unincorporated enterprise in which a single foreign investor maintains an effective voice by covering 10 per cent of ordinary shares or voting power in an enterprise or covers less than 10 per cent and yet maintains an effective voice in the management. An effective voice implies the ability to influence the management and not absolute control. The threshold equity, usually chosen, ranges between 10 per cent and 50 per cent of equity shareholding, which allows effective voice in the management. Ways of acquiring effective voice, other than equity share holding are turnkey arrangements, franchising, leasing, subcontracting, licensing and production sharing.

FDI could be desegregated into components of equity capital, invested earnings and intra firm loans.

Foreign capital can enter into the Indian market in any one or more than one of the following ways:

FDI: Companies may be formed in other countries with the specific purpose of operating in India, companies may start their subsidiary offices or branches and affiliates in India or foreigners may subscribe to stocks and debentures of concerns in India.

Foreign collaboration: It may take place between two private parties in India and abroad or between foreign firms and Indian government or between foreign government and Indian government.

Other means by which foreign capital can enter the Indian markets are through inter-governmental loans, loans from institutions and external commercial borrowings.

In the current wave of liberalization there has been worldwide shift in the forms of foreign capital. Firstly, direct foreign investment through involving equity capital of an existing or new undertaking has been rising. Secondly, intergovernmental loans and loans from institutions have been declining and external commercial borrowings have been rising implying a shift towards free market-based system of attracting foreign capital. Thirdly, technical collaboration involving payments for technology is not a much favoured mode. Indian firms are apparently opting for equity-linked technology transfer.[1]

New Global Trend: Mobility of Programmes and Institutions

There is a new global trend of the international mobility of programmes and institutions. In the present form of such operation, institutions open subsidiaries abroad or offer their educational programmes and qualifications via partnerships with host country institutions. The experience of some countries in this is worth considering. Malaysia planned to expand transnational programmes within the country to meet the excess demand and also to reduce the amount spent on education abroad. China made various enabling provisions in late 1990s to promote collaborative programmes to fast catch up with foreign knowledge and world standards. In 1996, the state-run Economic Development Board was put in charge to attract ten prestigious foreign universities to set up branch campuses in Singapore by the year 2008 so as to turn Singapore into an international education centre. In 1990s, the foreign providers redirected their attention at specialized sectors of the market like nursing and other allied health disciplines and meeting the insatiable market for business education in all its forms. Gradually, their presence increased. In 2001, about 150 foreign education institutions and 40 foreign professional bodies offered 645 courses in Hong Kong alone or with local partners.[2] The global trend of the mobility of programmes and institutions show that foreign investment in education is a growing phenomenon. Countries have established norms for operation of foreign education providers to facilitate FDI. It may be observed that foreign universities are investing capital wherever regulation facilitates mobility of programmes and institutions.

The school sector is also gearing up in terms of attracting FDI in the present context. The scope of such intervention is very high especially in those countries where domestic capacities to open schools are limited. The number of foreign schools is increasing in the Gulf and African countries. Potential for FDI in school sector is no less than higher education. The important rationale for such hypothesis is that in school sector the student mobility is quite low. Hence, the mobility of institution would help the users an access to international education at low cost. Besides, harmonization of standard at school level will facilitate entry in higher education abroad and also help developing countries to participate in global market.

FDI in Education

The policy of FDI in five sub-sectors of education services under GATS—primary, secondary, higher, adult and others—is through automatic route. This means that any foreign enterprise can invest in education sector either on its own or with Indian partner without permission of Foreign Investment Promotion Board. They can transact money through the RBI. In the present context, foreign investment in the educational sector is small. That's why it is included in the 'other' category of service sector. At the same time, there is no enabling domestic policy in education for allowing foreign education providers in any of the five sub-sectors.

In the absence of any policy in this sector foreign capital may flow in or out by means of off-shore foreign institutions' campus or through the tie-ups with the private partner in India. There is also no limit to foreign capital investment in education services. It may be noted that under the UGC Act, the degree granting authority rests with the universities established under central or state act. Foreign degree provider institutions, even allowing for liberal FDI through automatic route, cannot *ipso facto* operate. Hence, in the absence of enabling domestic regulation FDI through automatic route in higher education is ineffectual. In the primary and secondary education, there is no such regulatory requirement yet FDI is not forthcoming in practice as other enabling provisions for entry are not supportive. At present, the foreign education providers in higher education are coming in unregulated manner and unregulated inflow and outflow of foreign capital in education sector, as a whole, is a cause of great concern. It is now felt that FDI in education must be guided by certain norms and control as it is a sensitive sector and its implications should be examined before any FDI policy.

Rationale for FDI in Education

As a Source of Investment

Traditionally education is considered to be non-tradable. The government is used to fund education through domestic resource mobilization. Recently, universalization of elementary education required large foreign capital to be funded through World Bank loan. 1990s was the decade of falling percentage budgetary allocation on secondary, higher and technical education. The resource crunch in these sectors has adversely affected the public sector and promoted the private sector participation at almost all levels of education. To raise the participation rate in higher education and to ensure quality education is an uphill task in view of impending financial shortage. It may be argued that FDI may be used as a source of investment at least in some selected sectors in education.

One of the potential sources of FDI in education is NRI investment. NRIs have found investment in secondary schools quite lucrative. Many schools in recent years have come up in large cities affiliated to Indian boards or international boards. Australian investment in secondary schools on moderate scale is also present in India. They are affiliated to foreign boards. Students prefer to join such schools as these schools provide a gateway to higher education in advanced countries.

Against this view academia in education sector argue that foreign investment in education might lead to cultural imperialism. Therefore, education should be national agenda purely funded through domestic resources. The point, however, to note is whether certain sub-sectors of higher education may be kept open for foreign investment.

Quality Issue

Argument in favour of FDI in education is that foreign institutions can bring quality programmes with market orientation. Besides updated curricula, teaching-learning processes, evaluation processes may be internalized within educational institution in India. It may also reap the benefits of improved managerial and organizational skills to run the institutions. It is also argued that FDI could promote competitiveness in the education system as a whole.

The critics maintain that the quality could be maintained in certain specific sectors where FDI takes place, whereas in mass education sector the spillover effect of quality may not take place. In fact it might lead to dualism in education. Hence, critics point that there should be no liberal FDI policy in education.

Export

It is also argued that there is a positive correlation between FDI and export. Hence, it is argued that allowing FDI in education might lead to export of Indian education abroad. It is also argued that emigration of Indian students for foreign higher education leads to substantial outflow of foreign exchange leading to the flight of capital. Entry of foreign campuses on Indian soil would substantially reduce this flight of foreign exchange. Education may, therefore, turnout to be net exporter and earner of foreign exchange. FDI may be attracted in education export zone in India where students from South and South East Asia, Africa, Latin America etc., may be attracted to study. This channel is considered cost effective as the cost of education per student will turn out to be substantially lower than abroad yielding some sort of comparative cost advantage for education in India.

It is, however, maintained that foreign institutions would be interested to exploit the large market in India, rather than exporting education from India. There is also no empirical evidence to show the positive association between FDI and export. So far as the outflow of Indian students is concerned, commercial presence of foreign institutions would not check the emigration of Indian students as they go to study abroad also with a view to move out in the international job market.

Since nations cannot remain isolated in this age of globalization, the FDI policy should be linked to specific sectors and the specific objectives alone.

Why Reservations on FDI in Education?

Although rationales exist to support FDI policy in education, there are counter arguments why it should take a back seat even in an era of liberalization? The liberal FDI policy would invite foreign institutions and universities in areas that have employment potentials. Education offered by multinational institutes (MNIs) would be guided by market signals and it may not reflect the societal needs. Besides, fees charged by them may be exorbitantly high to restrict access to the majority. Another effect may be felt on public system of higher education. The public institutions may either feel the compulsion to raise fees or may not prove to be competitive enough, given the resource crunch. Public institutions may also suffer stability due to the faculty mobility that marketization may induce. As a result of the absence of level playing field, the commercialization of education will hit hard those who have not enough paying capacity. Hence, the argument is that social costs of the liberal FDI regime in education will be high and will far outweigh the advantages that it may carry in terms of quality and competitiveness. After having analysed its implications in terms of social costs, it is worth examining the sectoral contexts of FDI.

Sectoral Contexts

Basic education is the sole responsibility of the government. There is no question of allowing private foreign investment through FDI at elementary education level. However, government has been running programmes sponsored by external funding agencies to promote quality elementary education through inter-governmental loans and loans from institutions. At the secondary level in many states it has been declared as the responsibility of the state to provide free secondary education for all students or for girl students. At the secondary level, therefore, government may consider to raise resources from external funding agencies to enhance the basic infrastructure only and refrain at present from private foreign investment. At the higher education level, there are arguments to support the fusion of ideas through the mobility of programmes and institutions brought about by FDI. It is indeed a compulsion of knowledge society that universities promote networking among institutions in different areas of research. Hence, world-class research universities may be invited to collaborate with selected Indian institutions/universities. Similarly, established colleges and universities may either partner with higher education institutions or establish off-shore branches for teaching functions. This would certainly necessitate the inflow of foreign capital. Government may consider the appropriate FDI policy in this regard that may be partly funded by foreign institutions/governments but this part of the funding cannot be left to be determined by pure market forces for various reasons such as the possibility of rouge providers or the possibility of commercialization of education that is ruled out by the law or conventions of the land. Hence, FDI in higher education alone may be allowed strictly in preferred area and subject to the regulatory framework. There is also definitional issue relating to higher education. Should higher education include various non-degree courses as defined under GATS CPC classification head 923? There are requests from developed countries to include training and testing services under higher education. At present, training and testing services are not under the definition of higher education. Besides, FDI in training and testing may have commercial implication. Hence, FDI policy in training and testing though related to education can be considered only outside the purview of education.

Table 6.1

FDI in Higher Education

Purpose	Source of Financing	Extent of Partnership	Partnership Institutions in India
Research	Government/ Public Institutions	Up to 49 per cent FDI	Government/Public Institutions/Universities
Teaching	Public/Private	Up to 49 per cent FDI	Public/Private Colleges or Universities
Training/ Testing	Public/Private	Not to be allowed under 'education'	

FDI and GATS

In the background of GATS the policy on FDI needs to be discussed. GATS is directly not an investment agreement. It is a trade agreement in services that is multilateral and guided by minimum rules principles. Hence, institutional and legal interlinkages under GATS also necessitate the FDI gearing to fulfilling trade-based needs arising from interlinkages. It should be noted that investment is one of several different ways of gaining access to market. There is no investment protection provision as found in bilateral agreement.

Hence, if there is commitment to permit commercial presence in Mode III, no control in FDI is possible. The FDI follows automatically from what is there in the 'Schedule of Commitments'. If there are no Market Access (MA) and National Treatment (NT) limitations or any other horizontal limitations, FDI will also not be subject to any control. In case of limitation, say market access limitation, FDI will be restricted to those limitations only. There is no back tracking possible because of progressive liberalization of trade under GATS.

GATS not only addresses the terms and condition upon which a foreign investor may enter the market, but also deals with establishment 'trade' or in other words, the conditions of operating in the post-investment phase. As such FDI is not only one-shot affair, it happens to be a continuous phenomena as well.

The next important point is that both existing and future bilateral and regional investment agreements will need to take its provisions fully into account including strong MFN commitment. It means that opening any sector today for any country would mean opening the sector for all countries under GATS.

FDI in Higher Education

What are the various mechanisms in which foreign institutions would like to invest in higher education in India? The study on 'Foreign Education Providers in India' (NIEPA, 2005) shows that in an unregulated environment foreign institutions partner with the private institutions. The presence of foreign institutions is through the study centres, programmatic collaboration, franchising and twinning. In all the above modes of operation, there is the minimum stake and the risk of foreign institutions is minimal as the Indian counterpart supplies the infrastructure etc. Investment in branch campus is nil showing that in an unregulated environment no foreign institutions are ready to invest. As large amount of FDI is accompanied through the branch campus, the government may consider selective world-class universities to offer quality education programme in partnership with public or private universities and colleges.

Preconditions for an Effective FDI

Education in India is recognized and organized as a non-profit activity. The educational institutions will have to be established and run by a society registered under the Societies Registration

Act or as a public trust or under Section 25 of the Companies Act. All these prohibit educational institutions from making and appropriating profit.

FDI inflow depends on transparent government policy. The regulatory framework should be simple and a single window clearance should be in place for clearing projects in a time bound manner. The regulation must insist chiefly on quality assurance.

There is at present no assessment of potential FDI inflows in education. In most countries education is considered as a public good. Higher education, however, is oriented towards privatization due to resource crunch and other factors. Hence, willingness of foreign institutions to invest in India in branch campus is doubtful if not completely ruled out. In fact some universities from UK, USA, Australia have shown some preference but it can be turned into reality only when institutions are given autonomy with transparent regulation. An enabling provision for registration under the Societies Registration Act, 1860 and permission to purchase land to develop infrastructure for branch campus may have to be made. Similarly, a reasonable portion of earnings for the services being provided should be allowed for repatriation.

Hence, an essential precondition for an effective FDI is that though foreign investment should not be guided by free market principle, it should be regulated by domestic policies that should allow a normal return on investment. Income over and above normal return should be reinvested to improve the quality. Besides, a transparent policy of regulation should be in place.

Need for Domestic Investment Policy

A domestic investment policy in education that promotes the private providers needs to be built by lifting various controls for opening schools and colleges. It was noted earlier that FDI in education as an investment proposition is only of secondary importance. However, from domestic investment point of view rules for opening schools and colleges should be simple and investment friendly. Some of the deterrents are difficulties in obtaining a 'No Objection Certificate' from government and elaborate procedures for affiliation with the boards and the universities/institutions that have certificate and degree granting authority. These impediments also need to be worked out along with the incentives for promoting investment in education.

Proposals for Policy Consideration.

Proposals for FDI for Discussion

1. At the elementary and secondary level, foreign capital through inter-institutional/inter-governmental loans may be promoted for developing necessary infrastructure. No private FDI flows be accepted as a matter of principle.
2. There should be public-to-public FDI flow. For example, any foreign university willing to enter into a joint venture with public institutions in India may be freely permitted to enter into an agreement allowing FDI without any restrictions.
3. Any foreign universities—public or private—willing to open overseas campus in India may be allowed to do so under the regulatory control of government/government agencies. FDI should be guided by minimum investment norms decided by the regulating authority.
4. Any foreign public or private joint venture in partnership with Indian private sector may be permitted with majority stake in Indian partner. Besides, educational joint venture programme should be strictly guided by the norms fixed by the government/government agency.
5. Any foreign private-to-public joint venture programme may also be allowed without any restrictions so far as FDI is concerned as public institution in India is already covered by the national system of regulation.

Notes

1. See Basant (2000), for an overview of corporate strategies in 1990s relating to mergers and acquisitions, distribution of collaboration by level of control and types of collaboration.

2. See the study conducted by NIEPA (2005) on 'Foreign Education Providers in India' for a detailed account of new trends in higher education. It is worth understanding how these countries made enabling provisions for smooth flow of FDI as well as the mobility of programmes and institutions.

References

Basant, Rakesh (2000), "Corporate Response to Economic Reforms", *Economic and Political Weekly (EPW)*, March 4.

NIEPA (2005), Report on Foreign Education Providers in India, NIEPA, New Delhi.

III

Reform Process

CHAPTER 7

A Neo-Liberal Agenda of Knowledge Commission

Knowledge Commission has produced the report on higher education. It declares a 'quiet crisis' in higher education and recommends a systemic reform. Directions of reform support public investment. However, institutional reform supports neo-liberal agenda to reduce state control without going into the roots of the 'quiet crisis'. Some of the recommendations have far-reaching implications and need systematic understanding. The suggestion of an Independent Regulatory Authority for Higher Education (IRAHE) to accord degree granting power to institutions will not only centralize the decision making, it will go against the spirit of federal character of democracy, as legislative control of state to establish university will become redundant. Further, norm-based approach to grant license may support the expansion of private higher education, moving away from the need-based approach to establish universities.

The minimalist role of University Grants Commission (UGC) to disburse funds, driving all councils out of the functions relating to the maintenance of standards of institutions and establishment of IRAHE subsuming partly the role of all the councils is founded on misconceived facts and assumptions. For example, UGC provides guidelines of schemes and programmes for the utilization of grants. It advises universities on a number of issues that help to give broad directions to higher education system. University system has its own autonomy within a broad framework of accountability to the state and UGC's role in this has been that of a moral guardian suited to a democratic framework. The Knowledge Commission's indictment of the role of UGC on account of over regulation is not quite correct. Other professional councils have also issued norms and guidelines to maintain standards which the university as autonomous institutions are expected to follow. On the other hand, there is no reason to assume that IRAHE subsuming the role of all the professional councils will prove to be only efficient institution.

Supply constraint, lack of accountability to the students, and absence of competition are the chief premises on which critiques of the existing system for the deterioration in quality are based. The restructuring of institutions is based on the premise that regulatory control in the establishment of institutions needs to be simplified. Promotion of quality is based on the premise that excess supply of institutions will generate competition by being more responsive and accountable to students and providing greater choice to students.

It is assumed that the single window clearance will simplify the entry of institutions and competition will do the rest of the magic, as if by invisible hand, to achieve quality and excellence in higher education. There is, however, no road map. There is no reason, therefore, to believe that expectations will be fulfilled. On the other hand, there are dangers of overexpansion and falling quality. Another suggestion relating to salary differentials to attract talents will raise the cost of higher education adversely affecting access and equity.

The most important issue is the restructuring of universities. The cumulative underinvestment in higher education has been responsible for the restricted access and has affected quality adversely. The foremost concern, therefore, is to raise the plan support to a level that helps to realize commitment of the state to achieve 1.5 per cent of GDP in higher education. Given the commitment, mechanism needs to be found to update curricula, promote interdepartmental and interdisciplinary mobility of teachers and students, integrate information technology in governance, teaching-learning process and develop the capacity of teachers on a strong foundation of infrastructure and governance. A road map for this through plan may be developed.

Recommendations on a systemic reform in higher education contained in the report of the Knowledge Commission, therefore, need to be examined. The purpose of the chapter is to examine the issues of structure and governance suggested by the Knowledge Commission. Section II notes the theoretical backdrop of the recommendations of the National Knowledge Commission. Section III analyses the underlying assumptions of liberal and neo-liberal theories. Section 4 notes the structure and governance of higher education as given in the NKC. Section V spells out underlying assumptions behind structural reform. Section VI analyses the implications of underlying assumptions. Section VII notes the basic premises in the restructuring of universities and undergraduate colleges. Section VIII shows the emerging structure of institutions in higher education under the Knowledge Commission. Section IX examines the critical issues in restructuring of institutions.

II
Theoretical Backdrop

In the first half of 20th century, the period between two world wars saw the failure of market and the downfall of a period of liberal market ideology. The downfall of liberal ideology was followed by a new doctrine of welfare state in the immediate post second world war. The decades of 1950s and 1960s may be said to be the period of Keynesian policy of state intervention. Its failure to ensure the sustainable growth in the 1970s marked a new period of neo-liberal policies which established a synthesis of market and state interventions by invoking the principles of market in the functioning of state.

To understand the genesis of the recommendations of the Knowledge Commission on higher education, it would be necessary to understand the assumptions of liberal and neo-liberal systems of thought and practices. The genesis of the recommendations on the restructuring of higher education to support a knowledge society is based on the understanding that state cannot be an efficient allocator of resources. A political state, however, is the essential entity to balance the struggle of power and develop a democratic order to avoid the turmoil. Hence, state has to be a mediator and in the role of a mediator, it has to follow the principles of market. This neo-liberal stand-point which is inherent in many of the OECD countries in higher education policy cannot, however, be a panacea of the ills of the higher education system in developing countries. The reason, it is argued, is that a state in developing countries balances the struggle of power in the unpredictable way. For example, Indian state is based on an understanding of highly unstable coalition of political parties representing varied groups of industrial capitalist, rural peasantry and dalits. A consensus is difficult to arrive at and hence neo-liberal policies are neither desirable nor seem to be a practical solution, given the coalition of interests. Most of the recommendations will be taken by the bureaucrats in a casual and ad hoc manner without providing systematic directions to the higher education policies.

III
Analysing Liberal and Neo-liberal Doctrines

Classical liberalism was represented by the doctrines of the neo-classical economists—Walras, Jevons and Menger—in 1870s. They advanced the choice theoretic framework of a rational utility maximizing individual that formed the basis of demand and supply theory. The theory of market supply and demand was supposed to achieve equilibrium. It meant that market principle will achieve efficiency in the allocation of scarce resources. The competition was the mechanism to ensure the efficient allocation of resources. Competition meant that resources will be diverted towards high profit from the lower profit sectors till a uniform rate of profit is achieved. The grand principle of laissez faire rules out state intervention in the allocation of resources.

Within liberal thinking the state assumed importance in following functions—(i) the supply of public goods and services, (ii) to regulate the failures of market, (iii) to arbitrate between competing social groups and classes. Education of course was a public good and state's role in its supply was considered important. State provided education was also desired as the basis of liberal democracy as former provides the basis of informed choice necessary for a successful democracy (Mill, 1965).

Though liberalism is based upon the autonomy and freedom of individual, it is necessary that freedom of an individual does not interfere with the freedom of another individual. State intervention was thus desirable to ensure that freedom becomes non-coercive (Green, 1888). Market process may not ensure the right to education and may constrain the freedom necessitating the role of state in the delivery of education (Ritchie, 1895). Every liberty rests on a corresponding act of control to be provided by the state (Hobhouse, 1911). Under the liberal approach, market exists that ensures the choice theoretic freedom. However, state may also coexist to ensure freedom, to guarantee certain basic rights and to ensure the welfare of the people. Philosophically, however, individual's choice theoretic framework is the dominant discourse. Under liberalism, minimalist state exists with its own method of intervention—policy and planned approach and control and regulatory approach. State is negated in the sense of becoming a dominant discourse.

The neo-liberalism emerged as an important doctrine in the late phase of capitalism. Foucault's (1991) analysis of neo-liberalism reinforced the principles of market in following ways:

1. Market and competition to be engineered by the state.
2. Increase competitive forms throughout society, social and work relations to assume market form.
3. Supports active creation of social conditions for an effective market order.
4. Policies geared to create entrepreneuvial spirit and opposing bureaucratic initiatives.
5. To correct bureaucratic dislocations.
6. State itself subject to market laws.

Neo-liberalism reinforced the idea of individual rationality of liberalism. It also argued in favour of competition as the basis of market mechanism in achieving equilibrium. The further shift from liberalism to neo-liberalism means that state is supposed to intensify the market operations. It implies privatization of a part of services produced by the state. Neo-liberalism means that bureaucracy is to be replaced by new doctrine of managerialism, contracting and performance appraisal. It is assumed that self-interest of bureaucrats leads to corruption and inefficiency as there is nothing called collective self-interest. An individual as part of the state needs to be manipulated in such a manner that it becomes responsive to market signals and performance orientation.

The neo-liberalism argues that public monopoly should be abolished. Barriers to entry should be done away with and opportunities should be created for the private participants. There is greater role for the policy in favour of restructuring rather than planning by the state. Market-based incentives need to be promoted by the state. Thus role of state is not negated. State participates more and more not in the production of goods and services but in facilitating the production by the privatized mode. The neo-liberal doctrines were propagated in variants such as Human Capital Theory, Agency Theory, Public Choice Theory, Transaction Cost Economics and Conservatist Doctrine of Monetarism.

The neo-liberal doctrine rests upon the following maxims:

- Tariffs and subsidies should be abolished.
- Cost recovery should be made.
- Entry barriers such as legislative requirement should not exist.
- Competition should be generated through more and more players in the provision of services.
- Control in the export and import of capital as well as goods and services should be over.
- Argues against too many regulations as it prevents competition.
- Accountability should be generated through measurable yardstick and competitive pressures.
- Individual rationality is preferred to collective rationality; in fact collective rationality does not exist at all.
- Quality is maintained only when there is competition.

It is important to bear in mind that under neo-liberalism state is not negated. It actively constructs the market. Discourse of state management and control is authoritarian to invoke principles of market. It points to more effective means of social engineering. Control of state is more devolved and flexible. Decentralization of power and provision of services is preferred. It would be interesting to find that recommendations of NKC are influenced by neo-liberal doctrines.

IV
Structure and Governance of Higher Education

Many important recommendations of the Knowledge Commission pertain to the institutional restructuring. These are as follows:

Recommendations

1. Independent Regulatory Authority for Higher Education (IRAHE): (i) IRAHE to be established by an Act of Parliament with the responsibility to set the criteria for opening new institutions, to accord degree granting power to institutions, to monitor standards, settle disputes, grant license for accreditation agencies. (ii) Role of UGC to be redefined to focus on disbursement of grants and maintenance of public institutions. (iii) The AICTE, MCI and the DCI to work as professional associations only; their role as regulating education to be performed by IRAHE.
2. Restructuring the system of undergraduate colleges affiliated to universities: (i) autonomy to limited number of colleges or cluster of colleges, (ii) a number of affiliated undergraduate colleges could be remodeled as community colleges providing vocational/formal education, (iii) central and state boards of undergraduate education should be established to set curricula and conduct examination for undergraduate colleges that choose to be affiliated with them and (iv) new undergraduate colleges to be established as community colleges, be affiliated with boards of undergraduate education, or be affiliated with some of the new universities.
3. Restructuring Universities: New universities to be created to reach a total of 1,500 universities. New universities will

be smaller in size with, having undergraduate colleges affiliated to it. Some clusters of affiliated colleges could become universities.

4. National Universities: to be established to provide education of the highest standard. These universities shall train students in a variety of disciplines, including humanities, social sciences, basic sciences, commerce and professional subjects, at both the undergraduate and postgraduate levels. About 10 such universities in the next three years and a long-term target of 50 universities has been kept. These may be from among existing ones or may be established either by government or private sector.

V
Underlying Assumptions

The following assumptions are spelled out in the recommendations relating to structural reform in higher education.

(a) Barriers to entry, particularly for private institutions, through legislation prevent competition.
(b) Councils such as University Grants Commission, All India Council for Technical Education, Medical Council of India and Dental Council of India have created barriers to entry as 'the system of authorizing entry is cumbersome'.
(c) There is multiplicity of regulatory agencies where mandates are both confusing and overlapping.
(d) System as a whole is over regulated but under-governed.
(e) The large size of affiliating universities has become non-governable.
(f) The system of affiliated colleges for undergraduate education lacks autonomy to grow.
(g) Affiliated colleges cater to diverse groups with a uniform curricula and evaluation.
(h) There is an implicit assumption that a single regulatory body would regulate effectively the market expansion presumably by some transparent system of quality assurance and accreditation, the rest being presumed to be taken care by the market.

VI
Implications of Underlying Assumptions

The implication of assumption 1 in the report of the Knowledge Commission is that legislative process of establishing university under 2f of UGC Act 1956 is burdensome and creates barriers for establishing institutions. If the barriers need to be removed then it is suggested that 2f of UGC Act 1956 need to be repealed and it is proposed IRAHE that will be responsible to determine eligibility for setting up a new institution, based on transparent criteria, that will have degree granting authority.

Assumptions 2, 3 and 4 are invoked to argue that all regulatory councils have created barriers to entry and are inefficient (see reference on 12 where examples of engineering and business schools are given), under-governed and non-transparent. The implication is that good institutions are not allowed to be established. Assumption 4 means that over regulation "is not conducive to innovation or creativity in higher education". An independent regulatory body is, therefore proposed to grant license to any institution that meets some basic norms.

Assumptions 5, 6 and 7 imply that affiliated colleges under the control of university tend to produce inefficient outcomes for two basic reasons, there is lack of autonomy and unfortunately the large size of university is unable to enforce accountability as well.

The fundamental point of the Knowledge Commission is that the basic structure of the existing institutions is based on the control framework.

Knowledge Commission is against the control framework of higher education. First of all, it argues that state creates control through 2f of UGC Act, 1956, by restricting the universities to be established under state or central act creating barriers to the free entry and thus restricting competition. Second, the regulatory councils control the universities and professional institutions in a number of ways that again creates barriers to entry, prevents competition and restricts autonomy without creating responsible system of accountability thereby allowing inefficiency and inferior quality to flourish. Thirdly, universities' control framework further prevents competition as it does not allow the good quality institutions to enter and bad quality institutions to restructure or quit.

The solution suggested by the Knowledge Commission, therefore, is to dismantle the control framework. The concrete suggestion is that the legislative route to establish universities to authorize degree granting power to them should be done away with. Secondly, regulatory councils' power to maintain standards and issuing guidelines to such effect etc., in education should also be abolished. UGC should remain merely funding organization and should have no business in the maintenance of standards in higher education. Similarly, other professional councils should have no role in maintaining the standards of technical and professional education. They should restrict themselves to maintain the standards of professionals and to address other issues of respective professions. Then the Knowledge Commission suggests that universities and undergraduate colleges need to restructure in such a manner that the control framework of the universities is further dismantled.

VII
Restructuring Universities and Undergraduate Colleges

The basic premise of the Knowledge Commission in the restructuring of universities and undergraduate colleges is as follows:

1. Multiple structure of institutions not having the necessity to be affiliated with universities.
2. Universities themselves may be established with the permission from IRAHE and hence the legislative route is either redundant or unnecessary.
3. More appropriately scaled and more nimble universities, say 1,500 nationwide by 2015, but also that we need smaller universities which are responsive to change and easier to manage.
4. Universities should be able to attract the best talent whether teachers or students.
5. Sufficient choice of institutions to be made available to students.
6. Transparency through external accreditation of universities.

7. Universities must have the ability to compete.
8. Departmental divides and disciplinary boundaries should no longer prevail.
9. Universities must be flexible, innovative and creative.

VIII
Structure of Institutions Recommended under the Knowledge Commission

Based on the above premises for restructuring universities and undergraduate colleges the following structure of institutions is envisaged under the Knowledge Commission. Independent Regulatory Authority for Higher Education (IRAHE) will provide license authorizing degree granting power to four types of universities/boards thus satisfying premises 1 and 2 above relating to multiple types of institutions but a single body providing the license. It will presumably ease the barriers to entry. Restructuring of universities is suggested in a manner that appropriate size is ensured thereby increasing the number to approximately 1,500. Premises 4 and 5 mean that restructuring should be in a manner that quality is promoted through type 2 universities, shown in the diagram, consisting of an individual or cluster of good colleges. Besides, restructuring would imply relevance in terms of a right combination of undergraduate and community colleges, the latter promoting two-year vocational courses. Excellence is to be promoted through type 1 universities that would be truly world-class and would create a cadre of researchers working in the frontiers of knowledge. Premise 6 relates to accreditation as a form of quality assurance. IRAHE will provide license to creditable accreditors who will accredit institutions and probably provide the basis for benchmarking quality. The rest of the premises are the necessary conditions that should ideally prevail for the universities to be quality oriented. The role of the University Grants Commission (UGC) is reduced to disbursing public funds (see Diagram 7.1). Other regulatory councils are completely restricted to perform any function related to maintenance of standards in technical and professional education.

Diagram 7.1

Structure of Institutions Under Knowledge Commission Recommendations

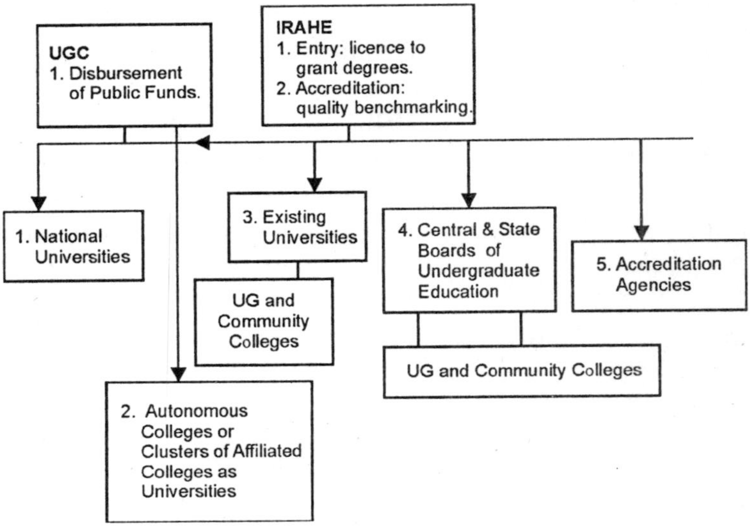

IX
Examination of Critical Issues in Restructuring

(i) *Role of state*: The role of state in establishing universities through legislation has put some checks on the growth of universities in the past. As a result, affiliating universities have overgrown in size. Knowledge Commission rightly points this out. This mechanism has, however, restrained the growth of institutions of inferior quality as well. In recent years, there has been greater demand by private education providers to allow them to establish institutions. In Chhattisgarh, more than 100 universities were established with the passing of an act permitting universities to be opened after the approval of state government. Many such universities were ultimately closed down under the directives from Supreme Court. In recent years, private universities are being established under state legislature. There has also been 100 per cent growth in deemed universities, mostly private, during the last five years. It shows that expansion has been restricted in the case of public universities due to financial resource crunch and self-financing private universities and colleges have increased to fill the void.

Expansion in higher education is necessary both from the point of view of increasing access and increasing competitiveness to improve quality. The traditional route has been to allow establishment of universities (public or private) through legislation and colleges to be affiliated with the universities. Thus, the expansion of colleges within the framework of public control of universities was always permitted. Additional mechanism was through deemed universities route. Knowledge Commission report says that control of state through legislative route is unnecessary. It will simply lead to decontrol of state and expansion of private higher education.

Given the resource constraint the privatization and commercialization of higher education is taking place. To check the commercial activity in self-financing institutions, there is the need to control commercialization. To control profiteering there is the need to pass legislation for admission and fees in private colleges and universities. Thus, entry of private institutions should be promoted. However, private institutions should be permitted within the framework of existing state control. The existing institutional mechanism should not to be disturbed. The present social configuration of communities in India needs an active state intervention and commitment of state rather than a free market-based approach to the expansion of higher education suggested by Knowledge Commission.

(ii) *Role of UGC and other regulatory councils*: Knowledge Commission argues that multiple councils have functioned in the past as mere instruments of control without facilitating the expansion of quality institutions and that they lacked complete coordination among themselves resulting in license raj that presumably created obstruction for the growth of private institutions of high quality. Has, therefore, UGC failed to fulfil its mandate? If it has failed the reasons responsible for its failure also needs to be analysed before any prescription of redefining the role of UGC and advocating the independent regulatory authority.

First, UGC was established by an Act of Parliament under the provision of the Constitution of India to maintain and coordinate the standards. However, UGC was not given sufficient teeth to give recommendation in the establishment of universities through legislative routes. State universities were purely in the domain of state government. Universities at present have degree conferring authority and UGC has no role to close down universities as long as state governments establish and maintain the universities. UGC, under the present provision, can only recognize the university for the purposes of providing plan grant. Out of 369 universities (including deemed universities) and 18,064 colleges, only 164 universities and 5,525 colleges are recognized under 2f and 12B and are eligible to receive UGC grants. Thus, it can monitor the schemes only against which it has provided the fund. To penalize any university or college UGC can only withhold the grant which in any case was pittance. In the absence of any power matching with its responsibility, UGC was reduced to a mere funding authority and could not exercise requisite power even to maintain standards.

It is precisely for the above reason that UGC was ineffectual to close down universities that were established under Chhattisgarh legislation. It is precisely for this reason that it has so far failed to control private universities, even though UGC has developed the guidelines to regulate them. It has only recommending role to the central and state governments and central or state universities. It provides guidance to universities and colleges and acts as guardian. Through numerous committee on governance, curriculum, examination reform, gender issues, eligibility conditions for the appointment of faculty, appointment of Vice-chancellors, the UGC has provided a direction to the higher education and this contribution should not be underplayed nor for any other deficiencies emanating at the level of universities, should UGC be blamed.

Thus, whatever UGC has so far achieved, it was due to its moral appeal and on this account its success is indeed tremendous, given the fact that plan funding per college allocated by the government was very small. The role of UGC in setting the directions of higher education through its numerous committees and the initiatives of the chairmen of UGC in a liberal democratic set-up should not be underestimated under any empiricist or propagandist statement that quality in higher education has gone down and that UGC failed to maintain the quality and therefore be axed. UGC in India is a household name. It has evolved over time and its legitimacy and moral appeal is accepted by all public institutions. It is only private (self-financing) institutions or universities that refuse to the appeal of UGC, as they engage in commercial educational practices.

UGC needs restructuring. There is no doubt about that. But the restructuring should be based on the following principles: UGC should be authorized to decide the norms, be given the authority to inspect before establishing new universities and be also given the authority to issue warning and finally closing down the universities if they do not conform to the minimum norms. Besides, UGC should establish a Higher Education Research Council that should provide information based on research findings to UGC on all aspects of higher education. A higher education information system, online monitoring, effective governance and adequate state funding of the order recommended by the Knowledge Commission can take care of the maintenance of standards.

(iii) *Coordination of the councils*: Given the control of state and an active role of UGC and professional councils to maintain standards in professional education there is the need to coordinate the various councils. This should be done by a high powered Higher Education Commission to be chaired by the prime minister with representation of various concerned ministers and chairmen of the councils. This would facilitate coordination. More importantly, the functioning of respective councils will considerably improve with greater teeth and under the overall supervision of the prime minister. The basic philosophy of higher education commission will be to reassert the role of state and guide the growth process that addresses the issues relating to inclusion. Any single regulatory commission that would reduce the role of state and would be created to regulate the market process facilitating its growth would create an imbalance and aggravate the exclusiveness. Worldwide the tendency has not been reduction in the role of state. State has, however, redefined its role to support the market expansion in higher education without mitigating its role and responsibility.

(iv) *IRAHE*: From above discussion it follows that there is no justification of any independent regulatory authority such as IRAHE. It will centralize the decision making. It will also take away the authority of state government to establish universities. Education is a concurrent subject and any central authority should not have sole authority to permit the entry of institutions in higher education. IRAHE will be against the spirit of federal character of democracy, as legislative control of state to establish university will become redundant. Further, norm-based approach to grant license may support the expansion of private higher education, moving away from the need-based approach to establish universities.

(v) *Restructuring institutions*: There are suggestions in the Knowledge Commission report regarding restructuring of universities. The suggestion of national university is an idea worth pursuing. In fact in the setting up of national university, the regional balance must be kept in mind. The size of affiliating university should be reduced to a level that can be managed. The idea that a cluster of good colleges can form a university is also worth considering. However, an autonomous college may continue and very few may be granted deemed university status. Feasibility of increasing the number of universities to 1,500 is so far based on the argument that small size universities will perform better. Education institutions in higher education can only evolve in a steady manner. On case-to-case basis respective state governments can decide which institutions need to be converted into autonomous institutions or into universities. The increase in the number of university should, however, be restricted to less than 1,000, as some of the state governments may not be willing to increase the number due to increasing infrastructural and cost requirement. Assuming 25,000–30,000 students on an average in the university, 1,000 universities can accommodate 25–30 million students in higher education.

The system of board of undergraduate education to deal with curriculum and examination is not a welcome idea, as it would separate the teaching and research functions. At present, universities have the authority to confer degrees. Colleges are affiliated to the universities. University can separate its governance system to deal with undergraduate and postgraduate independently. However, for the purpose of academic integration, UG and PG should work together. Restructuring of undergraduate colleges into vocational streams is again a welcome suggestion.

So far as quality assurance of higher education is concerned, presently NAAC is undertaking the task. NAAC has earned experience. It should create regional centres and ask these centres to make efforts for quality assurance in higher education. Universities must have quality assurance cell and these cells should work to improve and assure quality of PG departments and colleges.

(vi) *Quality in higher education*: Knowledge Commission makes important observations on quality in higher education. The perspective is again a neo-liberal one, as it argues in favour of state de-control. The logic of the argument is that barriers to the entry must be removed. IRAHE is suggested for a single window clearance of institutions. It argues that such mechanism will remove the barriers to entry. It then goes on to argue that an expansion of higher education which provides students with choices and creates competition between institutions is going to be vital in enhancing accountability. Accountability is then supposed to improve the quality of higher education institutions in India. Internal systems of evaluation are suggested to strengthen accountability in the teaching-learning process. Information is said to be important in reinforcing accountability. For this purpose, disclosure norms for universities and institutions imparting higher education are suggested. It would empower students and parents and enable them to make informed choices. It is noted that "information, along with competition, fostered by increased supply, will close the accountability loop". Salary differentials between and within universities constitute another important suggestion made by the Knowledge Commission. It also notes that diversity and differentiation need to be promoted, yet for excellence achieving distinction is suggested.

The theoretical underpinnings in achieving excellence through competitive pressures resulting from easing the barriers to entry may not necessarily promote quality. Quality needs institutional processes and mechanisms to be generated. University system in India cannot afford to ignore the equity dimensions. A market-based approach may act against equity objectives.

To conclude, it may be noted that the Knowledge Commission rightly calls for 1.5 per cent of GDP for financing higher education. However, the decontrol of state to allow entry of institution in higher education is a risky proposition. The suggestion of an IRAHE is not acceptable. The role of UGC and professional councils should be given due consideration in maintaining standards of education. There may be established a mechanism to take care of the coordination of councils. Finally, the role of state, the relative autonomy of universities and colleges and institutional reform should be clearly defined to make India a vibrant economy. A neo-liberal agenda of reforms suggested by the Knowledge Commission is not the right answer.

References

Foucault, M. (1991), "Governmentality", in G. Burchell, C. Gordon and P. Miller (eds.), *The Foucault Effect: Studies in Governmentality*, The University of Chicago Press, Chicago, IL, 87–104.

Green, T.H. (1888), *Works of Thomas Hill Green*, R.L. Nettleship (ed.), Longmans and Green, London.

Hobhouse, L.T. (1911), *Liberalism*, Williams & Norgate, London.

Mill, J.S. (1965), (New Edition), *Principles of Political Economy*, Vol. 2 of Collected Works, J.M. Robson (ed.), Toronto University Press, Toronto.

Ritchie, D.G. (1895), *Natural Rights*, Swan Sonnenschein, London.

CHAPTER 8

Yashpal Committee on Renovation and Rejuvenation of Higher Education

The Yashpal Committee Report (2009) is an important addition to a new perspective of knowledge management in higher education. It provides the conception of university suited to production of universal knowledge that benefits society. The fact that another report on renovation and rejuvenation of higher education after the National Knowledge Commission (NKC) report on higher education has been made available requires that both the reports are examined well to provide a clear guiding framework for renovation.

This chapter has four sections. Section I presents a structural functional framework to understand various contradictions inherent in industrial and post-industrial transformation. Section II examines the features of the Yashpal Committee Report (YCR) and section III attempts to understand the comparative perspectives of NKC and YCR. Section IV presents a critical appreciation of YCR.

I
Historical Phases of the University System

There is hardly any dispute over the idea of a university to generate knowledge, develop humanism and inculcate scientific spirit in the minds of people. University is a social institution that passes through several phases and in each phase it needs to be structured in a manner that serves its intended goal nearly completely. To serve such eternal functions western universities fought the domination of church and prevalent feudal order up to the late 18th century. During this period theologically-centred scholasticism was replaced with humanism. This was the period of Renaissance. The second transformation of the university system took place during the phase of industrial capital which brought with itself discipline-based knowledge in arts, science, commerce, technology and professional areas. The secular values, democratic ideals and nation building that universities promoted also signified this age (Patnaik, 2009). Mass education to serve the need of mass production is an essential feature of the phase. The mediating role of the state under the public good notion of higher education is significant in this transformation. The contemporary phase in the transformation of the university system is the age of globalization or post-industrialization, which is characterized by the IT revolution. Knowledge is produced at the boundaries of disciplines and is considered the significant driver of growth. Most importantly, the phase is witnessing an intense competition among capitalist nations where market is playing a dominant role. The neo-liberal state is not only supporting the market but also playing the important role in correcting the distortions of the market. Universities are again in the phase of transformation to support the generation of knowledge.

The scenario is little different in Indian context. Universities were established by the British government in the second half of the 19th century in order to strengthen its control. However, the western liberal education provided an opportunity to the Indian intellectuals to question the British rule and also became a powerful force in the freedom struggle to liberate the country from Britishers. After independence universities mainly stood for values of humanism and scientific spirit. India's late arrival in the industrial transformation and also the legacy of British rule meant that state-supported universities during the first phase of expansion after independence could support the transformation to a limited extent only. There is, on the other hand, the phase of globalization. Universities in India are thus facing dual transformation—industrial transformation as well as post-industrial transformation. It is this overlap that produces complexities in renovation and rejuvenation of higher education in India.

The above characterization of the historical phases of transformation is important, as it helps understand the essential institutional structure of the university system in India. It is, therefore, necessary to understand the features of both the transformations and the attendant structure needed for the university.

Structure of Higher Education in Industrial Transformation Phase

In this phase, the state supported universities to build the structure. In the beginning, at the time of the promulgation of the Constitution of India in 1950, education was a state subject, which was put in the concurrent list by the 42nd amendment in 1976. While a university having degree conferring authority could be established by an act—central or state—there was imposed a barrier to entry and the accountability of the university was almost complete to the state. Further, it was within central government jurisdiction to coordinate and determine standards of higher education institutions. To maintain the quality the central government was required to invest in the institutions of higher education. Hence, structures like the University Grants Commission (UGC) were created to maintain quality and provide central funding. Other professional councils such as AICTE were established to provide an orderly growth and maintain standards of technical and professional education. Some councils were also supposed to impose some ethical norms in the practice of professions such as medical, law, education, architecture, etc. This then gave rise to regulatory structure—a system of control of the centre and the states.

The structure of a university was guided by the Act and the statutes of the university. The appointment of the Vice Chancellor was almost the state prerogative and the functioning of the university through General Councils (Senate), Executive

Councils (Syndicate) and academic, research and other functional bodies was under the centralized authority of the Vice Chancellor. The governance of the university was bureaucratized. The postgraduate departments and research centres were directly under the control of university. This phase of expansion saw large number of colleges being affiliated and supervised by the university. The autonomy of the departments, research centres and colleges was limited under the rules and regulation of the university. It was more of a patron and client relationship. Decision-making was in the hands of university and finally in the hands of the state governments. This laid the foundation of regulatory framework which governed the functioning of universities.

There developed, however, several strains in the regulatory structure and the functions which universities were supposed to perform. Structure could not sustain beyond a point to enable universities to perform their expected functions. For any measures to suggest the rejuvenation of universities, it is worthwhile to consider the reasons for the structural failure.

Over-regulation and Under-governance

Various hypotheses are put forward for the failure. The first and foremost argument relates to the structure itself. The NKC (2006) notes that there is a multiplicity of regulatory agencies. They impose irrational and inconsistent conditions for the establishment of universities as well as the maintenance of standards of education. The system, as a result, is over-regulated but under-governed. To quote an example, the report notes that there are extensive rules after entry, as the UGC seeks to regulate almost every aspect of an institution from fees to curriculum. NKC also gives an example where approval of an engineering college or a business school is based on irrational considerations.

Shortage of Public Resources

Another hypothesis relates to the resource crunch (Tilak, 2004). Shortage of public resources weakened the infrastructure of public institutions. There was almost negligible investment in the educational processes that determine quality. On the other hand, scarcity of resources gave rise to the self-financing programmes in public institutions and created conditions for the growth of self-financing (private) institutions in professional disciplines. The resource crunch paved the way for privatization through the deemed universities route and also through private universities under the State Act. Universities granted affiliation to the private colleges in a liberal manner. The privatization of higher education could not be regulated in a proper manner resulting in the failure of universities to perform expected functions.

Decline of Professoriate

The failure of universities is also attributed to the decline of professoriate (Jayaram, 2004). Political pressures in the recruitment of teachers, liberal promotion policy, lack of autonomy, pressure of teacher unions and protective policies have contributed to this decline. Professoriate failed to perform in teaching and research in most of the universities. Universities had no policy to attract the best talents and defy any market pressure to deplete the pool of best researchers in the universities. It may be argued that the decline of professoriate is mainly due to structural factors that protected inbreeding and prevented the system to compete and promote meritocracy.

Affiliating System

Affiliating system is an important structural feature of the university system in India. The strain of the large affiliating system upon universities is yet another factor. Eleventh Plan (Planning Commission, 2008) notes the rationalization of large universities. The large number of affiliated colleges in a university exhausted the time and energy in managing them. As a result, the postgraduate and research level governance was neglected (Shah, 2005). Financially, the sustenance of universities was dependent upon the affiliation of private colleges and hence universities were liberal in granting affiliation to them but in turn adding to their burden.

Failure in Coordination

Singh (2004) notes that failure in the coordination of standards is rather an important factor that contributed to the growth of higher education without any meaningful direction. The Ministry of Human Resource Development could neither manage the coordination between professional councils nor provide UGC with sufficient powers and autonomy to deal with the issue. As a result, the over-expansion in teacher education institutions or engineering or medical or distance education centres could not be managed. The privatization without suitable regulation and quality supervision was the result of the failure in the coordination of standards. For example, UGC could only stop funding to its associated universities and colleges for the failure in the maintenance of standards. Besides, in the case of private universities, UGC has no direct control. In the case of private deemed universities it could only recommend derecognizing to the central government. It did not have absolute powers of derecognizing the state universities for the failure in the maintenance of standards.

To sum up, the traditional structure of universities developed strains to fulfil the expected functions of universities in the phase of industrialization. The failure of existing structure controlled by the state was explained by means of various hypotheses related to over-regulation, shortage of public resources, decline of professoriate, affiliating system and the failure in coordination. Therefore, existing structure needs to be reformed to carry on the expected functions of universities.

What is, however, important to understand is the newer functions that the 21st century's universities are expected to perform? The new functions require new structures in post-industrial transformation. This creates newer tensions between structures and functions. Let us now turn to understand the essential features of functions and structures of higher education in post-industrial transformation phase.

Functions and Structure of Higher Education in Post-Industrial Transformation Phase

Knowledge Economy

The present phase of globalization is characterized by the knowledge economy. The production of knowledge takes place at the boundaries of disciplines. Universities are expected to produce knowledge that is multidisciplinary. In the production of knowledge universities and its departments are supposed to network with other universities and departments. An important function of university is networking with a view to exchange knowledge, as it provides the basis of new knowledge. As knowledge is embodied in human resources, universities need to exchange students, teachers and researchers. This means that the internationalization of higher education is increasingly emerging as a new dimension of the functions of the universities.

Commodification of Knowledge

The commodification of knowledge is forcing universities to adopt the principle of market. The products of the universities need to be marketable—both knowledge produced as well as students embodying knowledge. Knowledge is private and needs copyright and patent for its protection. Universities in the process of creating knowledge can succeed by creating Intellectual Property Rights (IPRs). Efficiency and competition are the two important aspects of the functioning of market. Universities need to be competitive. It means barriers to entry and exit should be minimized. Recruitment and salary conditions of teachers will be guided by the market. Competition reflected in the demand and supply of students, teachers and institutions will produce equilibrium where wastages or inefficiency will be nil.

Learner-centred Approach

An important function of the university is to satisfy the learner who is considered as the client. Curriculum, delivery practices and evaluation must be designed with a view to optimize the learning. In fact, teachers' scholastic knowledge matters little. Teachers' performance will be evaluated by the students and the promotion of teacher should also depend on the evaluation by the students. Instructivist approach should give way to constructivist approach of learning. Since the demand for educated human resource is in global market place, students must learn to adapt to diverse situation and universities must create a global environment in their campuses for satisfying students. Accountability of a teacher is in the market place. He/she should be instrumental in designing a programme which is student-friendly. Greater autonomy should be given to the teacher and the department. However, autonomy is subject to fulfilling the competitive conditions of market.

Supporting Corporate Sector

Universities also need to serve the corporate sector. Hence corporate sector requirement of skill formation should be fulfilled. University and industry linkages are vital for the survival of the universities. New knowledge culture is emerging for the benefit of multinational corporations, the world of financial institutions and the market economy (Thomas, 2004). Universities, therefore, need to embrace the new knowledge culture.

Life-long Education and Training

The strategy of production in higher technology sector requires updating of knowledge and skill throughout the life. The restructuring of the company and management for flexible production becomes necessary. Hence job specification may keep on changing requiring not only higher skills with sound theoretical knowledge but also higher problem-solving ability may be required. Hence, to support knowledge economy, the traditional model of higher education of teaching and research must embrace the concept of life-long education and training

So far as structure of universities is concerned, the newer functions expected from the universities require that universities need to be entrepreneurial. Hence bureaucratic approach to governance should give way to corporate style of functioning. The Vice Chancellor of the university should be risk taker rather than risk averter. The decision-making process should be short and quick. It implies that the governance structure of universities should be less bureaucratic.

Universities should build competitive structure. It means students should be allowed admission on the principle of merit and not through affirmative action. The best of the faculty should be recruited on competitive basis. Differential salary to the teachers should be permitted. Universities should compete for research funding. Periodically research assessment exercises should be carried out.

Under the new structure university should be liberated from the control and regulatory structure of the state. University should also be allowed to raise funds from the market. Higher education is considered as a private good. As private benefits accrue to the students, there is a case for raising fees. If student is unable to pay fee, then, loan market needs to be developed to financially support the students.

Total quality management of the corporate sector should be practised in universities. The leadership role should be permitted for every teacher who should be free to take initiatives.

Contradictions between Structures and Functions

The above characterization of the structure and functions suited in the post-industrial transformation produces a lot of contradictions that need to be analyzed.

Tensions between Old Structure and New Functions

There exists a new tension between the regulatory structure which was supposed to serve the industrial society and the newer functions expected from the universities for serving the post-industrial society. Newer functions to serve the corporate sector, create knowledge through patenting, developing networking and internationalization etc. require entrepreneurship, competitive mechanism and flexibility which the regulatory structure is ill-equipped to provide. It means if universities are required to perform new functions, it should put in place new structure and dismantle old structure. A prescription for renovation and rejuvenation will require nothing short of this.

Tensions between Old Functions and New Functions

The tension consists of the fact that how is it possible for *homo academicus* to adapt the values of *homo mercantalis* in the phase of globalization? This presents a great challenge for the academia. Some might reject the latter function on the ground that there is potent danger in this transformation, as universities will tend to be undemocratic as they embrace and serve the global market place (Jarvis, 2001). Academic freedom will become a farce as universities are enslaved to market forces. Autonomy will be undermined both in teaching and research (Keast, 1995; Hartley, 1995). Notwithstanding the contradictions between the old and new functions, universities can hardly afford to neglect the newer set of functions as students will be forcing the universities to perform new roles.

Tensions between Old Structure and New Structure

Still there is a problem of superimposition of new structure onto the old structure. Can regulatory structure be set up afresh dismantling old structure or should keep adding elements of new structure? In the case of former entry or exit barriers will have to be removed so that competitive forces drive the system to move towards efficiency and quality. In the case of latter universities Acts and statutes need to be revised to modify the functioning of regulatory mechanism in favour of commodification, corporatization and internationalization.

There is thus a dilemma for renovation and rejuvenation of higher education. If regulatory structure is dismantled and new market-friendly structure is established, then, there is the danger that higher education will be elite-oriented. The democratic, egalitarian functions of universities will take a back seat. If old structure is continued, universities in a globalized scenario will loose their relevance. Hence, a practical approach needs to be developed to remodel the structure in such a manner that universities are able to perform twin functions where they satisfy the conditions for industrial as well as post-industrial transformations.

II
Yashpal Committee

The report of Yashpal Committee has come at an opportune moment. Higher education requires structural transformation.

The important features of the Yashpal Committee Report to bring about the transformation are analyzed in this section.

Concept of a University

The report brings to the light the concept of a university. Universities are places that provide opportunities to creative minds to work together in specialized branches of knowledge. The process of knowledge creation in university should not take place in isolation. Research and teaching are the two important pillars of the creation of knowledge and should go together. They should not be treated as watertight compartments. Community of scholars in the university must be primarily accountable to the society and hence should engage themselves in response to the needs of society. Universities should establish centres of culture, knowledge and research. They should provide practical training to the people based on new knowledge and in response to social and personal needs. University should be allowed for the diverse growth of knowledge but should not lead to fragmentation of knowledge. Hence uniformity and standardization of curricula and syllabi should not be attempted. Universities should be accessible to all irrespective of caste, gender, religious and economic considerations. The most important assertion about the university is that it is the responsibility of the state to fund it. Yet universities be allowed to retain the moral and intellectual autonomy from political authorities and economic powers. It should provide freedom in research and training.

Fragmentation of Knowledge

The report notes that growth in knowledge has begun to challenge the boundaries of disciplines, which so far have kept knowledge fragmented. This universal approach to knowledge demands that boundaries of disciplines be porous and scholars be constantly on guard against the tendency towards 'cubicalization of knowledge'. Fragmentation of knowledge has led to a tendency towards creation of 'stand alone' specialized institutions of higher education. A shift from discipline-based knowledge to a new interdisciplinary knowledge is, therefore, advocated by the report.

University system needs to respond to the challenges by creating structure that connects up the fragmented reality. University system must allow within itself the specialized institutions which need not be stand alone. It must interact with all areas of knowledge being pursued within a university. As structural necessity, the report notes: "Creative and flexible mechanisms that ensure the autonomy of the diverse institutional responses should not be curbed." It implies that autonomous institutions with little regulatory restriction should grow within a university rather than outside it.

The report furthermore notes that the undermining of undergraduate education is also the result of fragmentation of knowledge. The dichotomy that was created between the undergraduate affiliating colleges and university postgraduate departments is the result of a misconception that undergraduate education is a lower level of learning. The UG-PG hierarchy is the result of the fragmented knowledge system that was created. The basic questions, so crucial in the knowledge creation, are asked by students at lower stage of education. Hence, the university system should embrace both undergraduates and postgraduates and not create any hierarchy. An agenda of rejuvenation of higher education should not ignore this. The report concludes that "should be mandatory for all universities to have a rich undergraduate programme and undergraduate students must get opportunities to interact with the best faculty".

An important way in which the fragmentation of knowledge occurred was by creating the divide between research bodies and universities. The report notes that "this disjoint between teaching and research has led to a situation in which, on the one hand, most of the universities have been reduced to the status of centres that teach and examine masses and, on the other hand, more and more elite research bodies are being created where researchers have absolutely no occasion to engage with young minds". In a university teaching and research are inseparable for the holistic process of the generation of knowledge. Similar arguments are advanced in the context of Indian Institutes of Technology (IITs). They were treated as elite institutions and preferential policies were suggested. It was little realized that by doing so IITs grew in isolation with little connection to a humanist understanding of the society. Not surprisingly, many IIT graduates left the country. Fragmentation of knowledge—treating technological institutes differently than university—created more harm than good. Hence, the IIT should also be like a university "producing scholars in literature, linguistics and politics along with engineering wizards".

Multiplicity of Structures of Regulation

There are various arguments put forward against the multiplicity of regulatory structures in the Yashpal Committee Report.

Fragmentation of Policies

At the national level, the report notes the emergence of numerous national-level bodies, each looking after a separate area of professional education in isolation. Bodies like the AICTE, ICAR, MCI have led to a fragmentation of policies and a failure in coordination among them has led to chaotic growth of the institutions. Along with regulatory councils, central and state governments and their directorates' regulation without any coordination created difficulties in the approval, recognition, affiliation and accreditation of programmes and institutions.

Outdated UGC

University Grants Commission was set up as a statutory body with the mandate to perform an overarching function of steering higher education in the country. However, new structural necessities have emerged in the field of higher education, which could not have been visualized earlier while designing the UGC. It is suggested that to keep pace with the changes impacting education, the higher education sector in India would require a radically different and new regulatory organizational architecture replacing the existing ones, including the UGC and other bodies.

Think Beyond Regulation

Multiplicity of structures of regulation is considered to be an obstacle in the knowledge management. However, the report argues that there is need to even go beyond mere reform in regulatory system. The report notes that creative and flexible mechanisms that ensure the autonomy of the diverse institutional responses should be promoted. It implies that there is need for creating the condition for producing an environment that nurtures a democratic, tolerant and inquisitive mind, ready not only to engage with but also create new ideas, free of regimentation.

It is important to note that both NKC as well as Yashpal Committee Report argue against too many regulations. However, NKC provides efficiency argument and favours barrier-free entry and exit to promote competitive drive for quality improvement. Yashpal Committee also argues that too much regulation is an obstacle in the creation of knowledge. Knowledge creation requires creative and flexible mechanism and an environment for debate and discourse. Hence, there is need to think beyond regulation.

The report notes that the multiplicity of authorities and duplication of inspection and control have obstructed innovations of curricula, experimenting with the approaches to teaching and learning and establishing meaningful links with the society. A highly over-regulated system consists of interference by multiple agencies which tend to stifle innovation and creativity, increase inefficiency and breed corruption and malpractices. An under-regulated system encourages exploitation, contributions to disorder and erosion of social justice. Therefore, it is important to design a balanced regulatory system that is transparent and ensures accountability.

On Privatization and Commodification in Higher Education

The report notes that there is a substantial role for the private sector. While there exist some centres of excellence in the private sector, most private institutions, instead of helping rejuvenation of higher education, have become commercial entities with very low quality. The report admits that reduction in public funding and demand factors have propelled the growth of private colleges, deemed and private universities in recent years. The trusts managing these institutions had little understanding and experience in education. The trusts or societies that were formed largely consisted of immediate family members. They controlled admission, collected capitation and other fees and appointed teachers on low remuneration. Privatization benefited few who could afford to pay fees. Besides, private investment led to unbalanced growth limited to few states, programmes and disciplines. There was no doubt exception to such rules. However, in majority of cases, deficiencies in enforcement instruments were responsible for commercialization. Regulatory agencies failed to supervise their intake capacity, faculty quality, academic infrastructure and laboratories. Privatization has thus dealt a serious blow to the credibility of the Indian university degree.

UGC has failed to enforce its own guidelines for declaring an institution a deemed university under Section 3 of the UGC Act as "the institution should generally be engaged in teaching programmes and research in chosen fields of specialization which are innovative and of very high academic standards at the master's and research levels. It should also have a greater interface with society through extramural extension and field-action related programmes". The report suggests that it would, therefore, be appropriate to stop the practice of according *de novo* deemed-to-be university status to any institution. Other institutions wishing to get deemed university status should demonstrate special capabilities as was originally intended and should be rigorously evaluated to see if they fulfil the holistic and universal concept of university outlined in this report. The institutions, which have somehow managed to secure such status, should be given a period of three years to develop as a university and fulfil the prescribed accreditation norms failing which the status given to them would be withdrawn.

All private institutions, which seek the status of a university, will have to submit to a national accreditation system. An institution working with a motive of private profit does not have the right to be called a university.

III
National Knowledge Commission (NKC) and Yashpal Committee Report (YCR)

National Knowledge Commission (NKC) of the Government of India presented its report on higher education in 2006. The Yashpal Committee, appointed by the Ministry of Human

Resource Development, has presented its report in June 2009. It is interesting to understand the comparative perspectives within which the restructuring of higher education in India is being conceptualized in these reports. It shows how a complex picture is looked at from two different perspectives. In fact, the two worldviews of restructuring higher education are presented in these reports. It indeed poses a serious policy dilemma in higher education in India.

NKC and YCR note that higher education in India is over-regulated. However, both the reports make a departure in analyzing over-regulation. NKC notes that regulation has caused barriers to entry and exit. This puts restrictions in establishing new institutions, prevents competition and restricts quality. It advocates that if regulatory restrictions are minimized, the market will ensure competition and through greater transparency and accreditation institutions will improve quality. The process will create differentiation among institutions. In the long run, however, the best quality will survive.

YCR, on the other hand, argues that knowledge generation in a university system requires that different disciplines must grow in organic unity. Fragmentation of knowledge by creating boundaries of disciplines is not conducive for knowledge generation. University should be autonomous in allowing the balanced growth of various branches of knowledge. Over-regulation and interference in the functioning of university creates distortions in the knowledge generation and therefore be rationalized.

NKC feels that there was too much protection given to the institutions and the faculty in the past. This has caused inbreeding and inefficiency. The system needs to be exposed to competition so that a drive is created to improve quality. YCR feels that the institution of university suffered from conceptual and structural deficiency, as state failed to create conditions for a balanced growth of all disciplines in close unity with each other within university.

From the above basic differences in perception towards the process of knowledge generation arise further differences in understanding the problems of higher education. YCR argues that fragmentation in knowledge causes the dichotomy between the undergraduate affiliated colleges and postgraduate colleges and university. Fragmented policy has caused further distance in teaching and research institutions. With a porous disciplinary boundary, the unity of teaching and research and undergraduate and postgraduate departments functioning within a university would create conditions for further knowledge. What is required is the structure of a university where all knowledge from humanities, social sciences, basic sciences and applied disciplines fuse and grow together. Autonomy of the university and of the individuals should be guaranteed.

NKC asserts that different types of institutions/universities may coexist. In fact, it suggests Undergraduate Board of Education for the undergraduate colleges. Cluster of colleges may form a university. Autonomous colleges may be given the degree-granting power. What is required is greater transparency in the functioning of the system so that competition could be generated. Fragmentation in knowledge is not a problem so long as institutions respond to market signals through grading, evaluation etc. and strive for the quality and excellence.

It is important to note that both NKC and YCR argue in favour of autonomy. However, autonomy in NKC implies freedom to take decisions in response to market, whereas in YCR it means that freedom should be given to create knowledge that is not fragmented but is in response to the society. Most significantly, the former would treat higher education as merit good whereas the latter as public good.

Independent Regulatory Authority in Higher Education (IRAHE) in NKC is entrusted with the task of granting licence to institutions on transparent criteria. It is also expected to issue licence to accrediting agency so that the quality of the institution is made known to all. UGC's role is reduced to funding only. National Commission of Higher Education and Research (NCHER) in YCR is given a mandate to eliminate the fragmentation of knowledge and helping university to nurture knowledge by providing feedbacks. All professional councils including UGC are subsumed within NCHER. This is the most significant difference in recommendations of the two reports.

It is significant to note that none of the reports have analyzed the limits under which UGC has provided the institutional support to the university system in India. Autonomy of university should be analyzed along with the autonomy of UGC. UGC is an agency to provide guidelines to maintain standards in higher education to the universities. It also provides the plan support to development purposes. Only instrument of control with UGC is that it can stop funding to a limited number of institutions if they fail to comply with regulations for the maintenance of standards. State governments and universities under State Act are constitutionally independent under the federal governance. UGC has no power to interfere with the functioning of the university under federal structure. The problem compounded when private universities began to be established by State Act and central government failed to regulate through the legislation by Parliament. Besides, the liberal opening of deemed university route is also the result of the dominant lobby of private providers. UGC is simply a recommending body to the government, which finds it easy to serve the vested interests.

UGC no doubt became another bureaucratic organization rather than developing an academic outfit to guide the university. It is in need of restructuring in favour of greater academic role to perform the function mandated by the Constitution of India. It is not clear at all how the reduction in its role as simply a funding agency would serve the purpose. How new institutions suggested in two different reports are expected to take up the constitutional mandate. Certainly, the coordination function is being performed by the government and probably not so well. Hence, there is need to develop the institutional structure for coordination. This could be easily done by constituting a Higher Education Council with the Prime Minister of India as its Chairman and the HRD Minister as the Vice Chairman with members from different ministries engaged in supporting higher education and representation from councils dealing with professional disciplines. However, how could UGC be made more academic body to guide the standards in higher education is certainly a question that needs to be debated?

IV
Critical Appreciation of Yashpal Committee Report

The report notes that dichotomies of higher education are precisely because there has been fragmentation of knowledge and hardly has there been attempt to understand the principle of universal knowledge. Unless this epistemological understanding of knowledge is clear, the renovation and rejuvenation of higher education cannot be even conceptualized.

The report refers to various dichotomies in the higher education. Dichotomy between central and state university and between state university and affiliated colleges and between school and college level of education are principally the result of the fragmentation in knowledge that the policy has so far supported. University, if it is the creator of universal knowledge, cannot be differentiated among them on whatsoever is the criterion. State universities, therefore, cannot be given a treatment that is in any way inferior to central university. Similarly, undergraduate, teaching in affiliated colleges and postgraduate teaching in university departments and university colleges cannot be treated separately. Both should co-evolve together and be treated in terms of organic unity. In fact, undergraduate and postgraduate should be the part of university and knowledge created at both the levels should feed each other. The less favourable treatment to undergraduate level of education will impact postgraduate and higher levels of education and the same is true for school and college levels of education. There has been further dichotomy between teaching and research due to the fragmented way of looking at the creation of knowledge. Teaching and research should also co-evolve together. Teaching promotes research as creative minds work together and pose questions which cannot all be answered in the classroom but taken up for research and the research understanding further develops the teaching. This integrated approach leads to qualitative improvement among teachers, students and researchers and provides the basis for further knowledge. There have again been attempts at creating a distance between teaching and research institutions and this defies the principle of universal knowledge. Scientific and industrial research institutes are given mandate to create knowledge outside the university system which is not a desired direction the higher education system should move. A desirable course of action should be an integration of such research centres within university where fusion of different boundaries will create a more mature knowledge beneficial to the mankind. Biologists, chemists, pharmacists, engineers, doctors and technologists should develop a much more humanist understanding of knowledge in the university.

The conception of a university in the report follows from the understanding of the theory of knowledge. University is a place where universal knowledge is created in the unity of all disciplines. Even if the disciplinary boundary is created for the convenience of understanding knowledge, there should be full opportunity for interaction with other disciplines. A fragmentary and fractured understanding of knowledge is dangerous. Universities where all disciplines grow in a more or less unity provide the right place for universal knowledge. Universities may differ from each other in terms of emphases yet variety of disciplines adds perfection to the knowledge creation. It will prove to be more beneficial for the society. Within university there should be autonomy and intellectual freedom. Centres or departments must be provided enough flexibility and less and less of regulations so that individual creativity finds fullest opportunity to grow.

Regulatory framework to govern the universities should also be minimal. UGC and other regulatory councils for want of coordination in policies have created fragmentary and lopsided growth in higher education.

Idealism vs. Realism

Idealist conception: Description of a university in Yashpal Committee Report is guided by an idealist perspective. This is a conceptualization much closer to the ideals of Plato's democratic republic where the philosopher king rules. Academic culture thrives when there is self-regulation and self-discipline. Whenever the latter prevails accountability is naturally enforced. There is none to ensure it. Individuals within such institutions enjoy full freedom and autonomy. The distinction between the rulers and the ruled is blurred and, therefore, there is self-governance and no administration. The path to the creation of knowledge is not dictated by the state or the state regulating body.[1] As the individual consciousness is the social consciousness, societal concerns are automatically taken into account. Knowledge is, therefore, also self-regulated and caters to the mankind.[2]

University as a social institution: University is not a construct that can be developed independent of historical transformations. It is a social institution. Whatsoever the ideal and the humanist conception of knowledge is the construct of the university depends upon the stage of development of society. Universities passed through the stages of church, state and contemporary phase of market domination. The way university is structured to create knowledge in the phase of state domination is markedly different from the stage of market domination. We have already discussed in detail these structural differences during industrial and post-industrial transformations. In the latter phase the construction of knowledge is guided by the market mechanism whereas in the former phase it is state that may determine the directions in which knowledge construction should take place. In both the phases the knowledge construction may not be guided by societal interests. In fact, even during state domination, the knowledge construction may be guided by the interests of rich if state designs policy to favour them.

The point to note is that the Yashpal Committee Report failed to see the way in which knowledge is created in reality in different periods. The realist picture of knowledge and consequently the university may diverge from the idealist notion. It is for this reason that the Yashpal Committee Report suffers from lack of realism.

Knowledge generation ignores the role of market: Yashpal Committee Report is based on the humanist conception of knowledge. Knowledge belongs to humankind and therefore can be shared by all. It is also the responsibility of the state to support the generation of knowledge. University supported by public fund is then a suited structure to produce the knowledge for societal reproduction.

However, in a globalized phase of reproduction of the society, knowledge is no longer heritage of mankind. It is considered as property to be created by an individual or group or company and an institutional mechanism is being established to patent and protect it. It is argued that protection of knowledge will provide an incentive for the producers of knowledge to produce. Thus knowledge has an important dimension of commercialization and marketing. It means that universities will have to make effort to transform its implicit knowledge into an explicit knowledge, i.e., in forms in which it can be traded. Knowledge is thus a differentiated product whose demand is derived from the market. Given this conceptualization of knowledge the idealist notion of university breaks down and university becomes an entity that has to be guided by the dictates of the market. It then means that fragmentation of knowledge becomes a reality that university structure has to deal with. University cannot ignore the aberrations that are created by the market. Market dominance is so important that university cannot remain isolated from market interference and can in fact face the danger of its existence.

Ignores the dynamics of privatization: The private and deemed universities have grown rapidly in the recent years, as state failed to fund the state universities. Given the state's failure to fund higher education, how it is possible to adhere to the notion of an all-pervasive concept of an ideal university conceptualized by the Yashpal Committee Report. The privatization carries with it the commercialization. The only way to deal with the process of privatization is a strong regulation. However, apart from the aspect of regulation, it is not clear how the private state/deemed university will be an ideal university? In US system the private university is supported by the state in research funding. The relation of state with private, apart from the aspect of regulation, is not well analyzed in the report in spite of the acceptance of the role of private participation in higher education.

Faulty conception of individual and community of scholars: The notion of an individual as autonomous, concerned with societal interests and hence entitled to the freedom of decision-making without checks, is a dangerous assumption. It is indeed difficult to think of mass education where state being an important stakeholder may not enforce norms of accountability upon individual and the institution. Scholars point out the myth of self-governing community of scholars in today's context. University as an institution has evolved over time and represents a collective entity which may defy the conception of scholars conceptualized in the report. The conception of state as neutral and undertaking full responsibility in establishing universities is not well founded as the state finds it increasingly difficult to fund them. Suffice it to mention here that even in the American system of higher education "the myths of a community of scholars (Keller, 1983; Goodman, 1962) outlast actual behaviors, and the myth was sustained until the 1980's"(John, 2000: 32–33).

Heavy reliance of state as exclusive provider of higher education: Implicit in the conception of knowledge and that of the university is the role of the state in public funding. Given that state is expected to put no restrictions on the internal functioning of university. This is unrealistic assumption in the report. State cannot remain non-interventionist. As state is primarily responsible to the public and universities are only indirectly responsible to the public, the state needs to ensure the accountability of the university.

V
Conclusion

It was noted that there is a policy dilemma. The industrial and post-industrial transformations require that universities have complex role to play. The fundamental role of a university is to generate and disseminate knowledge. The needs of society are mediated through state and the market, yet the dynamics of knowledge generation and its benefits to the society in both the cases differ. Hence, the conceptualization of a university must take into account the elements of both the stages of development. It cannot ignore the dynamics of market influencing the process of knowledge. Universities in India will have to deal with the duality arising from both the industrial and post-industrial transformations.

YCR rightly highlights the humanist and scientific approaches to knowledge. Universal approach to knowledge defies fragmentation in knowledge and policies that create divide are opposed. However, this is an idealist approach and ignores the reality and, in particular, the role of market in the knowledge generation. The knowledge is in the market place and the role of private providers and corporate sector cannot be brushed aside while the state has to bear the major responsibility in shaping universities. The ideal view of university in YCR needs to be supplemented with the structures that permit the role of private sector in knowledge management under the regulatory structure of the state. Besides, it is important that UGC should build an academic structure with adequate powers and functions. We can also not be oblivious to the role played by professional councils in the maintenance of standards. The coordination between professional councils needs to be ensured by a high-powered body of Higher Education Council chaired by the Prime Minister of India.

It is also important to note that NKC's argument to establish IRAHE is equally non-tenable as it would amount to minimizing the role of state and regulation. The market dominance will be dangerous and the state has to regulate the market in higher education.

The path for renovation and rejuvenation of higher education in India essentially lies between maintaining the balance between the roles of state and market. State has built the institutions over the last 60 years and these institutions should prepare themselves to serve the society as well as accept the role of market and learn to exploit the role of market to be meaningful and relevant in today's world.

Notes

1. This classical model of self-regulating institutions is consistent with theories of knowledge such as the 'internalist' model of the development of science (Merton, 1973) and the notion that the

government of knowledge is conducted through the Republic of Science (Polanyi, 1962) rather than through government.

2. Within this framework the response to external influences are guided by " own intellectual and moral recognisances" (see Kogan, 1988).

References

Goodman, Paul. (1962) *The Community of Scholars*. New York: Random House.

Hartley, D. (1995) "The 'McDonalization' of Higher Education: Food for Thought?", *Oxford Review of Education*, Vol. 21, No. 4, pp. 409--23, December 1995.

Jarvis, P. (2001) *Universities and Corporate Universities*. London: Kogan Page.

Jayaram, N. (2004) "Higher Education in India Massification and Change" in Altbach Philip G. and Umakoshi Toru, (eds.). *Asian Universities Historical Perspectives and Contemporary Challenges*. The John Hopkins University Press, Baltimore.

Keast, D.A. (1995) "Entrepreneurship in Universities: Definitions, Practices, and Implications". *Higher Education Quarterly*, 49(3), 248–266.

Keller, George (1983) *Academic Strategy: The Management Revolution in American Higher Education*. Baltimore: The Johns Hopkins University Press.

Kogan, Maurice (1988) "Government and the Management of Higher Education: An Introductory" Review in *International Journal of Institutional Management in Higher Education*, 1988, Vol. 12, No. 1.

Levin, John S. (2000) "The Practitioner's Dilemma: Understanding and Managing Change in the Academic Institution" in *Managing Colleges and Universities* ed. by Hoffman M.A. and Summers R.W., London: Bergin and Garvey.

Merton R. (1973) *The Sociology of Science: Theoretical and Empirical Investigations*, Chicago: University of Chicago Press.

National Knowledge Commission (2006) Note On Higher Education, 29th November 2006. Website: www.knowledgecommission.org

Patnaik, Prabhat (2009) "Challenges Before Higher Education in Developing Societies", Keynote address delivered in Sub-regional

Conference of South, South-West and Central Asia on Higher Education—"Facing Global and Local Challenges: The New Dynamics for Higher Education" February 25–26, New Delhi.

Planning Commission (2008) Eleventh Five-Year Plan 2007–2012, Vol. II, Planning Commission, Government of India.

Polanyi, M. (1962) "The Republic of Science: Its Political and Economic Theory", *Minerva* 1: 54–74, 1962.

Shah, A.M. (2005) "Higher Education and Research: Roots of Mediocrity", *Economic and Political Weekly*, Vol. 40, No. 22.

Singh, Amrik (2004) *Fifty Years of Higher Education in India: The Role of the University Grants Commission*, New Delhi: Sage Publications.

Thomas, Elwyn (2004) "Knowledge Cultures and Higher Education: Achieving Balance in the Context of Globalisation", paper presented at UNESCO Colloquium, Paris, December 2004.

Tilak, J.B.G. (2004) "Absence of Policy and Perspective in Higher Education", *EPW*, Vol. 39, No. 21, May 22–28, 2004.

CHAPTER 9

Reform in Governance of Universities

Bureaucratic machinery to run the affairs of the academic life of the universities assumes importance in the governance of the university system. The internal life and the external environment of the university system are undergoing rapid transformation necessitating change in the governance structure. The chapter analyses the features of bureaucracy and different perspectives of university administration. The changing role expectation of the universities is reviewed and given the changes in the inner life of university, professional management of university system is advocated.

I
Bureaucratization of University Administration

The term 'bureaucracy' evokes in our mind a picture of rigid, non-professional, hierarchical institution. When it comes to managing the university system ideally characterized by the community of scholars, the bureaucratic tendencies in the university administration are assumed to be *naturally* unsuited. It is so because in a community of scholars, every individual is supposed to be master in his or her own field and so there is no scope for hierarchy. Individual is receptive to change and is supposed to take initiatives and hence there is no need for top-down guidance and supervision as in a bureaucratic set-up.

It is argued that much of the ills that plague the university system in India is due to heavy bureaucratization in the university administration as latter leads to delays, inefficiency and wastages and kills initiatives of the actors. The section analyses the objective conditions that gave rise to bureaucratization in the university administration and the consequent effects upon higher education system.

Characteristics of Bureaucracy

An important characteristic of bureaucracy is emphasis on job descriptions and on rules and regulations. It is an essential element of an organization. It leads to certainty in behaviour. It also does not permit favour. It works well in situations where the organization is large and some standardized practices are to be followed on a regular basis. When rules predominate uniform practices find ready solutions, however, new practices wait for a solution. Too many rules also sometimes lead to reinterpretation and misinterpretation thereby causing dissatisfactions.

Another feature of bureaucracy is that it is hierarchical and control system is centralized. In organizations where ranks matter and superior-subordinate relation, as in government departments, are present, orders flow from the top and bottom line officers merely obey and report. Hence, policy and planning is the privilege of the few at the top. Subordinates are responsible for implementation. There is no scope of disagreement.

The core of bureaucratic management is rational decision making. Manager collects and analyses the right data, understands the most efficient means by which goals can be achieved and devises control activity. The assumption of rationality as always making best choices creates troubles as ideals in terms of perfect information and coordination may not be achieved.

Bureaucracy is a neutral concept. It does not admit externalities. It is a closed world. If at all externalities occur then these are recorded, analysed and the solutions are found. If, however, the external influences are large and the machinery is not efficient enough to record then decisions get delayed causing dissatisfaction. We will observe that university administration failed to administer because of bureaucratization as the conditions for the working of an ideal bureaucracy was never created.

II
Four Perspectives of University Administration

Self-Governing Community of Scholars

This is an ideal perspective. This is a conceptualization much closer to the ideals of Plato's democratic republic where philosopher king rules. Academic culture thrives when there is self-regulation and self-discipline. Whenever latter prevails, accountability is naturally enforced. There is none to ensure it. Individuals within such institutions enjoy full freedom and autonomy. The distinction between the rulers and the ruled is blurred and, therefore, there is self-governance and no administration. The path to the creation of knowledge is not dictated by the state or the state regulating body.[1] As the individual consciousness is the social consciousness, societal concerns are automatically taken into account. Knowledge is, therefore, also self-regulated and caters to the mankind.[2]

Scholars point out the myth of self-governing community of scholars. However, in the past this might have been a reality in Nalanda or Vikramshila University or in ancient Oxford or Cambridge University. However, as an approximation to above ideals the governance in colleges or universities in European higher education institutions and also in India existed before the 'massification' of higher education. The generation of learned people who were students in 40s, 50s and even in 60s take pride in narrating the older memories of academic culture that prevailed in those days. The Vice-chancellor of a university was truly an academic leader. There was no problem in administration as academic community was equally powerful in terms of knowledge being the source of power. Traces of self-regulation exist even today in terms of 'Academic Councils' composed of deans and departmental heads although various other structures exist today to counter the autonomy of the community of scholars to which we will return later. Suffice it to mention here that even in American system of higher education "the myth of a community of scholars (Keller, 1983; Goodman, 1962) outlasted actual behaviours, and the myth was sustained until the 1980s" (Levin, 2000: 32–3).

From Self-Governance to State Control

Critics of the university system as the community of self-governance maintain that universities must come out of the 'ivory tower' as intellectuals should have a commitment to social problems. It involves a continuous review of the education system and a more careful planning of the content of education.[3] The upward economic and social mobility that is reflected in politics and in the instrumentality of state apparatus began to shape the future of universities. It was realized that higher education is the sphere that promotes the mobility, which, in turn, meant that higher education itself be subject to change.

The Gajendragadkar (1971) interpreted university autonomy as having two aspects; (i) autonomy within university, and (ii) autonomy in relation to agencies and authorities external to it, the most important of which is state. Thus, autonomy of universities was relative. It admitted that bossism of 'senior members' must be eradicated, effective participation of all members in various bodies be ensured and students must have legitimate representation.[4] The report notes, "The finances of a university are almost entirely provided from public funds .... This being so ... the universities and government (State and Central) have to and should work in close collaboration" (ibid.: 12).

Various committees, thereafter, maintain that the relative autonomy of the university should be the cornerstone of the governance of universities.[5] Yet the university administration was subject to excessive state control and hence to various pulls from external environment, on the one hand, and internal dissensions from within, on the other. This was the factor responsible for 'bureaucratization', which essentially meant deviation from the ideal typical notion of bureaucracy as conceptualized by Weber. Before examining bureaucratization in the university administration the relation between state and university needs further examination.

State regulation was not confined to the state being only policy and planning authority. State was responsible for deciding the appointment of Vice-chancellor. The recruitment of teachers, admission procedure, sanctioning of course, selection of nominees to Senates and Syndicates, determination of service condition and salary of teachers, tuition fees etc., began to be determined by the government. So long as public money is used to support university the latter was said to be accountable to legislature. Thus, tightening the grips over university was justified on financial grounds. It may be argued justifiably that state represents larger social groups than our community of scholars and, therefore, state has the legitimate right to direct higher education to meet the goal of social equity and raise the participation and quality to meet the demand for trained manpower.

However, state is not a neutral entity. It serves the interests of pressure groups. It also reflects the domination of superiors over subordinates. Democratic state in India is also said to be 'populist' and hence guided by short-term gains. Gunar Myrdal in Asian drama notes two features of Indian state. It is guided by 'soft' options as concessions predominate in budget that leads to fiscal crisis. Secondly, corruption is one of the highest in the world. In its relation with university, soft options meant that it prevented a rational fee hike. Appointment of vice-chancellor was guided by extraneous considerations and control amounted to interference in the internal affairs of the university. Universities were also starved of adequate grants. Following example is a case in point cited by Amrik Singh. Referring to Orissa Universities Ordinance issued on November 14, 1988, Amrik Singh notes that every single decision of the university is now subject to the control of the government as the category of ordinances has been done away with altogether and decision-making subsumed under the heading of statutes has been vested with the government (Singh, 1988).

From State Control to Market Hegemony

Professional Management: Excessive state control led to the bureaucratization[6] in university administration. However, fiscal shortage coupled with changes in external environment, namely, gearing to the diversified job demands such as in services sectors, globalization and privatization, in general, and marketization of education services, in particular, necessitated professional management in universities. The growth of higher education has also to be in tune with market demand. Hence universities must restructure the course, devise suitable teaching strategies, and provide adequate infrastructural facilities so as to yield placement results. Performance of institutions is, therefore, based on output rather than input. Universities must get high quality ranking. All these demand professional management of universities.

Professional management, however, can be ensured at a price. Besides, it requires autonomy of professionals as efficiency and competitiveness need to be ensured in professional style of management. Accountability through performance appraisal goes along with autonomy. The management also needs to ensure wide range of choice of products at competitive price. Governance requires transformation of higher education management from rigid bureaucratic to flexible system, from hierarchy to networking, from planned approach to entrepreneurial strategy and dogmatic to inspirational leadership.

New professional management can be ensured in a purely privatized set-up. The world over rise of private universities manifests the growing demand for privatized educational product whereby individual's cost-benefit approach dictates investment decision by an individual to join the course and the institution. The tendency is manifest albeit, on a modest scale in India as well. In Malaysia and Singapore, consequent commercialization and commodification of education led to a growing feeling of universities being a business enterprise and academicians being viewed as entrepreneurs (see Molly, 2002).

Hybrid of Bureaucracy and Professional Management

Governments both in developing as well as the developed world have stakes in higher education to fulfil the objectives of socio-economic development. Yet a combination of factors has led to market orientation of higher education services. This creates a growing tension in the university administration between traditional bureaucratic and professional management approaches to governance. Universities are now supposed to act as a 'hybrid' organization being called to operate in both public as well as private domain. They are supposed to fulfil public duties and developing commercial market activities.[7] They thus become a mixture of both a government or a quasi government institution and a commercial enterprise.

The tendency for the hybrid system is seen in many Western European universities who have been under close government control and are now pushed onto the open market.[8] Thus there has been a change in the climate from 'dependence' to 'exchange' and the universities are now being called upon to change the mindset towards professionalism geared to the market forces.

In Indian scenario, the governance in colleges and universities presents a complex picture. There seems to be developing a dualism in managing mass education at subsidized cost and managing elite education at non-subsidized cost.

III
Changing Role Expectation

Applied Fields and Corporate Settings

In the new context, the role expectation of universities is changing in response to knowledge economy. Significance of knowledge is increasing from national to global perspective of development. The value of knowledge has no more intrinsic importance. Knowledge is increasingly seen as potentially generating revenue in the global marketplace. This means that applied fields of knowledge are gaining prominence over basic disciplines. Hence the role expectation of universities is to produce knowledge in applied fields that have greater significance for global market. Humanities and arts subjects have to compete for institutional support with subjects that more evidently contribute to national and business agendas of wealth creation. Changing role expectations therefore, demand changing structure and functions of universities having implications for what Maurice has called the inner life of institutions (Kogan, 1988).

Universities as social institutions have educational commitments for preserving knowledge as public good, cultivating citizenship, transmitting cultural heritage, forming individual character and habits of mind. However, universities are now being viewed as quasi-corporate entities producing a wide range of goods and services in a competitive marketplace. This shift in the role from the university as social institution to university as industry is also creating a shift in the structure of institutions. Academic management is being guided more by managerial abilities.

Managerialism

Universities are increasingly seen as organization under labels like managerialism. University leaders are guided by maximizing efficiency. Various functions—academic, technical and administrative—are viewed to satisfy the clients. Students are seen as consumers. There is more an element of quid pro quo or direct benefits to the society. This means academics are no longer seen as luxury where the value of leisure is seen as adding to the creative elements. Academic or administrative personnel are busy performing multiple functions. They must know to coordinate different functions. They must know to manage time and class. They must consciously attempt to innovate. There has to be benchmarking and no one is assumed to fall below the standards set by means of benchmarking.. Under new managerialism, the institutional leadership role is increasingly viewed as most important.

The perspective of leadership to take initiative to maximize efficiency is the perspective that may not be always welcome. Universities as social institutions stand for social values rather than the value system that emphasizes universities as business enterprises. Yet managing the social affairs efficiently is something that cannot be ruled out. This change in the role expectation of universities, therefore, calls attention.

Increasing Social Demand

Universities have also to fulfil increasing social obligations. Another role in which universities have to function relates to serving as the location of near universal training and lifelong learning for population of knowledge society. This broadens the sphere of work for the universities, as the concept of education is no longer restricted to a particular age cohort. Technological change is taking place at a fast pace which also means that knowledge is getting outdated fast. Hence, universities have to keep abreast of advances in knowledge. It is then supposed to devise curricula that can serve the function of lifelong education and training to meet rising social demand from various age groups. The role expectation of university fulfilling the goal of lifelong education and training, too, needs to be analysed, as it may also have its effect on the structures.

IV
Failures of Bureaucratization in University Administration

In principle, university system consists of a self-regulatory system. University functions according to the Acts under which it comes into existence. The Act allows the university to formulate its own statutes and ordinances. While statutes deal with the role of the universities bodies and the officers of the university bodies, laying down the broad parameters for the functioning of the university, the ordinances deal with the various faculties, the duties of the deans and the heads of the departments, the preparation of syllabi, the conduct of examinations, the evaluation of papers etc. The Senate and the Syndicate, the academic council, the planning board and the finance committee carry out administration. There are various other bodies, which report to the university.[9]

The problems often encountered in the governance through these well-defined structures are that these often invite elaborate processes so that the speed and the decisiveness required for efficient and effective administration is lost. Technical objections quoting the books of law are pointed out that put obstacles rather than facilitate the Vice-chancellor. Senate and academic councils are large bodies that produce little result out of rational analysis.[10] There are numerous committees with a power to study, delay and veto. Senate becomes more of a bottleneck. University is such a loose federation where different components do not make an organic whole.

Gnanam (1990) notes some of the features of centralized administration in Indian universities and its consequent effects. It reports: "In the universities, most of the issues, however insignificant and unimportant they may be, are referred to the Vice-chancellor and it is generally said in the academic community that in most of the universities nothing moves without the signatures of the Vice-chancellor .... This practice, thus, leads to delays in decision making, unnecessary paper work, over burdening of the Vice-chancellor and authorities with the routine work, development of the sense of lack of confidence at the lower levels, which finally lead to a slow pace for the promotion of standards and achievement of objectives ... delays thus caused also add to the agitations amongst students, teachers and non-teaching staff when issues relating to their causes are involved" (pp. 87–88).

The point to note is that massification of higher education enlarged the parameters of participation in an effort to democratize the university life. However, bureaucratization in university administration along with the combination of forces has resulted into the crisis of higher education.[11] Mehta (2003) notes, "In our search for uniformity and standardization, we have become victims of centralization, uniformity and bureaucratization. A sound education system cannot be created on the basis of these characteristics".

V
Perspectives of Reform in Governance in Universities

In response to the role expectation, therefore, there is an urgent need for strengthening of the management (Meek, 2004). There is the need for the fusion of new managerial values with traditional academic ones (Clark, 1998). It implies that the traditional governance model needs to be reformed to accommodate the fast decision making mechanisms. These elements of change and reform process need to be discussed to fulfil the role expectations of universities.

Teaching and Learning

In the inner life of universities, the teaching and learning has been dominated by a focus on individual practitioner and change in the classroom. It was assumed that individual teacher will carry out quality improvement. At the institutional or policy level, quality improvement was not the dominant issue of reform. Quality assurance was the only agenda that was taken up at the government level. In recent years, the teacher centred management of teaching and learning has given way to the student centred learning. Researchers are now subject to research assessment exercises. Students' assessment of teachers, too, is being invoked into practice which was hitherto not known in academic institutions. This may also be considered as "part of a broader reconceptualization of the roles of universities in the student marketplace" (Mcinnis, 2005). It means that universities have to respond to a demand driven management ensuring professionalization of teaching and learning.

To what extent the universities will respond to the learner-based approach and introduce mechanisms for effective teaching learning processes will depend to a great extent upon the realization of academic leaders to the emerging demands of knowledge economy. So far developed countries have responded to the professional management of teaching and learning both at the level of research and practices. However, in developing countries the public universities have not responded to the demands of learner centred approach. In some of the deemed universities and private colleges, practices are observed to introduce a new model of teaching and learning. Research findings on these are, however, not available.

Disciplinary Boundary and Interdisciplinary Approach

The most important change that is occurring within universities relates to the blurring of distinctions between basic disciplines. Until the onset of mass higher education, the pure disciplines enjoyed pride of status. A new context affecting the inner life relates to the shift from mode I to mode II knowledge. Mode I emphasizes the discipline as the basis of knowledge production. Mode II knowledge production is through application, problem solving, multidisciplinarity and entrepreneurship. Knowledge must relate to the concerns of particular individuals, organizations and the societies. What it implies is that instead of firms, universities have greater role in innovations in knowledge-based societies. This demands an increasing networking between universities, industries and the government. The approach is known as 'Triple Helix' thesis that supports and indeed goes beyond the mode II interdisciplinary approach to knowledge production (Etzkowitz and Leydesdorff, 2000).

Will disciplines break the boundaries? Will colleges break the boundaries? Will universities break the boundaries? These questions are important to ask to inner academic fraternity. If knowledge production has to break the boundary and increasing reliance is to be placed on networks and communication with scientists and social scientists, with academic experts and pure managers and administrators and with experts and corporate leaders and NGOs, the inner life within universities has to undergo radical transformation with multiple functions and responsibilities. Concept of a good teacher and good researcher must also embrace itself with the qualities of a good leader and a manager.

Stumbling block on this line of thinking could be the mind-set of inner circles. No less important, however, are the rules and regulations that provide a rigid framework. Still another factor could be issues relating to the autonomy. Developed countries have made progress towards transdisciplinary approach to knowledge production and academics are being encouraged to pursue that. Academic circles within universities in India need to network and collaborate teaching and research programmes.

Academic Freedom

Restructuring the bureaucracy is just one solution. The complexities of today's world demand that there may be many more approaches to governance. As pointed out earlier, market is the most important external environment to coordinate. The objective of the post-secondary education is to prepare the students for job market. Hence, university governance requires the flexibility with which the curriculum, the teaching practices etc., could be developed in short time. Universities exposed to the market and international practices in teaching and research also need entrepreneurship because only those education providers who can innovate and be receptive to change can survive in the market and also can face external challenges. The model of bureaucracy and even those of reformed bureaucracy cannot just work. Some sort of corporate culture giving importance to the entrepreneurs, leaders, informal procedures, collegiality will have to be created within universities. Such corporate culture may be independently allowed for certain specific activities or it may even be allowed within a bureaucratic structure providing almost absolute autonomy to determine admissions, fees, teaching-learning, evaluation and establishing collaborations.

Bureaucratic Reform

As said earlier, mass education necessitated large structures to be managed through bureaucratic machinery. However, the bureaucratic machinery failed because it was unable to integrate large scale externalities and also the uncertainties that external environment imposed. The result of all these factors was that an ideal community of scholars disappeared and the structures superimposed to manage the university system could put in place the systems, the personnel and the processes that managed mass education but could not evolve to manage the quality. Other smaller structures allowing self-governance and autonomy emerged to manage the quality bypassing the university system. An ambience of teaching and research was lost in the universities and this is the real crisis that bureaucracy prevented the quality to develop. But this was inevitable, as quality cannot be managed only through rules, instructions and controls through monitoring.

Raising the participation rate from 7 to 20 per cent by the year 2020 is something that is talked about for India to achieve the knowledge superpower status. Given that compulsion, the bureaucratic machinery needs to be reformed to further manage the mass education. Thus, restructuring of bureaucratic machinery in administering the university is the solution that may further be tried out. In this connection, CABE Committee has considered the recommendations of the Gnanam (1990).

UGC (2003) notes, "More recently, with many additional functions being taken up by universities, two new cultures have now come up, viz., commercial culture and corporate culture. The former culture is useful to support activities like continuing education, testing and consultancy, distance education and publication/distribution of course material, which are important for revenue generation and time bound work. On the other hand, the latter culture emphasizes the leadership role provided by senior academics/officials and the top-down planning and monitoring practices, which may be introduced by them in the functioning of the university. However, such a mixed culture and its possible benefits have yet to be well accepted in the Indian university system".

The real problem is that Indian state is not receptive to those changes. There are political and social compulsions of mass education. State will find it difficult to move away from bureaucracy. As state will hesitate to move away or to provide space for corporate culture in any proactive manner, other non-government agencies will take advantage of the rising ambitions and demand of middle classes, which will then fill the void due to inaction by the state.

A Mixed Baggage of Policies

There is no clear line of thinking in policies. This needs a little analysis. In developing countries, the governments have to resolve the contradictions at multiple levels. In developing countries, increasing access and concern for equity are the demands of democratic societies. In a resource constrained situation, investment for quality and excellent infrastructure can be only on a selective basis. This is bound to happen during transition from elite to mass higher education. Hence the contradiction to manage quality in a mass higher education system will continue to persist.

The changing role expectation of universities may not be supported by the government to effect various changes at the level of policies. However, a greater accountability will be placed upon the traditional structure of universities without any change in governance pattern. The dynamics of the situation will then be high level of inefficiency. The traditional structure of universities will begin to show the signs of collapse.

high level of inefficiency. The traditional structure of universities will begin to show the signs of collapse.

Shift to Change Process

The essential question is: how should a shift to change process continue? The answer to this question is a complex one, as factors influencing institutionalization is still something not so clear to the policy makers. It may happen that universities themselves initiate process of change as a result of changes taking place elsewhere. In such a scenario, however, the trajectories of growth process may not be uniform. In India, there is a mixed baggage of policies which do not give a clear signal to the direction in which change should take place. It is also not clear how far policy-induced changes will have impact on organizational behaviour? Whether there is autonomous or induced shift, it is of utmost importance for the members of the academic community to understand the changing role perception of universities and define the inner life of universities in a changing context and design appropriate governance model for the university system.

Notes

1. This classical model of self-regulating institutions is consistent with theories of knowledge such as the internalist model of the development of science (Merton, 1973) and the notion that the government of knowledge is conducted through the Republic of Science (Polanyi, 1962) rather than through government.
2. Within this framework the responses to external influences are guided by "own intellectual and moral recognisances" (see Kogan, 1988).
3. See Gajendragadkar (1971: 8). The report further notes that "The organization of the university should, on the one hand, prevent the growth of an exclusive caste system of academics and administrators, and on the other, encourage mobility between the universities and the various sectors of national life and economy".

5. See Appendix-1. The summary points of the various committees are taken from a concept paper "Towards Formulation of *Model Act* for Universities of the 21st Century in India".
6. A study on governance structure of 131 institutions in western Europe shows that on an average about 80 per cent of all rules and procedures are laid down in regulations indicating high degree of formalization present in bureaucratic organization (see Boer and Goedegebuure, 1996).
7. See Twist and Veld (1999) and Koelman and Vries (1999).
8. See Kogan (1988).
9. "More often, the Universities have a culture that is a mix of academic and bureaucratic cultures. While the academic units like faculties, departments, colleges, schools are generally academic in their approach, the central administration manned by officials may not be so. And, it is often likely to be of the bureaucratic type. Sometimes, this can result in difficulties, as academic decisions being based on committees deliberations may not be always easy and practical for implementation by the concerned officials. In such situations, it is only the wisdom and positive approach of senior academics in the University hierarchy that can come to the rescue of the system" (UGC, 2003).
10. See Dubhashi (1995).
11. Molly (2002) notes that "This academic bureaucratic culture, as a result of too much direct government control over the universities, has degraded academia in Malaysia. The development of such a culture has also tightened the government's grip on the universities because academic bureaucrats turn to the government and to the political leaders for recognition and rewards that have nothing to do with academic achievements" (p. 161).

References

A. Gnanam Committee (1990), *Report of the UGC Committee towards New Educational Management*.

Boer, H.F. de and L.C.J. Goedegebuure (1996), *Bestuursstructuren Vergeleken: Een Internationaal Comparatieve Beschrijving van Bestuursstructuren* in Zeven Europese Landen, CHEPS, Enschede.

Clark, B.R. (1998), *Creating Entrepreneurial Universities: Organisational Pathways of Transformation*, Pergamon Press, Oxford.

Dubhashi, P.R. (1995), "University Administration", in *Journal of Higher Education*, Vol. 18, No. 2, Summer.

Etzkowitz, H. and L. Leydesdorff (2000), "The Dynamics of Innovation: From National System and 'Mode 2' to a Triple Helix of University-Industry-Government Relations", *Research Policy* 29: 109–123.

Goodman, Paul (1962), *The Community of Scholars*, Random House, New York.

Keller, George (1983), *Academic Strategy: The Management Revolution in American Higher Education*, The Johns Hopkins University Press, Baltimore.

Koelman, Jos and Piet De Vries (1999), M"arketisation, Hybrid Organizations and Accounting in Higher Education", in *From the Eye of the Storm: Higher Education's Changing Institution*, B. Jongbloed, Peter Maassen and Guy Neave (eds.), Kluwer Academic Publishers, Dordrecht.

Kogan, Maurice (1988), "Government and the Management of Higher Education: An Introductory Review", in *International Journal of Institutional Management in Higher Education*, Vol.12, No. 1.

Levin, John S. (2000), "The Practitioner's Dilemma: Understanding and Managing Change in the Academic Institution", in *Managing Colleges and Universities*, M.A. Hoffman and R.W. Summers (eds.), Bergin and Garvey, London.

Mcinnis, Craig (2005), "The Governance and Management of Student Learning in Universities", in *Governing Knowledge: A Study of Continuity and Change in Higher Education–A Festschrift in Honour of Maurice Kogan*, Ivar Bleiklike and Mary Henkel (eds.), Springer, The Netherlands.

Meek, V. Lynn (2003), *The Higher Education Managerial Revolution*, Centro de Investigacao de politicas do Ensino Superior, Kluwer Academic Publishers, London.

Mehta, V.R. (2003), Killing of Higher Education, UGC Golden Jubilee Series Lecture entitled at Ranchi University on 19th September, UGC.

Merton, R.K. (1973), *The Sociology of Science*, Chicago University Press, Chicago.

Molly, Lee N.N. (2002), "The Academic Profession in Malaysia and Singapore: Between Bureaucratic and Corporate Cultures", in *The Decline of Guru: The Academic Profession in Developing and Middle-Income Countries*, P.G. Altbach (ed.), Boston College Centre for International Higher Education and Palgrave Publishers, New York.

P.B. Gajendragadkar Committee (1971), *Report of the Committee on Governance of Universities and Colleges*, Part I, Governance of Universities.

Polanyi, M. (1962), "The Republic of Science: In Political and Economic Theory", in *Minerva*, 1.1.

Singh, Amrik (1988), "The Governance of Universities", *University News*, January 23.

Twist, M.J.W. van and R.J. van In 't Veld (1999), Public Organizations in the Market Place. Risk, Profit Opportunities and Conditions for Existence, NIG Working Papers, No. 99–5, Enschede.

UGC (2003), A Concept Paper towards Formulation of Model Act for Universities of the 21st Century in India. See www.ugc.ac.in

Appendix

D.S. Kothari

Model Act for Universities (1964):

- Variety in organization, so desirable in a large country like India;
- Autonomy from external control, for smooth functioning;
- Sufficient freedom to permit innovation/experimentation;
- Internal democratic administration to enable active role for faculty;
- Organization pattern to serve their true objectives;
- Constitution that is not stereotyped, with too many safe-guards;
- Structure in broad terms, with details in the Statutes/Ordinances;
- Personnel with responsibility and discipline, to set conventions.

P.B.Gajendragadkar

Governance of Universities and Colleges (1971):

- Autonomy, both within and in relation to external agencies;
- Student participation in administration and academic affairs;
- A grievance redressal system to take care of students, teachers, staff;
- Flexibility in organization: essentials in act and details in Statutes;
- Possibility to bring in a sense of belonging among all the constituents;
- Ease of coordination with the UGC;
- Zealous pursuit of knowledge and commitment of higher education.

A. Gnanam

Towards New Educational Management (1990):

- Autonomy, coupled with responsibility and accountability;
- Well-defined powers and responsibilities among the authorities/bodies;
- Role perspectives with effective linkages with other social subsystems;
- Depoliticization of the campus for a healthy academic environment;
- Decentralization of the decision-making process;
- Debureaucratization of the administrative set-up.

Soneri

Review of Gnanam Committee Recommendations (1995):

- All the items recommended by the Gnanam Committee, except: paras relating to:
  - (i) Statutes on Administrative and Financial Matters (No.141); and
  - (ii) Central Legislation on Universities Governance (No.144).

CHAPTER 10

Academic Reforms: Choice-Based Credit System

The suggestion of the National Knowledge Commission (NKC) to introduce course credits as a measure of academic reform is noteworthy. Choice-based credit system provides 'diversity and more flexibility in course structures'. It presents also with a freedom to the choice of course to the students. NKC also notes that through the transferability of credits the mobility of students can be increased across colleges. It would also provide an opportunity to introduce continuous assessment. In September, 2007, the issue of the introduction of credit system was raised at the Vice-chancellors' conference organized at the regional as well as at the national level. With its multiple advantages, it is necessary that academic reform relating to credit system should be introduced in Indian universities. The chapter explores the issues relating to credit system. It discusses the concept of credit system, its advantages and some of the limitations in introducing the system.

Concept

An academic credit is defined as the unit by which an institution measures its course work. The number of credit hours is defined by the number of hours per week in class and the number of weeks in a semester. Thus, a course of three credits means 3 hours per week in class usually for 16 weeks in a semester. It amounts to 48 hours (16 weeks × 3 hours/week) of class for 3 credits of a course.

Choice-based credit system allows the students to choose the course among a large number of electives within a department or outside the department or even outside the faculty. Greater number of choice for a student enables him to acquire relevant interdisciplinary knowledge besides the core competence in the subject in which he is undertaking undergraduate or postgraduate qualification. Credit system, introduced in US in the late 19th century, is a recent phenomenon in Indian universities. JNU, IITs and lately Pondicherry University in 1993 are the early precursors of choice-based credit system. Since then colleges and universities in Tamil Nadu, Karnataka, realizing its importance, have begun to adopt the system.

According to Philip Altbach, "the credit system is simply a way of accounting for time spent on academic work. It is the central currency of student academic work. Students accumulate credits and when they have earned a sufficient number of credits in course or other academic work that is approved for the award of a degree or certificate, the specific academic programme is considered complete, and a degree is awarded" (Bridges and Tory, 2001). Another definition of credit is given as follows, "The credits provide a basis for establishing equivalence between different modules and programmes and, in terms of academic recognition, are complementary to the certification of qualifications" (Altbach, 2001). The award of credit enables students to transfer from one programme to another, within or between institutions through articulation arrangement thus reaping the maximum advantages of learning from different academic cultures or environments. Credit used in conjunction with a modular structure is a powerful instrument in enhancing curriculum design, particularly in developing flexible programmes suitable for lifelong learning. According to Bridges and Tory, credit system helps to define academic standards if incorporated into national curricular framework. Altbach, however, differs from above standpoint. He states that the system is suited for a mass system and credit system is not a way of measuring the quality of hours and thus the standards of education. The task of assessing the quality or standard of education is supposed to be done by accreditation agency such as NAAC in India.

Academic Credit in US and India

In US colleges and universities, the first degree, the associate's degree, normally requires a period of study of two years, the bachelor's degree four years, the master's degree an additional one or two years, and the doctor's degree another two to five years. A typical four years' bachelor degree consists of 128 credits. It means 32 credits per year or 16 credits per semester. The 16 credits consists of 12 hours of laboratory exercises (= 4 credits i.e.; 1 credit = 3 hr/week lab. work) and 12 hours of lectures and seminars (12 credits). Thus, 4 courses in a semester may consist of 4 credits in each course.

In India, a postgraduate of two years consists of 72 credits in Pondicherry University. M.Phil course consists of 36 credits in addition to the course requirements. Credits get accumulated from semester to semester ending up with requisite number of total credits to earn a degree (see Annexure I).

Credit Transfer

Transfer of credit may take place from one department to another within a university or between the universities in a country or inter-university transfer between two countries.

In Pondicherry University, for a postgraduate the hard-core subject requires a minimum of 48 and maximum of 60 credits where soft-core option requires a minimum of 12 credits. Thus, minimum 12 credits and maximum of 24 credits may be earned by a student in another department or in IGNOU, which may get transferred to Pondicherry University. The choice-based credit system allows the students to take interdisciplinary courses.

At the beginning of a semester, a student has to register for a minimum of 9 credits and maximum of 30 credits (Rajendran, 2004). Some of the universities in India which have recently offered choice-based credit system are as follows:

The Manonmaniyam Sundranar University offered PG courses under choice-based credit system from the academic year 1996–97. This is based on the cafeteria system. In this system, the real choice is given to students to choose the courses he/she wants in a semester. All the PG courses in Madurai Kamaraj University are offered under choice-based credit system which incorporates sufficient flexibility so that students can opt for elective courses from other departments to enhance their individual career plans. Choice-based credit system (CBCS) that lays emphasis on a continual internal evaluation is adopted to prepare the students to face the challenges in the new millennium in Annamalai University. At present, the Periyar University offers 109 courses in the affiliated colleges. Seven Postgraduate courses are offered under choice-based credit system in the university department, viz., mathematics, commerce, MCA, bioinformatics, biotechnology, applied botany (medicinal plants) and environment sciences.

Grading System

In Pondicherry University, there is 50 per cent weightage for continuous assessment and 50 per cent weightage for end semester examination. External assessment is followed for end semester examination. Department declares the result. The grading system is on 7-point scale. S=10, A=9, B=8, C=7, D=6, E=4, F=0. F only means failure. A Cumulative Grade Point Average (CGPA) of 5 or above is necessary to pass a programme.

Advantages of Choice-Based Credit System

Flexibility

A student may accumulate 72 credits for postgraduate degree by offering courses in economics equal to 48 credits, in mathematics equal to 24 credits or in economics equal to 48 credits, mathematics equal to 12 credits, statistics equal to 6 credits and philosophy equal to 6 credits. Thus, it provides flexibility with which a student can think of combining various optional subjects. He may not have to commit at the beginning of two years about the choice of subjects. As the semester progresses, at the beginning of each semester he has the option to choose the electives. Summer assignments may also be included into course to accelerate their studies. An employed may earn the degree over a long period pursuing course on part-time basis. The emerging knowledge paradigm requiring interdisciplinary ability can be fulfilled under choice-based credit system. Besides, quality of education may be substantially enhanced if a student gets the chance to acquire partial credit from reputed institution in which it has specialization. UGC should promote the inter-university transfer of credits to allow flexibility and even twinning in offering a degree programme.

It is also possible to add flexibility to the curricula. If market signals the need for introducing a new course, then without changing the complete curricular structure, a new course may be offered. Thus, course offering in a particular department may be cut where there is low demand and the vice versa.

Example 1

In UK, Credit Accumulation and Transfer Scheme (CATS) introduced in 1986 contribute towards wider access and of quality enhancement in higher education (Regel, 1992).

Example 2

Another example is European Community Action Scheme for the Mobility of University Students (ECASMUS) to increase student mobility among community countries, thereby providing the possibility for more students to spend part of their studying in another member state. At the core of the programme is the establishment of degrees and course units, known as the European Community Course Credit Transfer System (ECTS) whose central objective is to make credit transfer an effective currency of academic recognition by providing universities admitting students from other member states (Dalichow, 1991).

In this way, the use of credit system allows twinning and transfer programmes to be developed by higher educational institutions. These programmes often offer a potential student an opportunity to obtain foreign degree, both at the undergraduate and graduate levels, without incurring redundant expenses by reducing the number of years spent abroad.

Example 3

Many private institutions in India such as Indian School of Business, Hyderabad are twinning with 3 foreign universities. This is possible because the school has adopted the curriculum and course of studies of its twinning institutions. Through the use of credit transfer, the twinning programme allows IBS students to pursue their degree by starting the course at their own campus at Hyderabad but fulfilling the credit requirements by acquiring the credit from foreign institutions.

Learning Effectiveness

Choice-based credit system provides an up-to-date record of progress towards a degree and a plan for student's entire educational experience. The year-long experience of students in India through an annual examination is utterly frustrating. There is an examination anxiety to cram the course content. Students' discontent leads to the postponement of examination. In such scenario, the choice-based credit system through semester system and continuous evaluation enables students to absorb the content in more meaningful manner.

Through a variety of learning experiences to be creditable towards a degree, the educational experiences of students are broadened. The learning effectiveness also increases because the teachers offer variety of instructional designs to the students so that learning is more attractive than dull.

Examination Management and Cost Effectiveness

Higher the problem of examination management; higher is the failure rate in any system. In choice-based credit system, failure in one course does not mean failure for a whole degree programme. Student can repeat a course and improve the grade. Besides the teachers themselves mostly do the examination management at the departmental level, the university examination department does not have to bother about the examination. It is thus a cost-effective system that reduces dropouts and raises the internal efficiency of the education system.[1]

Vertical Mobility

Choice-based credit system by itself does not allow the flexibility. It is important that the curriculum be so designed that it allows a student to move to different levels of qualifications say, from a six month certificate to one-year diploma and further to an advanced diploma of two years and to the three-year first degree course. In the planning for career development, a student may earn diploma and get relevant work experience and then again come back in the educational system to earn two-year advanced diploma or three-year degree course. The curriculum should be so designed that the vertical mobility towards higher level of qualification could be permitted to a student.

Other Advantages[2]

(i) The course credit system may also permit educational institutions to collect fees based on credits earned. Thus, it provides the objective basis of assessment of fees. A graduate programme will then have uniform fee structure if the credits earned are uniform.

(ii) The workload of the professoriate may also be organized on the basis of credit. The norm for research-oriented universities, PG teacher, UG teacher, vocational college teacher, science teacher; teacher with administrative responsibilities may be determined on the basis of credit.

(iii) Choice-based credit system promotes accountability. It measures students' progress and keeps them informed periodically. It provides accountability for the teaching staff as well as it provides an easy and consistent means of measuring the work of professoriate. There are various decisions such as the allotment of fund that may be made on the basis of credits produced by the department.

To conclude, choice-based credit system permits flexibility and mobility of students nationally and internationally. It permits wider choice to the students. It is an effective means of measuring academic work, student's progress and teachers' workload. The system proves to be efficient and the one congenial to promote the quality.

However, choice-based credit system is not free from errors and the problems. Although in today's knowledge society, the interdisciplinary knowledge is essential, it may sometimes lead to a fragmentation of knowledge if the choice-based credit system is not properly planned. For example, the basic knowledge of a subject may be made compulsory. The accumulation of credits upto a certain limit in a subject should be binding before the choice of electives from various other disciplines. Another weakness of the system is that it does not distinguish the quality. Sometimes, students may only look at the attainment of degree by accumulating credits and the learning outcomes become secondary. There are also many complex issues involved in the transfer of credit. High-ranking institutes rarely oblige the students from low-ranking institutes to transfer the credits. The decision is mostly based on the quality of the sending institutions. Providing autonomy to teachers in internal evaluation may lead to favouritism and discontent among students. Critics point out that choice-based credit system may not promote 'educated person', although it may produce persons having skill and employability.

Crucial Assumptions for the Success of Choice-Based Credit System

(i) Autonomy of teachers.

(ii) High moral standards of teachers.

(iii) Well-defined syllabus and the uniformity of the content of syllabus across different courses. For example, all course, of 3 credits for 16 weeks imply 48 academic hours of syllabus for all courses.

(iv) Academic culture should be congenial for the adoption of choice-based credit system. There is least scope for students' unrest and disturbances in the campus in the choice-based credit system. The smooth continuity of the course must be ensured throughout the semester.

(v) The rules and the procedures should be clearly laid down and should be known to the students, teachers, educational administrators.

(vi) There should be proper guidance to the students regarding the electives.

(vii) Credit transfer depends on the networking of institutions/universities to allow the credit transfers. Advantage is limited if there is partial adoption of choice-based credit system.

Preparatory Stages for the University to Adopt Choice-Based Credit System

(i) A workshop with experts and departmental heads of university should be convened and feedbacks received in a questionnaire format on various aspects of CBCS.

(ii) Study of feedbacks and a committee of five members to frame the regulations.

(iii) Regulations may then be discussed with the experts and the PG heads and finalized.

(iv) Approval of regulation in the academic council and the notification by the registrar on the approval of the vice-chancellor of the university.

Regular Monitoring Bodies

(i) Departmental committee at the department level.

(ii) Advisory council of CBCS at the university level.

(iii) Internal quality assurance cell.

Notes

1. See the successful Indonesian experience where beginning in 1984, the credit system was gradually introduced in the entire higher education system saying goodbye to the traditional single entry and single exit system in Woodhill.
2. See Altbach (2001).

References

Altbach, Philip G. (2001), "Measuring Academic Progress: The Course Credit System in American Higher Education", *Higher Education Policy* 14, 37–44.

Bridges, P.H. and J.H. Tory (2001), "Credit, Qualification and the Fluttering Standard", *Higher Education Quaterly*, Vol. 55, No. 3, July, 257–269.

Dalichow, F. (1991), "European Community Course Credit Transfer System (ECTS): A Learning Concept for Trans-European and Trans-Atlantic Student Exchange?" *Higher Education Policy*, Vol. 4, No. 3, 991.

Rajendran, M. (2004), "Choice-Based Credit System: Decision Input, through Process and Output Approach", *University News*, Vol. 42, No. 25, June 21–27.

Regel, O.M. Pam (1992), The Academic Credit System in Higher Education: Effectiveness and Relevance in Developing Countries, Education and Employment Division, Population and Human Resources Department, The World Bank.

Woodhill, Maureen, Turning Points in the Development of Higher Education in Asia: A Comparative Study of Alternative Patterns of Provision, Financing and Governance, 1960–90, The World Bank, Washington DC.

Annexure I
Pondicherry University (A Central University)

Choice-Based Credit System

From the academic year 1992–93, the university has introduced a Choice-Based Credit System (CBCS)

- Under this system, the students have a good deal of freedom in designing their own curriculum to suit their needs.
- The students can take any course offered in any department as long as they fulfil the prerequisites for that course.
- The students can also take as many courses as they can handle subject to a maximum of 30 credits in any semester.
- Students who have difficulties may choose a slower pace while brighter students may complete the programmes in 3 semesters instead of 4.
- Each course [(except MBA (tourism), MBA, MA (econometrics), offered at Mahe centre and M.Sc (marine biology) offered at the Andaman centre] is associated with a credit value and this accrues to the student when he/she successfully completes the course. A student, to earn an MA/M.Sc./M.Com./M.P.Ed. degree needs to score 72 credits and should score 108 credits to earn the MCA degree.
- Each programme will have a set of courses that a student must complete to get the degree. These are called hard-core courses.
- There is also another set of courses called soft-core courses where limited choice is given and the student may choose from this restricted set.
- In addition to these, the student will be allowed a minimum of 12 credits for courses of his/her choice, and this is left completely to the student and his/her advisor.
- Each student soon after he/she joins the course will fill a plan of study detailing the courses he/she plans to take. Depending upon the availability of the courses every

semester, he/she registers for a set of courses before the semester starts by filling in the appropriate forms. Each student should submit the registration card to the Head of the department on or before the last date prescribed for the same.

- To enable the students, the university will make available to each student a bulletin listing all the courses offered in that semester well in advance.
- The performance of the students is indicated by letter grades based on relative grading follows:

Grade	*Points*	*Description*
S	10	Excellent
A	9	Very Good
B	8	Good
C	7	Above Average
D	6	Average
E	4	Satisfactory
F	0	Failure
FA	0	Failure due to lack of attendance

- A student is deemed to have completed a course successfully and earned the appropriate credit if and only if he receives a grade of E and above. A grade of F or FA denotes failure in the subject. A subject successfully completed cannot be repeated at any time.
- A student is expected to maintain minimum standards to be eligible to continue the course of study. Students may refer to the guidelines and regulations available in the university library.

All M.Phil courses are offered under choice-based credit system (CBCS). A student to earn an M.Phil degree needs to score 36 credits and 30 credits for P.G Diploma course.

CHAPTER 11

Promoting Doctoral Research in India

The place of doctoral study in research management assumes importance in the context of knowledge society. The institutional role of universities is recognized to explore ideas and knowledge. Doctoral level research is the chief instrument through which universities allow to cultivate knowledge and disseminate it through two domains—teaching and research. The research emerging from universities should be viewed as primarily contributing to national development. Yet at the level of practice the share of the higher education sector in the total Research and Development (R&D) expenditure is a meagre 2.9 per cent,[1] as per the survey conducted by the Department of Science and Technology (DST), Government of India in the year 1998–99. In the field of research, the concentration of resources in bodies outside the universities in research laboratories under Council of Scientific and Industrial Research (CSIR), other research institutions and industries both in the public and private sectors is responsible for a rather low expenditure on R&D in higher education sector. Low R&D expenditure in the higher education sector not only affects the doctoral level of research but also is responsible for the low level of basic research in the universities. At the same time, poor university-industry linkages have not induced doctoral education in the universities to contribute in terms of applied research either.

Nonetheless, the place of doctoral study cannot simply be evaluated in terms of R&D expenditure in higher education sector and its contribution in basic and applied research at the level of doctorate research alone. In India, the view is taken that successful doctoral candidates are the finest human resources; they have acquired the highest levels of knowledge in the relevant field. Success at doctoral level means the development of a continuing aptitude for independent scientific inquiry and therefore those with a doctorate should have great potential to serve as good teachers or scientists or leaders in all sectors of development.

The objective of the present chapter is to examine the doctoral practices in universities in India. Given the primary role of doctoral research, the recognition of the importance and enhanced funding at the policy level is desired. Of great importance is the fact that universities plan a structural reform and introduce best practices to promote the standards of doctoral research. This would provide a firm basis to support the quality of teaching and research in universities and support the knowledge management of a country in a much more fundamental way. The paper explores the various facets of doctoral programme and suggests some ways in which the doctoral research can be improved.

I
Doctoral Process and Practices

Recruitment

Postgraduation is the minimum qualification for admission to the doctoral programme. Although M.Phil is seen as a preparatory stage to the doctoral degree in some universities, in majority institutions there is a provision of direct admission and registration at the university department. A candidate is required to submit a research proposal to the university department. The Board of Studies of the University Department, in a meeting of experts, examines the research proposal and if it is found satisfactory in terms of relevance of topic, research design, etc., a supervisor is allotted to a doctoral student. The research proposal is then finally approved by the university and the candidate is then asked to register for the doctoral programme with the topic of the research.

The question with respect to the recruitment that arises is whether Ph.D. programme should be restricted to highly selected ones to maintain standard at the outset or anyone who is eligible to do a Ph.D. programme should have the opportunity to register. It is due to the latter provision and lack of serious scrutiny by the university that the most mediocre students find their way to the Ph.D. programme. It is mostly in the case of fellowship that competitive entry to the programme is made.

Another issue relates to the capacity of an individual faculty or the department to support the doctorates in terms of faculty strength, research infrastructure and environment. It may be noted that in most university departments the intake of students for Ph.D. programme is not fixed in relation to the faculty strength or infrastructural facility. In such departments, the mediocrity may take a toll of the programme due to the faulty recruitment policy into the Ph.D. programme. As a matter of policy, the access to Ph.D. programme should be made attractive for the brighter students to pursue doctoral research.

Doctoral Process

After a doctoral candidate is registered for a Ph.D. programme there should be well laid down processes to be followed by a doctoral student. In most of the PG departments, there does not exist any process outlines except for the fact that the candidate has to keep interacting with the supervisor and on the basis of self study and supervisor's feedback, he has to manage the writing of the dissertation.

Doctoral process must have a well-defined objective. In defining the objectives it should be clarified whether doctoral study is a research certification or it is meant for preparing the professional career as well. In the case of latter, whether it is for preparing the doctorates for academic profession or for non-academic profession. So far doctoral study is considered only a research certification and consequently the doctoral process does not concern itself with academic and professional preparation of the students. Doctoral process, therefore, should ensure itself with academic internship to add value to the doctorates.

At the beginning of the doctoral process, there should also be an induction training of the doctoral students to apprise them of the course work, rules of the departments, ways of contacting supervisors, research facilities available to the students, research ethics, details about research and job opportunities and the funding arrangements.

During doctoral process opportunities need to be given to the doctoral students for participation in the workshops/ seminars, collaborative academic activities and interdisciplinary interactions, wherever required. This would expose researcher to the wide range of academically useful activities rather than becoming an ivory tower researcher.

Supervision

Supervision of doctoral study of a student by the teacher is a critical element of doctoral programme. Quality of doctoral work is said to depend upon the quality of supervision. As soon as the proposal for research for doctorate is approved, candidate is allotted a supervisor from among the teachers of the department depending upon the specialization of the teacher. Students may sometimes have the option to choose a Supervisor depending upon their research interest and supervisor's willingness to guide the student. There is also flexibility for a research student to choose an external supervisor with the consent and approval of the departmental research committee. The practice of the team supervision is not widely prevalent in Indian universities. There are also no qualifications, except the one that he should be a teacher, laid down for the supervisor.

During the period of supervision, a Ph.D. scholar works on a part of the study in continuous interaction with the supervisor and shares the findings of the research in a seminar. The six monthly progress reports prepared by the student are to be approved by the supervisor. Scholars should also be encouraged to publish their research findings. Finally, after the dissertation is submitted the report of the supervisor, among other requirements, is the basis for evaluating the dissertation.

In terms of actual practices, there is no transparency in the supervision process. The regular interaction between the supervisor and the student may not take place and as a result the aspect of mentoring may be completely absent. To ensure transparency of the supervision process, there should be well-laid down code of practice for the supervision and a register should be maintained by the department whereby the student should enter the details of issues discussed in each interaction.

The quality of supervision depends on the knowledge and expertize of the supervisor. Sometimes the topic of the dissertation may fall outside the expertize of the supervisor. As a result, the student may be deprived of expert comment on the findings of the research from the supervisor.

Ph.D. Examination

In Indian universities, the tradition of viva in the Ph.D. examination process holds the key to the maintenance of standard of doctorates. There are following key processes involved in the Ph.D. examination.

1. Evaluation of the thesis by supervisor/internal examiner.
2. Suggestion of a panel of external examiners by the supervisor.
3. Selection of two external examiners from amongst the panel by the academic council of the university.
4. Evaluation of the dissertation by external examiners and submission of the report.
5. Analysis of the report by the appropriate body/academic council.
6. Rejection/revision of dissertation or in case of positive recommendation, the holding of viva by external and internal examiner.
7. Process of the conduct of viva and defence of the dissertation by the candidate.

8. In case of revision, further submission of revised draft and holding of viva.
9. Recommendation for the award of Ph.D. degree.

The process of Ph.D. Examination may have variability of procedures, but the selection of external examiners and written report and the conduct of viva are two important steps which are so non-transparent that begs many questions on the system of Ph.D. examination and lack of quality assurance on the above account.

Selection of Examiners

Selection of external examiners by the university out of the panel of examiners suggested by the supervisor is the tradition followed in Indian universities. It is sometimes argued that selection of examiners is highly subjective and is not guided by the objective consideration of expertize in the area of study. There is a need to make the process of selection of examiners more transparent and a code of practice may be laid down for the selection of examiners. Examiners should also be given the guideline to be followed while examining the dissertation. In my view, the system of selection of examiners should be changed. National panels of examiners with high academic standing may be created subjectwise with their area of specializations.

Viva

Viva is an oral examination of the student who writes the Ph.D. dissertation. External examiners authenticate the dissertation of the student. The role of viva is crucial in the evaluation of the Ph.D. Some of the issues related to viva are: non-transparency of procedure and as a result the objective of holding Ph.D. viva to ensure the high quality of doctoral work and the authentication of dissertation may get defeated. The framework of best practice in the doctoral viva has been suggested in the academic literature (see Park, 2003). For holding viva, there should be a guiding framework that should discuss the objectives, role of external examiners, supervisor, student and other faculty members in the viva, record keeping, timing, viva report, process of conducting viva, appeal process and so on. Quite often the time consumed between the submission of dissertation and final viva voce examination of the candidate may be too long. This time gap, too, needs to be minimized to the possible extent.

Although in terms of procedure the process of evaluation is rigorous, in my view there are many loopholes in the system that need to be plugged if doctorates of high quality need to be produced.

Funding Arrangements

A hard reality is that less than 1 per cent aspirants undertaking the NET examination get necessary funding support from the UGC/CSIR for doctoral research. There are other research councils which provide some fellowships to the doctoral students. Therefore, many of the potential aspirants join a doctoral programme without funding support. At the level of the universities the funding support to promote doctoral research is completely lacking. Funding support for doctoral research in the universities by the central government needs to be substantially stepped up. State government, philanthropic support and industrial support should be garnered and efforts may be made to provide some financial grants to all doctoral students. Any such effort for financial help by the faculty should be acknowledged.

The Task Force for Basic Scientific Research in Universities has recommended that the number of Ph.Ds from Indian universities should increase fivefold within a span of ten years with proper standards. It has also recommended that in addition to research fellowship awarded by different national funding agencies, every university shall be provided, for pursuing doctoral research, 50 fellowships in basic sciences based on past performance of departments. Post-doctoral fellowships should be introduced for a maximum period of two years on a highly selective basis.

II
Critical Issues

India has one of the largest higher education systems in the world with over eleven million students enrolled in universities across the sub-continent. Of these 65,491 (0.66%) are enrolled in doctoral study. In the year 2002–03, 13,733 students were awarded doctoral degrees, of which 30 per cent were in professional subjects, 33 per cent were in science and 37 per cent were in arts subjects. The concerns have been raised on the quality of doctoral programmes in India (Paul and Ramanathan, 2001; Daftuar, 2001; Bandyopadhyay, 2003). Various issues arise in relation to doctoral programmes in India. First there is the issue of mediocrity in doctoral research. Therefore, a significant effort should be made to attract the talented fresh postgraduates into doctoral programme. In the selection of the topic the issue of relevance in doctoral research needs to be addressed. So far as the doctoral process is concerned, the doctoral experience should be one of intense interactions with scholars in related area providing opportunities for the academic growth of the researcher. During the period of doctoral research, skills relating to research and teaching should also be perfected. The process of supervision and evaluation are other important areas that require attention for improving the standard of doctorates in India. There are various critical issues that require attention.

Structural Constraints

Barring few, universities in India suffer from infrastructural constraints, such as lack of journals, equipments, laboratories, libraries and IT facilities. Besides, the teaching workload in departments in relation to available faculty is high. Even after spending four years at doctoral level there is no guarantee of a secured job. Though it also speaks of, sometimes, low quality, yet the market, too, has distorted the situation. Most of the education and research institutions being controlled by the government are unable to offer the salary and perks that corporate sectors pay to their employees. As a result, there is no incentive to successful doctoral candidates in terms of secured jobs and higher salary structure. Some of the structural constraints that refer to the facilities need to be removed.

Quantity vs Quality

University system consists of graduate (three years of first degree level) and two years of postgraduate. Expansion at the graduate level has adversely affected postgraduate and research by taking heavy time for managing the first-degree level. The recommendation of the Task Force for Basic Scientific Research in Universities notes that the number of Ph.Ds from Indian universities should increase five-fold within a span of ten years with proper standards.[2] A further expansion, however, demands that universities must concentrate on developing the standards at the postgraduate and doctorate level and a separate system should be created for managing the graduate colleges in a university. This will reduce the load on universities.

University-Research Institutions Linkages

Doctoral candidates register themselves only in university departments. The doctorates are then supposed to man research institutions to work on various research projects. This means there is one-way linkage between the university and research institutions and research laboratories. The decline in the standards of research in the universities is then bound to affect the research institutions/laboratories as well. If it would be possible to create the reverse linkages as well between research institutions/laboratories and universities, expertize available in the former could be used to upgrade the quality of doctorates in the universities. As a matter of general principle, mutual relationships and linkages would help to develop the quality of doctorates. In the Indian context this requires that UGC, ICSSR, CSIR, CHR, CPR, ICAR should develop two-way linkages between universities and all research institutions engaged in different disciplines and professions.[3]

Monitoring and Evaluation

Monitoring during the period of doctoral programme suffers from a number of deficiencies. Normally, the supervisor who has guided the maximum number of scholars is approached by the student for the guidance. As a result, he/she is overburdened and does not devote adequate time for the supervision. Besides he/she suggests repetitive studies with difference in titles so that the same methodology may be applied in number of studies supervised by him.[4] In order to improve the quality of dissertation, there should be some minimum conditions relating to the research credentials of the supervisor and the number of doctoral candidates that a supervisor can guide simultaneously.

There appears to be a mutual obligation of examiners to approve the thesis on reciprocal basis without going into the merit of the thesis. There are also several instances in which the examiner is chosen without requisite specialization in the topic. Due to the weak supervision and evaluation process there are instances of plagiarism. Even if such instances are found there is no awareness to book the culprit to the court. Measures therefore should be taken to ensure that evaluation of the dissertation is not simply a formality.[5]

Funding

It is a matter of great concern that government funding for doctoral fellowships is showing a downslide reflected in the falling number of qualifying students in UGC-JRF test eligible for fellowship.[6] Besides, the amount of fellowships offered to the doctorates is too small to attract the best talent for the doctoral research in the universities. This is becoming increasingly difficult with higher salaries being offered to even the lowest executive in the corporate sector. In fact research is attracting second and third grade talent. This is a matter of concern for the policy makers. I suggest that the present dilemma can be solved by the following means: (1) by raising the number and value of fellowship, (2) by linking the output of doctorates to the industries and in turn getting funding support from the industries, (3) doctorates may be linked to the project supported from the government and civil societies, (4) by shifting the preference of funding from research institutions to the doctorates in the universities. In other words, the doctorates may partly be linked to the applied research and be treated as potential income and not as a means to potential income in terms of better job prospects.

Sustenance of Universities

There is a dilemma both from the national as well as international perspectives. The finest human resources that India has may be attracted towards industries and they may not advance their careers in the universities and research institutions. As a result, diffusion of doctoral level knowledge may take place in different sectors of the economy but the sustenance of universities in terms of pool of researchers may be threatened. At the same time, advanced countries also attract the highest talent and that poses a danger in terms of so called 'brain drain'. In the current context of a knowledge economy, my own view is that the outward mobility of doctorates should not be prevented by means of any policy design. However, universities should be able to attract talents so that inward mobility of aspirants for doctoral study compensates to a great extent the loss of talent due to any 'brain drain'. From an international perspective therefore, there is a need to raise the infrastructure and facilities for doctorates in the universities to retain existing talent and attract new talent in the universities in the overall policy design of research to secure the place of doctoral research in future national development.

Role of UGC and Competitive Fellowship

UGC introduced the National Education Testing (NET) in 1984 as a requirement for securing junior research fellowship and later in 1988 for eligibility for the post of teacher. The move was introduced to improve standards of teaching and doctoral programme in the country by providing entry to the teaching profession and to the doctoral programme through competitive fellowship. The condition of NET for an entry to the teaching profession has recently been relaxed. As a result, the standard of teaching very much depends upon the standard of doctorates. Although the NET is still there to determine the award of fellowship for doctoral study, the policy of NET alone cannot improve the standard of doctorates unless there is systemic intervention. Merely conducting NET is not sufficient to ensure the quality and seriousness of researchers. There is also anecdotal evidence that Ph.D. degree holders are ill-equipped to handle analytical problems in professional careers. Various professions are undergoing sea change and the practices within doctorates should be examined not only to improve the standards but also to produce professionals capable of applying knowledge in the present context.

In this regard, the role of UGC should be to develop the code of conduct for each and every process of Ph.D. recruitment, supervision and examination to maintain the standard and direct NAAC to evolve the procedure to monitor through the process of assessment of standards. UGC should also enhance the funding for the doctoral programmes in the universities.

III
International Best Practices[7]

In UK, the Quality Assurance Agency for Higher Education (2004) has developed code of practice for the assurance of academic quality and standards in higher education for the postgraduate research programmes (doctoral programme). The code is a statement of good practice and is designed to guide institutions on the development of institutional codes of practice in the area of postgraduate research programmes. Best practices refer to institutional arrangements, research environment, selection, admission and induction of students, supervision, progress and review arrangements, development of research and skills, assessment of students' representation such as complaints and appeal process. The codes are, however, not the statutory requirements. A code is the best practices statement to ensure quality of doctoral programmes and assumes that each institution has independent system to maintain quality of doctorates.

Skill training regarding research quality is an important focus in UK and there is also a joint statement on the skills training requirements for research students by the research councils and the Arts and the Humanities Research Board (AHRB). Both the bodies play an important role in setting standards and identifying best practices in research training. The purpose of the statement is to give a clear message to the university that high standards of a doctoral programme can be maintained only if the research environment and research management ensure the appropriate research skills to be acquired by the doctoral candidate.

Mentoring the Graduates

Mentoring or close supervision is one of the most important aspects of the doctoral programme. Washington University in US prizes not only traditional classroom and research activities but also recognizes the intense, one-on-one relationship that is the hallmark of graduate education. The Distinguished Graduate Mentor Award, established in 1999, is one of the most prized awards given at the Washington University. The University of California, Davis Academic Senate recently announced a new annual award to honour the mentor through Distinguished Graduate Mentoring Award. The Graduate Student Council at Harvard University's Graduate School of Arts and Sciences established the Excellence in Mentoring Award in 1998 to recognize faculty who truly go out of their way to mentor graduate students, honouring faculty for efforts which often go unrecognized.

Recipients of the award are faculty members who have made outstanding contributions to the education and guidance of graduate students. A successful mentor is one who actively guides students' research and training, supports the graduates at a personal as well as a professional level, respects students' goals and helps students to work towards them, seeks financial support for students' graduate study, actively involves students in professional conferences and publications, assists students in career preparation and helps them to secure post-degree employment. Awards inspire the community of scholars to promote the best mentoring practices.. Students of these mentors act as role models for other young professionals in their fields.

Academic and Professional Internships

Doctorates are the finest human resource. During the period of doctoral research they need to be exposed to the world of work in both academic as well as professional settings. The internship during doctoral research exposing students for academic careers adds value to doctoral programmes. Graduate School at the University of Texas—Austin offers both academic and professional internship courses. Students enrolled in the academic internship course work one-on-one with the faculty of the collaborating partner institutions of the University of Texas. Examples of internship activities include: observation of teaching, lecturing classes (with student and mentor feedback), grading, constructing course syllabi, attending departmental meetings and events, directing lab sessions, discussions with faculty and students, assisting with student advising and mentoring, and working with students on research projects.

Internship is particularly useful for doctoral students in humanities and social sciences who opt for jobs in non-academic settings. Their value lies in analysing problems, communicating and writing well. Their finely-honed research skills may be utilized in professional work. Internship training in actual work environment during doctoral phase of research, therefore, is one of the best practices being followed in the US universities. Teaching assistantship is also offered to the students and during this period the faculty also supervises the doctoral student and exposes him to academic life environment. This is a fairly widespread practice in the US universities and needs to be adopted in Indian universities.

Assessment of Doctoral Dissertations

At the Michigan State University in the US, there is an annual practice of reviewing and discussing dissertations submitted over the past three to four years by a team of faculty. The objective is to select exceptional dissertations and analyse the difference between the acceptable and the exceptional dissertation. The purpose is to examine the level of performance during the dissertation process and to learn from the experiences of the students who produce exceptional work.

Alliances for Graduate Education and the Professoriate (AGEP)

All doctoral students at Howard University who have been funded through the AGEP Programme are required (after having completed 30 graduate credits) to participate in the Preparing Future Faculty Programme. This programme consists of coursework (issues in contemporary college teaching), seminar and workshop series (preparing a syllabus, handling classroom situations, ethics, etc.). This two-year commitment culminates in a supervised teaching experience. Students can choose from a variety of different types of experiences ranging from a week-long intensive experience at a local university to a year-long experience at such diverse institutions as Hope College, The University of New Hampshire, The University of Wisconsin or the University of Texas—El Paso. Students who complete 12 credits of specified work in this area can also receive a certificate in college teaching. All departments in the science, mathematics, or engineering fields at Howard University are required to present to the dean their action plans demonstrating how all graduate students within the department will be provided with a teaching experience.

The practice is occurring through the Alliances for Graduate Education and the Professoriate Programme at Howard University and through the office of the dean of the graduate school.

Graduate Select Admission Programme University of Texas (UT) Austin

The goal of the Select Admission Programme is to keep UT's best and brightest undergraduates on campus for graduate study by: (1) extending an 'early' (i.e., preemptive) offer of admission and financial aid, (2) removing financial and other costs associated with regular application; and (3) potentially reducing the total combined number of semesters (and therefore total number of dollars expended) needed to obtain an undergraduate and graduate degree (without reducing the hourage requirements for either). In making an early commitment, it may be possible to keep some of Texas' most capable undergraduate students from entering the competitive graduate school application market. This programme also may assist efforts to promote diversity by inducing UT's best minority students to remain on campus for graduate study.

IV
Recommendations

Recruitment

1. Admission process should be clear, demonstrate equality of opportunity and should be well-advertized by the university giving all the procedural details.
2. It should demonstrate that only qualified students having research aptitude and with sound research proposal are admitted to the doctoral programme.
3. Admission process should clearly mention schemes to attract fresh and bright postgraduate students for doctoral research.
4. Postgraduate departments fully prepared in terms of faculty strength, research infrastructure such as library and equipment should be permitted to admit students under doctoral programme.

Doctoral Process

1. Objectives of doctoral process as certification of research and developing academic and professional exposure should be clearly laid down. As such the doctoral process must include not only the research methodology training but also academic and professional training for varying periods.
2. Mechanism for induction training should be in place after admission into doctoral programme. Induction should focus on information and guidelines to be followed during doctoral process. Research ethics, IPR potentials of the research etc., should be known to the students during induction.
3. Doctoral process should provide opportunities for seminar presentation, interdisciplinary interaction and collaborative networking with other academic bodies at national and international level.
4. Doctoral process should also provide opportunities for acquiring potential jobs after successful completion of the doctoral programme. University and the respective

departments must make efforts to retain doctorates with exceptional merit on suitable teaching and research assignments.

Supervision

1. The university should develop code of practices for the supervision to be followed by the supervisor.
2. Every department must maintain a register where an entry should be made by the student for each interaction along with the ideas discussed with the supervisor.
3. As a matter of best practice an award may be instituted by the university for the mentoring. This is practiesd in many US universities.
4. The university should arrange the periodic workshop of supervisors to discuss the best practices and roles of supervision during doctoral research.

Examination

1. The process of selection of examiners should be transparent and a code of practice may be laid down for the selection of examiners. Examiners should be given the guideline to be followed for examining the dissertation.
2. National panels of examiners with high academic standing may be created subjectwise with their area of specializations.
3. Objective of holding Ph.D. viva to ensure the high quality of doctoral work and the authentication of dissertation should be ensured.
4. There should be a guiding framework that should discuss the objectives, roles of external examiners, supervisor, student and other faculty members in the viva, record keeping, timing, viva report, process of conducting viva, appeal process and so on.

Funding Support

1. Funding support for doctoral research in the universities by the central government needs to be substantially stepped up

during the 11th Plan. If each registered doctorate is financed for three years (extendible upto one year) and a target of financing 10,000 doctorates is kept each year then at the rate of Rs one lakh per year per student, the total financial allocation under the 11th Plan would be around Rs 1,200 to 1,400 crore.

2. Funding support for doctoral research needs to be generated by the universities through philanthropic support and support from the state government and from benefiting (benefits arising out of particular research) industries on a case-to-case basis in a substantial way.
3. All funding support should be performance linked and should be rigorously monitored by the universities.

NAAC

1. NAAC should develop a code of practice for the assurance of academic quality and standards for the doctoral programme in Indian universities. It should help put a check on the sub-standard doctoral programmes in India.

Conclusion

Attempts should be made to put in place systemic interventions to improve the standard of doctoral programme in India. As a priority step, UGC may constitute a committee to look into all aspects of doctoral programme. The 11th Plan should allocate larger amount of resources to finance doctoral research in priority areas. NAAC should develop a code of practice for the assurance of academic quality and standards for the doctoral programme in Indian universities. Universities must develop diversified strategies to promote the doctorates and particularly the best talents for research and teaching.

Notes

1. Department of Science and Technology (2002).

2. Governments of India (2005).
3. See Shah (2005) for analysing some of the dynamics in the relationships between university and research institutions.
4. See Mulimani (2003).
5. See Dahiya (2003) and Kapoor (2003).
6. The number of qualifying students of UGC conducted NET has come down from 550 in June 1993 to 347 in December 1999 and further down to 340 in December 2003. See Bandyopadhyay (2003).
7. For a list of best practices at the graduate level of studies in US universities visit the following website http://www.grad.washington.edu/envision/practices/promprac_ inst.html (last seen on 8th June 2006).

References

Bandyopadhyay, Madhumita (2003), Quality Control of Doctoral Research: Role of Research Fellowship, Scientific Research in Indian Universities, Association of Indian Universities (AIU), New Delhi.

Daftuar, Chittaranjan N. (2001), "Indian Universities: Temples of Learning or Warehouse?", *University News*, Vol. 39, No. 7, February 12, 1–4.

Dahiya, L.N. (2003), Quality of Doctoral Research in India: Some Monitoring and Control Issues, Scientific Research in Indian Universities, Association of Indian Universities (AIU), New Delhi.

Department of Science and Technology (2002), Research and Development Statistics 2000–01, Government of India, Ministry of Science and Technology, New Delhi.

Governments of India (2005), Task Force for Basic Scientific Research in Universities, published on the web at: www.ugc.ac.in.

Kapoor, J.N. (2003), Raising the Standard of Ph.D. Programmes: Some Suggestions, Scientific Research in Indian Universities, Association of Indian Universities (AIU), New Delhi.

Mulimani, V.H. (2003), Standards for the Ph.D. Degree, Scientific Research in Indian Universities, Association of Indian Universities (AIU), New Delhi.

Park, Chris (2003), "Levelling the Playing Field: Towards Best Practice in the Doctoral Viva", *Higher Education Review*, 36 (1): 47–67.

Paul, Justin and A. Ramanathan (2001), "UGC-NET: A Valid Test", *University News*, Vol. 39, No. 4, January 22, 5–6 and 9.

Quality Assurance Agency for Higher Education (2004), Code of Practice for the Assurance of Academic Quality and Standards in Higher Education, Section 1, Postgraduate Research Programmes, September.

Shah, A.M. (2005), "Higher Education and Research: Roots of Mediocrity", *Economic and Political Weekly*, May 28–June 4, website: www.epw.org.in.

IV

Plan Support and Financing

CHAPTER 12

Financing through Plan

The paper notes that there is deceleration in the public financing of higher education. It shows how neo-liberal policies of the state prevented it from implementing its own commitments of 6 per cent of GDP on education fuelling the crisis in the financing of higher education. Secondly, the role of UGC in financing and maintaining the standards of higher education is analysed. After having achieved the lowest plan contribution, there is a renewed effort during the 11th Plan to step up plan expenditure. The 11th Plan's intervention to support higher education is analysed.

I
Trend of Public Expenditure in Higher Education

Phase of Deceleration Since 1980

Pattern of public expenditure in higher education constitutes two important phases. A phase from 1951 to 1980 is a high growth phase of public expenditure and the second phase from 1980 to 2004 is a low growth phase of public expenditure in higher education. The compound annual rate of growth of central plan and non-plan expenditure in the former phase has grown at 17 per cent and it has declined sharply to 10 per cent in the second phase. The compound annual rate of growth of state plan and non-plan expenditure in the former phase has grown at 15 per cent and it has declined sharply to 11 per cent in the second phase. Thus, the decline in the rate of growth of public expenditure by the centre has been much sharper in comparison to the decline in the rate of growth of public expenditure by the state. The former phase in the growth of public expenditure was a high growth phase in spite of the fact that the rate of growth of GDP was much lower in the former phase at 3.35 per cent as compared to the 5.42 per cent rate of growth of GDP in the second phase. The second phase is therefore the phase of deceleration of public expenditure of higher education (see Table 11.1).

Table 11.1

CARG in Public Expenditure in Higher Education and GDP

	1951–52 to 1979–80	*1980–81 to 2003–04*
Total State and UT	15	11
Central Total	17	10
Grand Total	15	11
GDP	3.35	5.42

Note: Calculated from the MHRD (1950–51 to 2005–06).

From Rising to the Declining Central Financing

An important point to observe is the contribution of the centre and the state in the financing of higher education. The trend since 1950s provides an interesting picture. So long as education was under state list till the 42nd Amendment in 1976, the central government increased the share in the financing of public expenditure on higher education. Centre contributed 37 per cent in the total financing of higher education in 1965–66. Thereafter, even though education was put under concurrent list in 1976 thereby placing greater

Chart 11.1

State Share to Total Public Expenditure

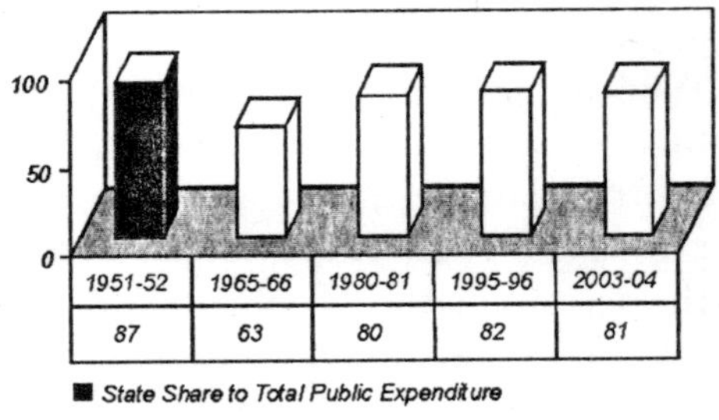

responsibility upon the centre, the share of centre to the public financing of higher education went on declining. Share of centre to the public financing of higher education declined to 19 per cent in 2003–04 (see Chart 11.1).

Centre's declining share is one of the important reasons for the deceleration in the public funding of higher education. States were constrained by fiscal shortages and they found it difficult to invest in plan funding to improve the quality of higher education.

Nominal and Real Public Expenditure per Student

The past trend of nominal and real public expenditure per student tells us a completely differentiated picture of the role of government in financing education. In nominal terms, the public expenditure per student in elementary secondary and higher education stands at Rs 2,162, Rs 6,852 and Rs 12,518

Table 11.2

Nominal and Real (Base year 1993–94) Public Expenditure per Student

(in Rs)

Year	*Elementary*		*Secondary*		*Higher & Technical*	
	Nominal	*Real*	*Nominal*	*Real*	*Nominal*	*Real*
1993–94	825	825	3,748	3,748	8,961	8,961
1994–95	893	793	4,040	3,588	9,821	8,722
1995–96	1,052	865	4,517	3,715	9,384	7,717
1996–97	1,220	959	4,890	3,844	8,438	6,634
1997–98	1,361	1,025	5,221	3,932	9,003	6,779
1998–99	1,654	1,175	6,285	4,467	10,238	7,276
1999–00	1,792	1,233	7,392	5,087	13,219	9,097
2000–01	1,900	1,220	7,153	4,594	13,956	8,963
2001–02	2,047	1,269	6,699	4,153	12,099	7,501
2002–03	1,977	1,185	6,641	3,982	12,294	7,370
2003–04(R)	2,162	1,229	6,852	3,896	12,518	7,117

Source: In terms of index of real public expenditure per student, the decline in public expenditure in higher education is equal to 21 percentage during 1993–94 and 2003–04 (see Chart 11.2).

Chart 11.2

Index of Real Public Expenditure Per Student

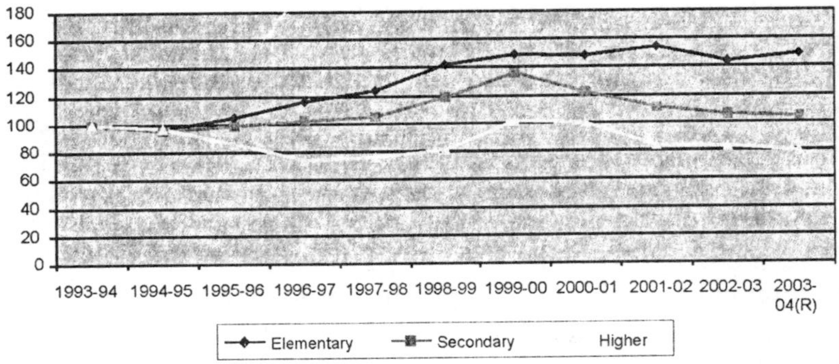

respectively in 2003–04. The trend analysis shows that the increase is not that marked if we consider the growth in enrolment. In fact the nominal public expenditure per student in higher education has gone up only by 40 per cent during 1993–94 and 2003–04. In real terms, however, public expenditure per student in higher education has declined from Rs 8,961 in 1993–94 to Rs 7,117 in 2003–04. In elementary education, the public expenditure per student has increased from Rs 825 to 1,229 only during the same period. In secondary education, public expenditure per student has remained almost static during above period at little below Rs 4,000 (see Table 11.2).

Some more facts can be established by breaking the component of per capita public expenditure. It may be noted that on an average during 2002–05, the central plan and non-plan expenditure per student amounts to only 7 per cent and 13 per cent respectively, whereas the state plan and non-plan expenditure per student amounts to around 5 per cent and 75 per cent respectively. Thus, total plan expenditure of centre and states constitutes only 12 per cent. The bulk expenditure is on account of non-plan expenditure. It is important to note that there has been a consistent decline in the planned resources per student for higher education (see Table 11.3 and Chart 11.3 below).

Table 11.3

Distribution of Total Public Expenditure Per Student in University and Other Higher Education

	Public Expenditure Per Student		
	2002–03	2003–04 (R)	2004–05 (B)
Central Plan	720	621	656
Central Non-plan	1,316	1,333	1,192
State Plan	501	455	487
State Non-plan	7,763	7,642	6,900
Total	10,300	10,051	9,235

Source: Computed from Analysis of Budgeted Expenditure, MHRD and Selected Educational Statistics of different years.

Chart 11.3

Per cent Distribution of Public Expenditure Per Student in University and Higher Education (2004–05)

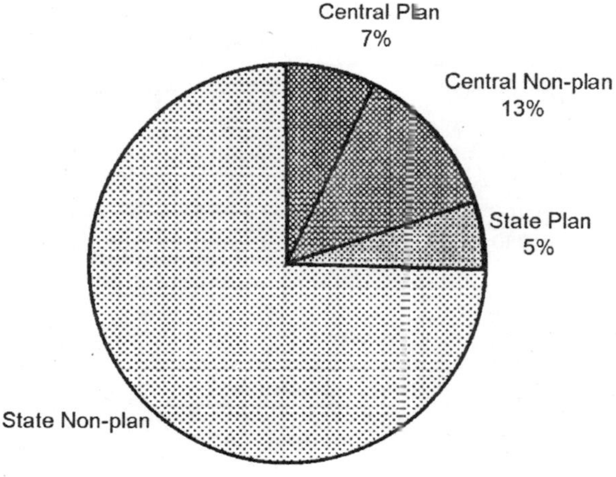

Factors for Deceleration in the Growth of Public Expenditure in Higher Education

This is a point of great significance that in spite of higher growth of GDP, state is finding it difficult to step up the public expenditure in higher education in the period since 1980. There is a systematic tendency towards deceleration. As public expenditure is showing signs of deceleration, it is worth pondering the reasons behind it.

Deceleration in Public Sector GDP

There are three plausible reasons for the deceleration in the growth. Firstly, the rate of growth of public sector contribution to the GDP has fallen from 7.73 per cent during 1960–61 to 1980–81 to 6.33 per cent during 1981–82 to 2002–03. On the other hand, the rate of growth of private sector contribution to the GDP has increased from 2.45 per cent during 1960–61 to 1980–81 to 4.94 per cent during 1981–82 to 2002–03. It means that in spite of high GDP growth since 1980 the private sector has increasingly become the important contributor to the growth (see Table 11.4).

Table 11.4

Public and Private Sector GDP and Growth Rates

	1960–61	*1980–81*	*1981–82*	*2002–03*
Public Sector GDP at 1993–94 Price (Rs in crore)	18,555	88,719	93,206	359,651
Private Sector GDP at 1993–94 Price (Rs in crore)	1,87,548	3,12,409	3,31,867	9,58,670
Public Sector GDP Growth Rate 1960–61 to 1980–81	7.73	—	—	—
Public Sector GDP Growth Rate 1981–82 to 2002–03	6.33	—	—	—
Private Sector GDP Growth Rate 1960–61 to 1980–81	2.45	—	—	—
Private Sector GDP Growth Rate 1981–82 to 2002–03	4.94	—	—	—

Source: National Accounts Statistics, various years.

Declining Tax to GDP Ratio

Secondly, the total revenue as a percentage of current expenditure and particularly tax revenue as a percentage of current government expenditure also shows a decline in the second phase. The former has declined from 117 per cent in 1950–51 to a level of 61 per cent in 2004–05. The latter ratio has declined from 102 per cent to 45 per cent during the same period. It means that the contribution of the private sector to the capacity of the state to spend has also declined. As a result, there has been fiscal constraint to public sector expenditure. The rise of the rate of growth of private sector contribution in the GDP and state's inability to tax the private sector are two clear trends that show the neo-liberal nature of state irrespective of political parties in power (see Table 11.5).

Table 11.5

Total Revenue and Tax Revenue as a Percentage of Current Government Expenditure (at current prices)

Year	*Total Revenue as a per cent of Government Expenditure*	*Tax Revenue as a per cent of Government Expenditure*
1950–51	117.08	102.99
1960–61	106.20	88.37
1970–71	105.16	77.13
1980–81	88.21	64.55
1985–86	81.54	59.38
1990–91	75.64	56.39
2004–05	61.49	45.16

Source: Chandrasekhar and Ghosh (2006).

Crowding Out Public Expenditure for Higher Education

Another important feature of public financing of higher education has been the crowding out of public financing of higher education by the elementary education in the second phase. It may, however, be argued that in the first phase it is the higher education that has crowded out elementary education. Therefore, the crowding out argument acquires significance only when there is acute shortage of financing due to fiscal resource constraint as in the period since 1980s.

It is observed that between 1951 to 1979, the compound annual rate of growth of public expenditure for elementary, secondary and higher education respectively was 13.7 per cent, 15.9 per cent and 15.2 per cent. The growth rates in public expenditure in elementary education increased marginally to 14.7 per cent and declined to 13.5 per cent in higher education during 1980 to 2003. Thus, crowding out as a whole does not seem to be an important factor. However, the phenomenon of crowding out is quite prominent with respect to central government expenditure on elementary, secondary and higher education. The growth rate of central expenditure on elementary education increased from 8 per cent in the former to the 31 per cent in the later period and from 10 per cent to 20 per cent in the case of secondary education. However, in the case of higher education it decreased from 19 per cent in the former period to 11 per cent in the later period (see Table 11.6).

Table 11.6
Compound Annual Rate of Growth

	1951–52 to 1979–80	*1980–81 to 2003–04*
Elementary total	13.7	14.7
Secondary total	15.9	14.5
Higher total	15.2	13,5
Elementary central	8.8	31.8
Secondary central	10.5	20
Higher central	18.7	11.1

Note: Calculated from the Analysis of Budgeted Expenditure, MHRD.

Projected Public Expenditure in Higher Education in 2007–08, Assuming 17 per cent Growth Rate in the First Phase (1951–52 to 1980–81)

Had there been state's active role in financing education, opposed to neo-liberal stance of the state, and in the period since 1980 had there been 17 per cent rate of growth of public expenditure on higher education, as observed in the former phase of centre financing, it would not have been difficult to achieve the target of 1 per cent of GDP for financing higher education.

The projection exercise shows that at the rate of growth of 17 per cent, the public expenditure on higher education could have reached a level of Rs 20,941 crore in 2002–03 and given GDP of Rs 22,49,493 crore, percentage share of higher education expenditure to the GDP would have touched a level of 0.93 per cent in 2002–03. In the first year of the 11th Plan, percentage share of higher education expenditure to the GDP would have touched a level of 1.1 per cent (see Table 11.7).

Table 11.7

Projected Public Expenditure in 2007–08

Public Expenditure on Higher Education 1980–81 (Rs crore)	483.66
CARG Public Expenditure 1951 to 1980	17%
Projected Public Expenditure on Higher Education in 2002–03 (Rs crore)	20,941
GDP in 2002–03 (Rs crore)	22,49,493
Per cent of Public Expenditure on Higher Education to GDP in 2002–03	0.93
Projected Public Expenditure on Higher Education in 2007–08 (Rs crore)	39,241
Gross Domestic Product 2007–08 (estimated)	34,67,441
Per cent of Public Expenditure to GDP in 2007–08	1.1

However, instead of stepping up the public expenditure in higher education, it went down steadily and compressed the ability of UGC to address the quality issues specifically for state universities and colleges.

II

Disbursement of Planned Resources for State Universities and Colleges

Meagre Allocation to State Universities and Colleges

It is interesting to observe that during the first three years of the 10th Plan in the university sector, UGC spent 39 per cent of planned resource (Rs 553.36 crore) for the development of central universities, 12 per cent for inter-university centres (Rs 168.79 crore), 6 per cent for deemed to be universities (Rs 82.53 crore). Mere 43 per cent of planned resources amounting to Rs 599 crore were spent on the development of state universities during the first three years of the 10th Plan. Under college development, 97 per cent amounting to Rs 486 crore was spent on colleges under state universities and 3 per cent of planned resources was spent on colleges of the central universities. Thus, of the total plan allocation of Rs 1,907.05 crore, state universities and colleges received Rs 1,085 crore during the first three years of the 10th Plan whereas the central university, inter-university centres and deemed universities received Rs 821 crore (see Chart 11.4).

Chart 11.4

Planned Expenditure in Universities and College Under Different Categories (First three years of 10th Plan)

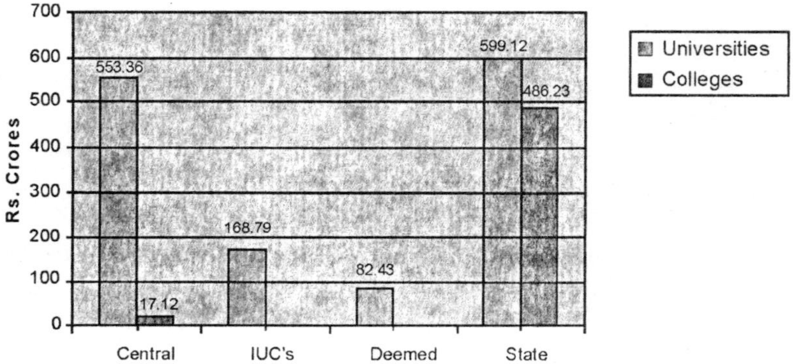

It is thus important to note that for a country of India's size that has 211 state universities and 17,625 colleges, mostly under state universities, a central plan size of Rs 1,085 crore for state universities and colleges during the first three years of the 10th Plan is grossly inadequate and, therefore, constitutes an important reason for deterioration in the quality of university and higher education. Lack of planned resource with the UGC is the most important reason for the oft repeated crisis of higher education (Mehta, 2003).

The educational planners of the country must think of committing a much larger plan resources for university and higher education in view of the emphasis given in education policy and the recent thrust of Prime Minister Manmohan Singh before the Knowledge Commission.

Utilization of Plan Grants for Universities

Utilization of plan grants for universities and colleges during the 10th Plan provides an idea of the magnitude and direction of investment. Major objectivewise utilization of plan grants by UGC for the universities are given in table below. General

Development Grant of university constitutes a major proportion of plan grants to the university. UGC provides plan assistance for staff, equipment, books and journals, buildings, campus and programme development. Sixteen central universities, 23 deemed universities and 113 eligible state universities are supported and the assistance is aimed at improving the infrastructure and basic facilities and to develop excellence. Development assistance,of the order of Rs 1,990.41 crore (61%) helps to achieve the major objectives of access, equity and promoting quality. Separately looking at the objectivewise plan assistance, UGC has spent Rs 145.28 crore (4%) for enhancing access and equity, Rs 211.24 crore (6%) for promotion of relevant education, Rs 481.13 crore (15%) for quality and excellence, Rs 428.55 crore (13%) for strengthening of research respectively during the 10th Plan (see Table 11.7).

The point to note is that UGC is bound to address the infrastructural deficiency of the universities in a major way. As a result, majority of the plan resources, 61 per cent, are spent on the general development of the universities. It was noted above that majority of the General Development Grant is disbursed to central universities. Therefore, two conclusions emerge. (i) Large number of state universities is left high and dry for support under general development grant in spite of greater per cent plan allocation under this head. (ii) Universities were left with very little (only 39%) under plan support to specifically address the issues of access, equity, quality and research.

Utilization of Plan Grants for Colleges

Similarly, major objectivewise utilization of plan grants by UGC for the colleges are given in table below. General Development Grant of colleges constitutes a major proportion of plan grants to the colleges. UGC provides plan assistance for staff, equipment, books and journals, buildings, campus and programme development. Out of 17,625 colleges, only 5,808 colleges are recognized by UGC under Section 2(f). Out of 5,808 colleges only 5,386 colleges are eligible to receive central assistance under Section 12(B) of the UGC Act, 1956. Development assistance helps to achieve the major objectives of access, equity and promoting quality.

Table 11.7

University Plan Grants

(Amount in Rs crore)

Scheme	*2002– 03*	*2003–04*	*2004–05*	*2005–06*	*2006–07 (BE)*	*Total*	*% to total*
General Development Grant to Universities	242.64	259.02	307.74	341.66	839.35	1990.41	61
Enhancing Access & Equity	2.91	9.02	26.84	22.27	84.24	145.28	4
Promotion of Relevant Education	31.75	27.17	37.46	27.20	87.66	211.24	6
Quality and Excellence	55.12	65.42	90.49	121.20	148.90	481.13	15
Strengthening of Research	84.17	81.28	87.19	66.26	109.65	428.55	13
Other	0.001	0.0019	—	—	—	0.0029	0
Total	416.591	441.9119	549.72	578.59	1269.8	3256.613	100

Source: UGC (2003a, 2004a and 2005a) and UGC (2003b, 2004b, 2005b, 2006 and 2007).

It may be observed that out of Rs 4,208 crores, 77 per cent was spent on the universities and therefore, colleges were left with very small kitty of plan assistance, of the order of Rs 951 crore. Out of which again Rs 450 crore was spent on general development due to serious infrastructural deficiency of the undergraduate colleges in India. Separately looking at the objectivewise plan assistance, UGC has spent Rs 121.27 (13%) crore for enhancing access and equity, Rs 140.96 crore (15%) for promotion of relevant education, Rs 147.77 crore (16%) for quality and excellence, Rs 90.68 crore (10%) for strengthening of research during the 10th Plan. UGC has disbursed Rs 951.45 crore as plan grants to 5,386 colleges during the 10th Plan. On an average, this amounts to Rs 20 lakh per college for five years. With this amount of support for the colleges, it could be anybody's guess what impact it would have on colleges to improve the access and quality?

Table 11.8

College Plan Grants

(Amount in Rs crore)

Scheme	*2002–03*	*2003–04*	*2004–05*	*2005–06*	*2006–07*	*Total*	*% to Total*
Development of College	85.35	103.43	90.34	99.56	72.00	450.68	47
Enhancing Access and Equity	4	3.59	23.94	51.74	38.00	121.27	13
Promotion of Relevant Education	24.74	29.43	30.37	30.42	26.00	140.96	15
Quality and Excellence	19.33	17.43	34.12	25.39	51.50	147.77	16
Strengthening of Research	9.47	18.23	22.76	22.72	17.50	90.68	10
Other	0.09	—	—	—	—	0.09	0
Total	142.98	172.11	201.53	229.83	205	951.45	100

Source: UGC (2003a, 2004a and 2005a) and UGC (2003b, 2004b, 2005b, 2006 and 2007).

III
Salient Features of 11th Plan Intervention in Higher Education

A dominant framework in the financing of higher education was guided by the philosophy of almost exclusive reliance on the state. As a result, the higher education's place as a principal claimant on public treasuries was recognized almost everywhere in countries—rich or poor. The above paradigm in financing of higher education was quite successful, in varying degrees, in making transition from elite to the phase of mass higher education—the phase that was necessitated by the growth of industrial society in terms of the demand for skilled and professional workforce.

The success of the state paradigm may be attributed to the rapid growth process and the ability of the state to siphon off the surplus through the instrumentality of tax. Taxable resources could finance the public provision of higher education whereas the private cost of higher education was financed by the household/parents. The economic crisis that was reflected in recession and the stagflation in 1970s and early 1980s, however, constrained state in many ways to sustain the funding of higher education without any limit.

It is heartening to note that the second wave of institution-building announced by the Prime Minister Manmohan Singh has finally got reflected in the 11th Plan. The priority in allocation for higher and technical education is amply testified by the sheer size of the 11th Plan under the head in financial terms which is of the order of Rs 84,943 crore at the current prices as against Rs 9,500 crore of allocation and actual expenditure of around Rs 8,000 crore during the 10th Plan. It is almost nine times against the allocation for and ten times against the actual expenditure of higher and technical education during the 10th Plan. The 11th Plan's objective approach to inclusive growth of higher education also deserves mention. Government's commitment to raise public expenditure on higher education to 1.5 per cent of GDP has been in the background of the 11th Plan proposal.

The priority in allocation and objective approach has given rise to a targeted expansion plan of large number of institutions and growth in enrolment of students from different social groups. The emphasis on reducing regional imbalance and the growth of quality and excellence of higher education institutions are the important hallmarks of the strategy of the 11th Plan.

An important assumption of the approach followed in the book that state has the primary responsibility to finance higher education seems to be testified in the 11th Plan allocation for higher education. The first two years of the 11th Plan allocation in the university and higher education of around Rs 5,800 crore is a substantial jump compared to total 10th Plan expenditure of Rs 4,183 crore in university and higher education. However, it remains to be seen how the rest of plan allocation of Rs 34,000 crore is provided for in the three years of union budget? The 11th Plan intervention is reviewed as it is bound to be an issue of great importance in the coming years.

Access and Expansion

Enrolment Target: 11th Plan envisages an increase in enrolment from 14 million to 21 million by 2012—additional 8.7 lakh in universities and 61.3 lakh in colleges—by 2012. It amounts to an annual growth rate of 8.9 per cent. This will help to achieve 15 per cent GER by the end of the 11th Plan and finally the enrolment is projected to the level of 21 per cent target GER by the end of the 12th Plan. Alongside above enrolment target, the plan document refers to disparities in GER based on census results. The disparities refer to rural-urban, gender and across social groups. Enrolment targets have not been mentioned, although reduction in such disparities 'holds the key to achieving GER of 15 per cent', as per the 11th plan. Inclusive growth also demands that expansion of higher education institutions take place in 370 districts having less than average enrolment. The 11th Plan does not specifically mention the imbalances in enrolment across levels and disciplines, although there may arise the need for increasing the enrolment at the postgraduate and doctorate levels and also in science, technical and professional courses.

Strategy

Approach of the 11th Plan to meet the enrolment target and other disaggregate targets for quantitative expansion is noteworthy. During the 10th Plan, enrolment is estimated to go up from 9.5 million during 2002–03 to 14 million during 2006–07, i.e., an addition of 4.5 million. Past growth may have been constrained by supply factors. It is assumed that given excess demand for higher education, if the supply constraint is removed, it is possible to increase the enrolment by 7 million during the 11th Plan. The 11th Plan points out following steps for expansion to achieve the target of additional 7 million enrolment.

1. Thirty central universities—16 in uncovered states and 14 of world-class standards—are planned to be set-up through special plan for higher education at an estimated allocation of Rs 7,500 crore. This also includes setting up of 30 medical and engineering colleges in central universities.
2. Eight new IITs, 20 NITs, 20 IIITs, 3 IISERs, 7 IIMs, 2 SPAs are planned to be set-up at an estimated cost of Rs 6,000 crore.
3. Creation of new state-funded universities and colleges, notably 370 colleges in districts with less than average GER. Nearly 370 colleges will receive central assistance of Rs 782 crore.
4. Expansion of existing institutions—both government and private under special plan for higher education, incentivising state governments for expansion, inclusion and excellence is given allocation of Rs 6,200 crore. Additional assistance to already covered universities (160) and colleges (5,500) of Rs 3,000 crore and supporting uncovered state universities (150) and colleges (6,000) of Rs 7,000 crore. An aggregate sum of Rs 16,200 crore is being allocated for expansion of existing institutions.
5. Promoting institutions in underserved regions, minority concentration districts and creating capacity for additional enrolment of backward classes. The 11th Plan proposes Rs 2,141 crore in higher education, Rs 1,000 crore in technical

education for reduction of regional imbalance/social gaps and promotion of inclusiveness and another estimated Rs 5,000 crore for 54 per cent additional seats in centre supported institutions.

6. For skill development through vocational training, Rs 4,400 crore of allocation has been made. New polytechnics and community polytechnics, support to engineering colleges for diploma courses, 210 community colleges and women's hostels are some of the new initiatives in the 11th Plan.
7. Around 50 per cent of additional enrolment is estimated to be in private institutions. Hence, it is proposed to increase the number of private and deemed universities and colleges by removing barriers in creation of new universities and colleges.

Thus, there is a clear indication of another wave of institutional expansion supported by government. The 11th Plan has allocated a little under Rs 40,000 crore for creating additional enrolment of 3.5 million whereas the equal number of enrolment is proposed to be raised by attracting private investment in higher education. All the measures listed above, technically speaking, may be sufficient to meet the enrolment target. The strategy is a perfect example of a pragmatic approach that puts state and market on equal footing in the expansion plan.

It is important to note that the financial support of state government is implicit in the approach of the 11th Plan. There is an explicit mention of matching contribution in the case of setting up of 370 colleges and for supporting already covered and uncovered universities and colleges worth around 11,000 crore. Incentivising state governments will also require state plan of around Rs 6,000 crore for expansion, inclusion and excellence. There is the conditionality of the availability of free land for central universities as well as for various technical and management institutions. Altogether the commitment of all state governments of an equal order or in the range of Rs 30,000 crore to Rs 40,000 crore will be required to meet the expansion plan for an additional enrolment target of 3.5 million in the public sector and the rest in the private sector.

Financial arithmetic and state governments' commitment to ensure supply side management of expansion is one side of the story, well-conveyed in the 11th Plan approach. However, it is important to understand that realizing the plan expansion requires managing men and materials and some of the challenges on this account are worth considering.

Some important challenges are coordination with state governments to acquire land and infrastructure for institutional expansion, to follow some of the legislative measures to establish universities/institutions, to retain fresh postgraduates and researchers in academics, to attract scholars of national and international repute in institutions of excellence, to invite visionaries in leadership positions and to design market-friendly regulation to attract private investment in higher education. It would be important to get views from academics to understand the ways in which the above expansion plan could be productively implemented.

Inclusiveness

Inclusiveness is not a hollow slogan or mere ideology. It is the approach and the strategy with a clear target backed by financial allocation in the 11th Plan. This is to be achieved through the following measures. Some of the new measures are—Setting up of 370 degree colleges and incentivising state government for expansion, inclusion and excellence; promotion of inclusiveness and reduction of regional imbalances/social gaps in higher and technical education, new polytechnics in unserved districts, 500 new community polytechnics, new 210 community colleges and various programmes of UGC under ongoing schemes. Allocations under the 11th Plan have been made to implement Oversight Committee recommendations and Sachar Committee recommendations. Construction of girls' hostels and women's hostels in 500 polytechnics has been given allocation worth Rs 1,500 crore. Thus, we notice that inclusiveness has a definite strand of thought as well as action in the 11th Plan.

An important aspect of inclusiveness is the affordability. Without affordability it is not possible to increase access and promote inclusiveness. In rural India, 95 per cent of population has average per capita annual consumption expenditure below Rs 14,000. In urban India, 95 per cent of population has average annual consumption expenditure below Rs 30,500. Thus, affordability will have to be ensured through special measures. The 11th Plan notes that scholarship for Rs 1,000 crore will be given to 2 per cent of total students. Rs 4,000 crore have been allocated under education loan interest subsidy through Higher Education Loan Guarantee Authority. There is also research fellowship for NET qualified and non-NET qualified Ph.D. students of Rs 2,300 crore. On the issue of fees, the 11th Plan has a cautious stand. It notes that fee levels should be increased gradually subject to the upper limit of 20 per cent of the operating cost of general university education. As operating cost of technical and medical education is higher, therefore, fees will have to be higher in those institutions. Affordability of higher education is least in the case of private higher education, as recovery of cost through fees implies a level of fees which may be beyond the capacity of the most of the people in India. In such a case, subsidized loan may partly be an answer to affordability. However, other options could as well be the reservation of certain number of seats in private institutions and the targeted scholarship in private institutions.

Thus, inclusiveness in its various dimensions finds a well deserved place in the 11th Plan with not merely intentions but a clear-cut strategy and action-oriented programmes with adequate plan allocation.

Quality and Excellence

Quality and excellence, sometimes referred to as the third vertex of a triangle alongside access and equity, deserve special mention. There are various facets of quality. Quality higher education is the one that ensures the fulfilment of all objectives of education—be it the values, the job skill or the higher order cognitive abilities. However, the end result can be ensured through right inputting and processing of the product. The 11th Plan proposes to do it in various ways and it needs analysis.

New Quality Institutions: 11th Plan does not simply mention the creation of central universities. It also provides basic features of a model central university to make it an institution of excellence. Central university system should emerge as an Indian model of knowledge hub with education and research in multiple disciplines. The vision is that they should be counted as top world-class attracting talents from all over the world having complete academic autonomy to compete for research funds and train students. The mechanics of its operational details need a careful understanding. Plan does mention the project team, implementation in a creative mode and in an evolutionary process. There are already existing models of central university (JNU), IITs, IIMs, IIS. The quality institutions and not just institutional accretion is the focus of the 11th Plan.

Upgrading Quality of Existing Institutions: Upgrading quality is one of the most challenging issues of higher education in India. The 11th Plan points out a detail reform agenda. The reform agenda points out the introduction of credit system, internal evaluation, semester approach, competitive entry and curricular revision. The plan also mentions three-point formula for external quality assurance—mandatory accreditation, multiple rating agencies and departmental ratings. Recruitment of quality teachers, capacity-building of teachers through their training and research facilities are mentioned. A new initiative in the 11th Plan with respect to the optimum size of universities and number of colleges affiliated to the university and the creation of a higher education policy research institute deserves mention.

Issues are known but implementation difficulties in introducing academic reforms need to be sorted out. The difficulty is that there is not much demand from below and on some pretext or the other reform is deferred. There is need to remove administrative barriers in implementation, develop orientation among key personnel and also link development funding to academic reforms—a step that is emphasized in the plan document as well. However, we need to ponder over the issue of autonomy and accountability as well. The 11th Plan's central focus is that internal accountability needs to be built and monitored by an apex, independent regulatory mechanism. It is not clear whether it endorses the recommendations of IRAHE advocated by the

Knowledge Commission or refers to the UGC assuming that role. As NAAC already exists as an independent body created by the UGC to evaluate performance and outcomes, it is a logical conclusion that UGC should consider the recommendation of NAAC on all such matters and alert universities and colleges to develop internal accountability. The plan document mentions further academic, administrative and financial autonomy with meticulous details. Quality and excellence can be developed only with sufficient autonomy. This is well known. However, pursuit of freedom and academic culture has been threatened in the past from excessive control and external interference. The 11th Plan document suggests a mechanism through creating governing board and academic council for each institution which should be empowered to take all decisions with transparency.

So far as financial allocation is concerned, the allocation for existing schemes by UGC for university and higher education (including Oversight Committee recommendations) have been increased to Rs 14,129 crore. Excluding OSC recommendation UGC will land up getting Rs 8,000 crore approximately. A part of which will be continuing quality improvement schemes. However, special plan for higher education mentions Rs 16,200 crore for state universities and colleges. There is a need to give thinking to the component of special plan for higher education to develop approach and its implementation strategy which is so far not spelt out in the plan document.

Information and Communication Technology: National mission in education through ICT will be launched to increase ICT coverage in all higher education institutions. Fully electronic universities and digital campuses will be set up. There will be availability of e-books in English language for most of the subjects. Video contents of teaching-learning materials will be generated, there is also move for national knowledge network connecting all educational institutions, R&D institutions, hospitals, libraries and agricultural institutions. There is an allocation of Rs 5,000 crore for this mission to be operational.

The success of the 11th Plan depends on many other crucial factors. They are as follows: (i) Central universities will be set-up through a single umbrella central legislation and will be subject to the state providing land free of cost and signing MOU for a minimum set of educational reforms in its university system. (ii) Uncovered state universities and colleges will be provided assistance under the plan on the condition that corresponding funds from the states are made available and there is also willingness to raise funds internationally. In addition, assistance to covered state universities and colleges will also be subject to the commitment of academic reforms from the state and the institutions. (iii) Centrally-sponsored scheme will be launched with a centre-state funding pattern of 1:2 (1:1 for special category states). (iv) 2,000 hostels at unit cost of Rs 1 crore will be constructed subject to the recurrent expenditure being borne by states/beneficiaries of hostels. (v) In establishing new IITs, NITs, IIITs, IISERs, IIMs and SPAs public-private partnership will be explored. (vi) In seven selected technical institutes for upgradation MOU will be signed on commitments making reforms. Also, to strengthen the capabilities of 200 state engineering institutions, one-time assistance will be subject to performance and state government accepting a minimum set of reforms. (vii) Coordination of the Planning Commission with the Finance Ministry and MHRD will be required to set-up higher education loan guarantee authority. (viii) Empowered committee and technical advisory committee will be constituted for a national mission in education through ICT. (ix) 700 new polytechnics will be opened through PPP and private funding.

Thus, PPP model, state's contribution and commitment to academic reform, coordination with different ministries and state governments are vital to the success of the 11th Plan.

IV
Conclusion

From the point of financing, higher education received a priority till early 70s. The mass higher education in the 80s, 90s and the early phase of the present decade witnessed a fall in public expenditure on higher education. University Grants Commission was constrained to finance adequately and the result could be seen in the deterioration in the standards of higher education. The trend in financing shows neo-liberal approach. The private investment in higher education filled the void as demand for higher education supported the private investment. There has been a growing realization that neo-liberalism needs to be supported with a massive investment in higher education to allow India to be an effective player in the globalization process. It is this realization that led to a substantial jump in the central plan allocation in higher education. The review of the 11th Plan suggests that state has to efficiently manage the implementation of the 11th Plan. There are serious challenges in terms of the shortage of faculty, ensuring the matching contribution of state government, implementing the public-private partnership and the above all creating partnership with academic community for effective implementation of the 11th Plan.

References

Aruchami, M. (2006), Reply received from Dr M. Aruchami regarding 'Criteria for Fee Fixation in Private Colleges', vide letter dated June 3.

Chandrasekhar, C.P. and J. Ghosh (2006), Macroeconomic Policy, Inequality and Poverty Reduction in India and China, The Ideas Working Paper Series, Paper No 05/2006. Online at www.ideaswebsite.org/working/oct2006/05_2006.pdf. Last visited on 25/04/2007

Government of India (2004), National Common Minimum Programme of the Government of India, May.

Government of Punjab (2005), Higher Education in Punjab: Vision 2020, Department of Higher Education, April.

Kothari Commission (1964–66), Report of the Education Commission (1964–66), Education and National Development, Ministry of Education, GoI, June 1966.

Mehta, V.R. (2003), The Killing of Higher Education, UGC Golden Jubilee Lecture Series, 2002–03.

MHRD (1950–51 to 2005–06), Analysis of Budget Expenditure on Education, Ministry of Human Resource Development, GoI.

National Knowledge Commission (2006), Note on Higher Education, 29th November 2006, Website: www.knowledgecommission.org

NIEPA (2000), 'Study: University Finances in India: A Profile', conducted by Tilak J. B.G. and Geetha Rani, November.

NIEPA (2005), Financing of Higher Education in India, with Special Reference to the System of Financial Management, New Delhi, February.

NIEPA (2005a), Report of the CABE Committee on Financing of Higher and Technical Education, New Delhi, June.

NIEPA (2005b), Report of the Committee on NCMP's Commitment of 6 per cent of GDP to Education, NIEPA, New Delhi.

Report of the Group for Central University to Oversight Committee (2006), August.

University Grants Commission (2003a), Annual Report 2002–03, UGC, New Delhi.

University Grants Commission (2003b), Annual Accounts 2002–03, UGC, New Delhi.

University Grants Commission (2004a), Annual Report 2003–04, UGC, New Delhi.

University Grants Commission (2004b), Annual Accounts 2003–04, UGC, New Delhi.

University Grants Commission (2005a), Annual Report 2004–05, UGC, New Delhi.

University Grants Commission (2005b), Annual Accounts 2004–05, UGC, New Delhi.

University Grants Commission (2006), Annual Accounts 2005–06, UGC, New Delhi.

University Grants Commission (2007), Annual Accounts 2006–07, UGC, New Delhi.

CHAPTER 13

Conclusion

Higher education in India faces challenge of rapid expansion. The expansion path furthermore has to take account of inclusion and regional balance. In the past, the institutional capacity and the enrolment of students has increased manifold. In the second wave of changes in higher education, building up of institutional capacity remains a major objective. There are, however, issues of great concern relating to quality. There are other concerns of directing the growth process in the light of recent developments such as privatization, globalization and liberalization. These new developments that necessitate qualitative shift along the path of expansion pose a real challenge confronting higher education.

The book attempts to provide solutions both at the policy level and at the level of practices to the desired qualitative shift in higher education. The role of state in financing and in determining future trajectory is crucial. It is also important to note that market cannot determine the trajectory, although the existence of market should be fully taken into account in future trajectory. The second wave of policy changes and institutional initiatives are summarized in the concluding chapter. The summary becomes necessary as the issues which might have remained hidden come to the surface in the final reading. Thus, the chapter looks back and tries to find the central points that the author wishes to communicate.

Expansion and Restructuring of University

At the highest priority is the expansion of institutional capacity of higher education. The past growth pattern has seen expansion in terms of affiliating state universities, the arbitrary manner of establishment of central universities, the increase in the number of deemed universities, mostly private and the emergence of private universities. The problem of oversize of state universities, under-governance of colleges and inadequate attention of postgraduate and research departments have been issues of concern. The expansion is characterized further with increasing student-teacher ratio and low paid contract teachers which are symptomatic of financial crisis facing higher education and also the shortage of high quality teachers.

Oversize of state universities is said to be related to entry barrier. However, in my view the rationalization of the size of state universities should be decided by respective state governments under UGC guideline of suggested framework. UGC should financially help state governments in restructuring and rationalizing the size of state universities. Every large state should also have central university which must have national character in terms of admission policy and faculty recruitment. UGC should also provide a guideline to the state governments to follow in the establishment of private universities and deemed universities. Restructuring should facilitate the expansion of institutional capacity. The expansion should take into account rural location of colleges and remove social and gender imbalance.

Quality Strategies

Various explanations have been given to the lower average level of quality of Indian higher education. Financial crunch, lack of planning to restructure university, policy failures, bureaucratization and excessive controls killing individual initiative and autonomy are some of the arguments advanced to explain lower average quality. Author's perception is that quality responds to the way in which a teacher is supported and works in pursuit of advancement of knowledge. Thus, it is the structure that constrains a teacher. Teacher needs to respond to change to adopt new practices in teaching-learning strategies and in the management of knowledge. There are two ways in which a new structure will facilitate a teacher. The first refers to competition model in which all institutions compete against each other forcing teacher to adapt to the change process. The competition model may, however, work through market signals and strategies. It means that institutions be given freedom to charge fees, fix remuneration of teachers and remove controls. This would provide a solution that may not produce social optimum. Hence, an alternative strategy would be to think of institutional mechanisms to invoke competition among teachers to respond to new situations.

Alternative strategy should be a mix of strategic initiatives by the UGC and the university system whereby the competitive spirit among teachers should be generated through sensitization, reward and punishment system facilitation and above all providing autonomy and space for initiatives. In terms of policies, UGC should come out with a rigorous monitoring mechanism for the recruitment and promotion of teachers. Quality should emerge as a culture of the new wave of institution-building. NAAC should emerge as an institution with various performance indicators and rankings inducing institutions and individuals to perform better.

Privatization and Policy Concerns

Last couple of decades has seen some new trends having far-reaching implications. The process of privatization is reflected in the growth of private professional colleges, deemed and private universities. There have been some unrecognized private institutions collaborating with foreign universities. The private foreign capital is also expected to flow in the country in education. This has created some distortions that need to be addressed through policy measures The distortions relate to excessive fees charged by private colleges and universities that lead to commercialization of higher education. Further, distortions are absence of a quality assurance framework of the most private institutions. The private institutions have also launched job-oriented courses that serve the purpose of preparing human resources for a job market. However, the teaching and research in basic disciplines are languishing for want of neither market supporting it nor state sufficiently providing resources. The foreign education providers have begun to collaborate with private players to market the programmes. The educational collaboration with state/central universities is non-existent in the absence of regulation. The issue of private foreign capital in education sector suffers from policy contradiction. The state has not been able to correct above market distortions through appropriate policies. As a result, some of these issues have necessitated judicial interventions due to executive and legislative failure.

Above issues have been analysed at great length in section two on emerging issues. The establishment of private universities under state legislation is a new phenomenon. State government has not established any specific institution to monitor the private universities. It is the responsibility of central government under the constitutional mandate to maintain standards. Hence, UGC must have an effective voice in the establishment of private universities. UGC should have an effective quality assurance control through NAAC. Central government should also come up with guidelines on private universities that state government should be obliged to follow. Guidelines should of course be aimed at controlling commercialization and maintaining effective check on quality. The private deemed universities have also not been effectively monitored by UGC once it comes into existence. An effective monitoring mechanism needs to be developed by UGC and the reports should be placed in the public domain for discussion.

It is ironical that central government issued a draft bill on admission and fees in private professional colleges and private deemed universities in 2005 and later withdrew it. The policy initiative on this seems to have subsided without settling it. The problems continue. There are recruitments through entrance examination and through arbitrary management quotas. The students have to appear in a number of examinations conducted by different private institutions and states. There is no centralized admission and fees policy that could guide different states to follow basic principles. This requires an urgent attention of central government.

Globalization has produced impact on higher education in a number of ways. The commercial presence of foreign universities in India is slowly becoming a major force. Foreign universities collaborate with private institutions in a number of ways. The mechanics of its operations is commercial. It is also in the absence of entry regulation an illegal activity. The regulation on fees, admission and quality assurance is non-existent. The draft bill could not be tabled in parliament. It was withdrawn by the government at the last moment. There is again indecisiveness on the entry and the manner in which control over foreign universities should take place. Though there are advantages in allowing the entry of foreign universities through collaborative partnership with Indian universities, the uncontrolled operation at present is purely commercial. The internationalization of higher education has various dimensions of knowledge creation and dissemination and therefore needs to be properly understood and promoted in a manner suited to the interests of the wider sections of society.

The policy on private foreign capital is highly ambiguous. Almost 100 per cent FDI in education through automatic route is continuing with regulatory controls in education making it practically impossible to attract foreign investment in education. The present uncertainty gives rise to unregulated flows of FDI due to absence of regulation on the entry of foreign universities in India. An essential precondition for an effective FDI is that though foreign investment should not be guided by free market principle, it should be regulated by domestic policies that should allow a normal return on investment. Income over and above normal return should be reinvested to improve the quality. Besides, a transparent policy of regulation should be in place.

Reform Process through Market

The absence of policy to effectively regulate privatization in higher education is one side of the story. It is creating distortions that adversely affect the social fabric and harms the long-run interests of the country. Another side of the story is that a reform agenda for public system of higher education is also proposed to be guided by the market principle as contained in the report of the National Knowledge Commission on Higher Education. State's control regime is said to be strangulating to the private participation and state's failure is said to be corrected by invoking market principle. Let state manipulate the interests of different sections of society in the political battlefield. In the provision of goods and services, however, state should run the system through market principle and let invisible hand serve the collective interests.

With this approach, the institutional restructuring is suggested where the minimalist role of state exists. The establishment of universities will require the permission from a central body called Independent Regulatory Authority in Higher Education (IRAHE) only. The legislative route would then become redundant. Once entry barrier is removed a lot of restructuring within is suggested to allow for individual initiative and putting an end to oversized affiliating system. It is, however, suggested by the author that a rational approach to such restructuring would be to cut the size to manageable limit under the guideline and financial support from UGC. Respective state governments should, however, undertake the task.

The author suggests that UGC should establish a Higher Education Research Council that should provide information based on research findings to UGC on all aspects of higher education. A higher education information system, on-line monitoring, effective governance and adequate state funding of the order recommended by the Knowledge Commission can take care of the maintenance of standards. Author further suggests that there is the need to coordinate the various councils. This should be done by a high-powered "Higher Education Commission" to be chaired by the prime minister with representation of various concerned ministers and chairmen of the councils. This would facilitate coordination. More importantly, the functioning of respective councils will considerably improve with greater teeth and under the overall supervision of the prime minister. The basic philosophy of Higher Education Commission will be to reassert the role of state and guide the growth process that addresses the issues relating to inclusion.

Reform Proposals

It is interesting to observe the trends in the governance of universities from administration based on community of scholars to bureaucratization and further to managerial form. In Indian case, the massification of higher education enlarged the parameters of participation in an effort to democratize the university life. However, bureaucratization in university administration along with the combination of forces has resulted into the crisis of higher education. Too much centralization has adversely affected the autonomy and killed the initiative of scholars. In the Indian context, it is suggested that traditional governance model needs to be reformed to accommodate the fast decision-making mechanisms. University administration should be governed by demand-driven management ensuring professionalization of teaching and learning. There should be increasing networking between universities, industries and the government. Progress towards transdisciplinary approach to knowledge production and academics should be encouraged. Academic circles within universities in India need to network and collaborate teaching and research programmes. University governance also requires the flexibility with which the curriculum, the teaching practices etc., could be developed in short time. The essential point is that bureaucratic reform along with autonomy to academic professionals should be the cornerstone of reform in governance of universities.

The second academic reform proposal is towards introducing choice-based credit system. It needs to be understood that credit system in notional term amounts to simply switching from marks to grade and that course is defined in terms of credit. At a much deeper level, however, its introduction amounts to shift to semester system, providing choice of subjects to students and flexibility with which a student progresses towards accumulating credit. It also makes the assessment more transparent thereby making teachers accountable to the learner and to the teaching learner process. It makes interdepartmental and inter-university mobility of students possible. It is suggested that university system in India should gradually move towards choice-based credit system.

The last but not the least important is to undertake reforms of the doctorate programme in Indian higher education. Doctoral level research is the chief instrument through which universities allow to cultivate knowledge and disseminate it through two domains—teaching and research. The present position is that the condition of NET for an entry to the teaching profession has recently been relaxed. As a result, the standard of teaching very much depends upon the standard of doctorates. Although the NET is still there to determine the award of fellowship for doctoral study, the policy of NET alone cannot improve the standard of doctorates unless there is systemic intervention. Merely conducting NET is not sufficient to ensure the quality and seriousness of researchers. Recruitment, supervision and the examination are the three important processes for a doctoral study. Doctoral programme suffers from deficiency at all the three levels. Suggestions have been advanced towards doctoral reforms through a model code of conduct. UGC should present the model of conduct to the universities. International best practices have also been suggested for the universities to be followed in India.

Hike in Plan Finance

Commitment of the government in the second wave of institution-building is clearly visible in the 11th Plan support to higher education. During 11th Plan, the biggest gainer will be education sector with the draft proposing to increase the allocation to 19.36 per cent of the Gross Budgetary Support (GBS) from 7.68 per cent in the previous plan. In absolute terms, the central government will be spending Rs 2,75,000 crore (Rs 2.75 trillion) on education during the 11th Plan as compared to Rs 62,238 crore (Rs 622.38 billion) in the 10th Plan. The Prime Minister in his independence day speech announced the setting up of 6,000 new high quality schools—one in every block of the country; 370 colleges in various districts, 1,600 new industrial training institutes (ITIs) and polytechnics; 10,000 new vocational schools and 50,00 new skill development centres. The government also plans to set up 30 new central universities; 5 new institutes of science education and research (IISERs); 8 new Indian Institutes of Technology (IITs); 7 new Indian Institutes of Management (IIMs) and 20 new Indian Institutes of Information Technology (IIITs).

It is suggested to raise resources partly through fees and establish institutions for financial support to the needy students. CABE Committee on the financing of higher education has suggested establishment of Higher Education Finance Corporation. It is also suggested to establish a higher education fund through contributions from philanthrophists and industrialists to help universities and colleges.

It is hoped that with hike in the plan finance and mobilizing resources from multiple sources, state will be able to provide the needed direction for higher education.

Index